Music Theory for Singers

Level Nine

Second Edition

Sarah Sandvig

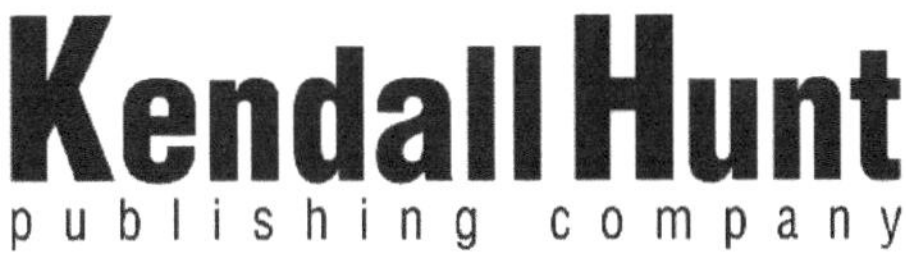

Cover image © Shutterstock, Inc. Used under license.
Back cover image and all keyboard and hand images
provided by the author.

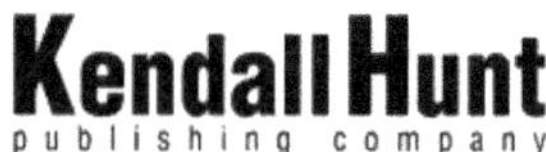

www.kendallhunt.com
Send all inquiries to:
4050 Westmark Drive
Dubuque, IA 52004-1840

ISBN 978-1-5249-1444-8

Published in the United States of America

FOREWORD

In Sarah Sandvig's *Music Theory for Singers*, voice students and their teachers finally have a singer-friendly primer for musicianship and music theory that is directly applicable to voice training. Mrs. Sandvig has capitalized on her experience as a successful private voice teacher to create this comprehensive workbook, which, in clear, concise language, lays out an easy-to-follow lesson plan progressing from basic through advanced skills. *Music Theory for Singers* is equally applicable in a college or high school classroom setting as in the private studio, and voice teachers will especially appreciate the inclusion of international musical terminology, and music history which their students are likely to encounter in vocal repertoire. For teens studying voice for the first time, as well as for life-long adult singers, *Music Theory for Singers* will become a valued adjunct to any level of vocal study.

Juliana Gondek
Metropolitan Opera soloist and
Prize-winning international recording artist
Professor and Chair, Division of Voice Studies
UCLA

I am beginning my first semester as a BFA Musical Theatre Major at The Boston Conservatory at Berklee. I used Sarah's theory books throughout high school from levels 5 through 10, and they have prepared me immensely for this first semester – and beyond. For example, I recently went through a music theory and sight singing placement test: I was so amazed how comfortable I felt with both the written and singing portions. It was everything I had already learned from these theory books – key signatures, scales, rhythm, solfege, and more. In addition, I became so familiar with the fundamentals of music and a piano keyboard (even through utilizing the vocal theory books) I was able to test out of a whole year of beginner piano. All of this creates the possibility for me to move on to higher levels and be more challenged than if I had to start from the basics. Not to mention all of the composers and terms that are necessary knowledge to be successful in professional music classes and settings. It feels good to know that if I am ever unsure about what I am learning in class, my theory books are right there on the bookshelf to help me out.

Sofia Ross
Musical Theatre Major
Boston Conservatory

Thank you to the following people for their help and guidance in writing these books: Mary Beard, Melissa Caldretti, Sally Curry, Sharlae Jenkins, Vanessa Parvin, Connie Venti & my dad, Ken Watson.

Thank you to my husband Darren and sons Aiden & Caleb for their love, support and patience throughout this writing process.

NOTE TO TEACHER:

These books are a supplement to private, group or classroom voice lessons, and though I feel they can stand alone, they are not meant as a replacement for a good teacher who ensures student learning and understanding of music theory, history, and sight-singing. Each book includes reviews of subjects with a review test (with answers) at the end. You may also purchase the Answer Key, which has answers to all pages in each level, 1-10. Composers, terms, IPA and solfege are unique elements of these books that make them especially helpful for singers.

I hope these books are a useful addition to the many tools you already utilize to teach young singers in your studio or classroom.

TABLE OF CONTENTS

Review of Concepts in Level 8 1
Lesson 1: Melodic minor Scale 4
Review: Lesson 1 8
Lesson 2: Major & minor Key Signatures 11
Review: Lesson 2 13
Lesson 3: Rhythm Review 20
Review: Lesson 3 21
Lesson 4: Triads and Inversions 24
Review: Lesson 4 25
Lesson 5: The Dominant 7th Chord 26
Review: Lesson 5 28
Review: Lessons 1-5 31
Lesson 6: The diminished 7th Chord 34
Review: Lesson 6 36
Lesson 7: Vocal Harmony 40
Review: Lesson 7 47
Lesson 8: Transposition 49
Review: Lesson 8 51
Lesson 9: Ornaments 53
Review: Lesson 9 56
Lesson 10: Conducting Patterns 58
Review: Lesson 10 61
Review: Lessons 6-10 62
Lesson 11: Vocal Diction & IPA 64
Review: Lesson 11 68
Lesson 12: Italian, Latin, Spanish, German & French Diction 70
Review: Lesson 12 74
Lesson 13: Sight-Singing 75
Review: Lesson 13 77
Lesson 14: Musical Terms 79

Review: Lesson 14 80
Lesson 15: Spotlight on Composers (Barber, Beach & Tchaikovsky) 82
Review: Lesson 15 85
Level 9 Review Test 86
Level 9 Review Test: Answers 93
References 98

MUSIC THEORY FOR SINGERS

LEVEL 9

Review of Concepts in Level 8

Rhythm & Scale Review

Time Signatures

3 beats per measure | 7 beats per measure | 5 beats per measure | 7 beats per measure | 5 beats per measure

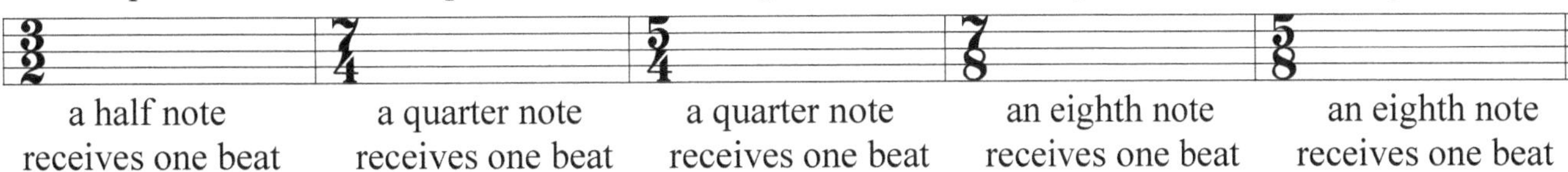

Harmonic minor Scale

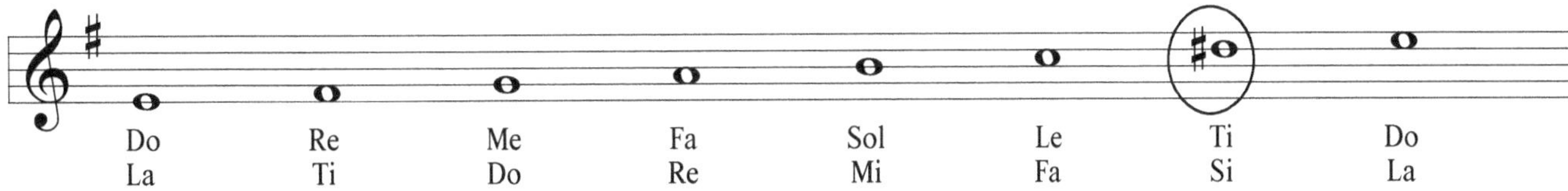

The 7th note is raised by a 1/2 step.

Key Signature & Triad Review

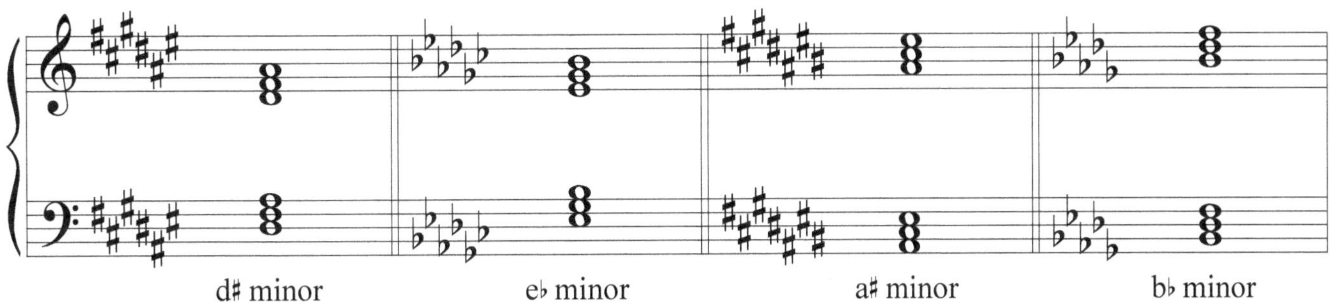

Ornaments: Musical Embellishments

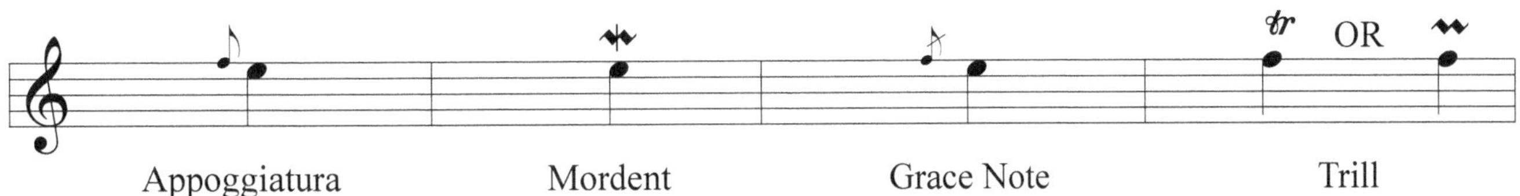

Modulation

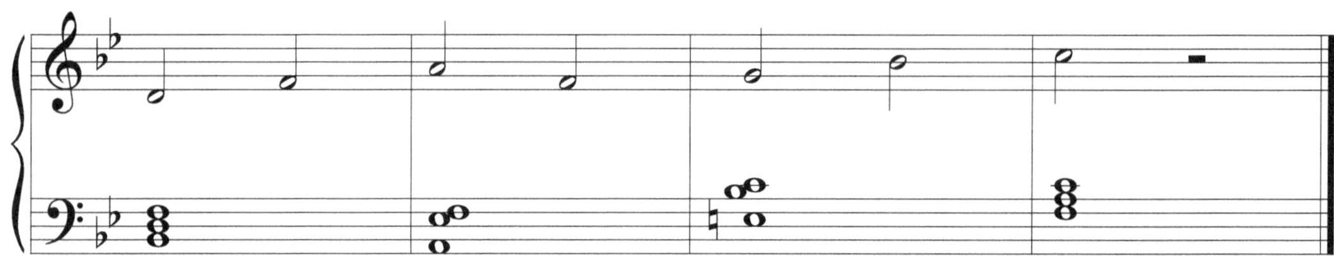

Dominant 7th Chord

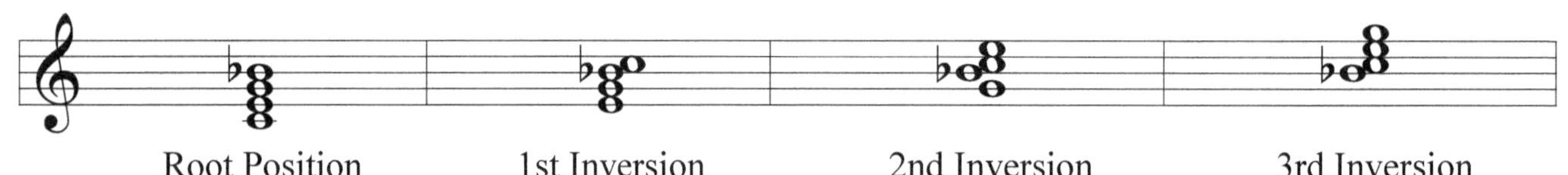

Cadences

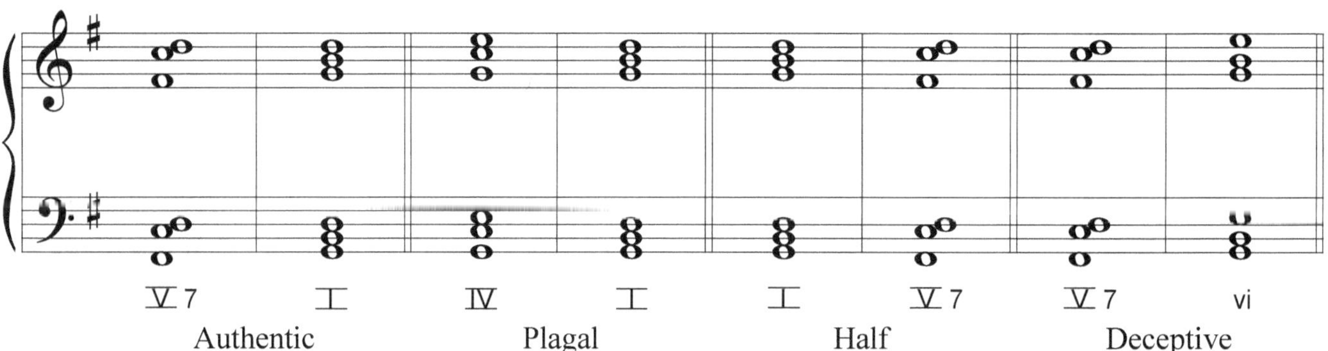

Chord Progressions

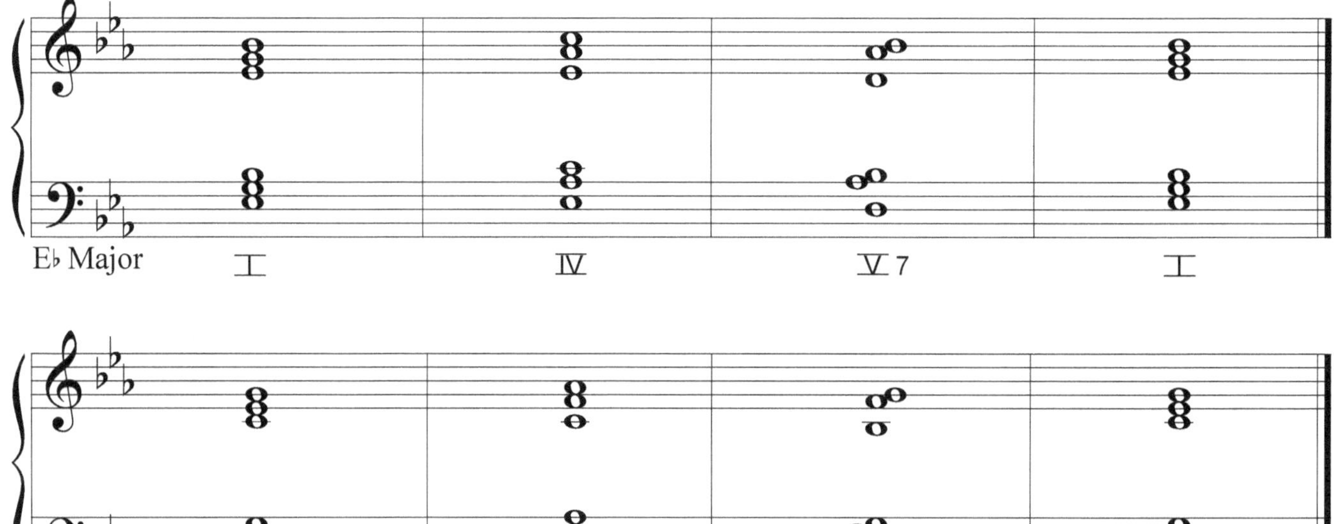

c minor i iv V7 i

IPA/Diction Review

IPA SYMBOL	UMLAUT EQUIVALENT	FOREIGN LANGUAGE WORD EQUIVALENT	TONGUE/LIPS PLACEMENT
y	ü	German: "über" French: "fut" Does not exist in Italian or English	Center of tongue is high Lips are rounded say "Ee" with "Oo" lips
ø	ö	German: "schöne" French: "feu" Does not exist in Italian or English	An open sound as in "hook" or "hurt" with taller lips, shaped like "oh."
ɛ	ä	German: "hätte" French: "belle" English: "fed" Italian: "bello"	Low tongue Lips relaxed

Sight-Singing Review

Rhythm

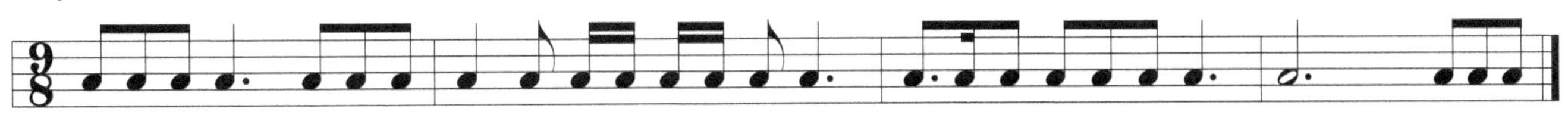

1 2 3 4 5 6 7 8 9 1 2 3 4 & 5 & 6 7 8 9 1 2 & 3 4 5 6 7 8 9 1 2 3 4 5 6 7 8 9
La La La La - La La La La - La La La La La La La - La - La La La La La La - La - - - - - La La La

Major

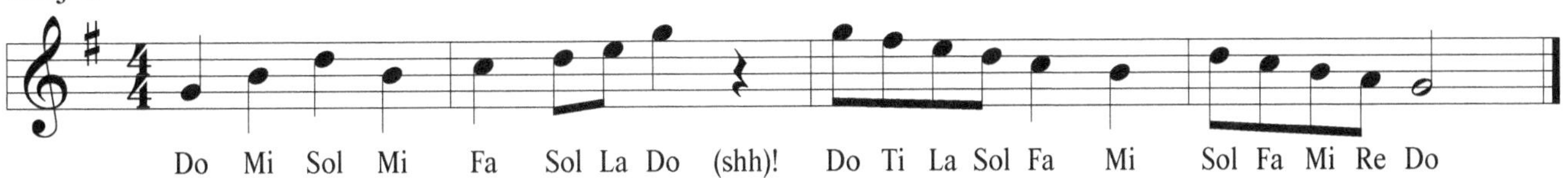

Harmonic minor

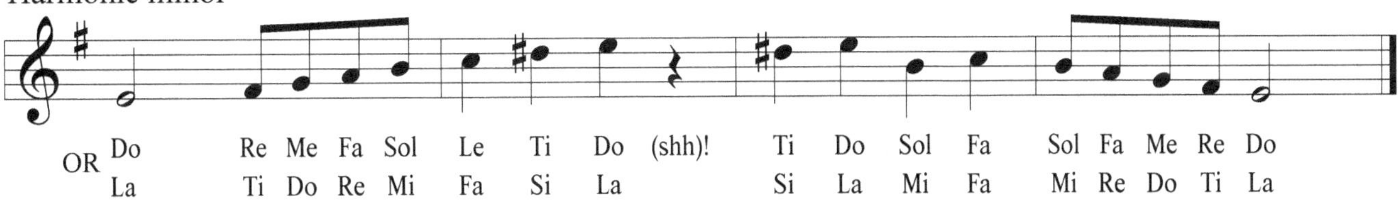

Lesson 1: Melodic minor Scale

In music, a Key Signature is a series of sharp (♯) or flat (♭) symbols placed on the staff immediately after the Treble and Bass clef. The Key Signature also creates the tonal center (Do) for a piece. If a piece is in D Major, D is Do.

The key signature shows which notes are to be sung a half step higher (sharp) or a half step lower (flat) for the duration of the piece.

Every Major key has a "relative" minor key. The easiest way to understand the difference between the sound of songs in a Major and minor key is:

Major key = Happy minor key = Sad

In order for a scale to be in a minor key, the notes must follow a specific pattern of half steps and whole steps.

The pattern of half steps and whole steps that make up a natural minor scale (8 notes) is as follows.

Whole - Half - Whole - Whole - Half - Whole - Whole (W - H - W - W - H - W - W)

Take a look at a c minor scale on the staff below. The E♭, A♭ & B♭ must be added in order for the formula (pattern of half steps and whole steps) to be correct.

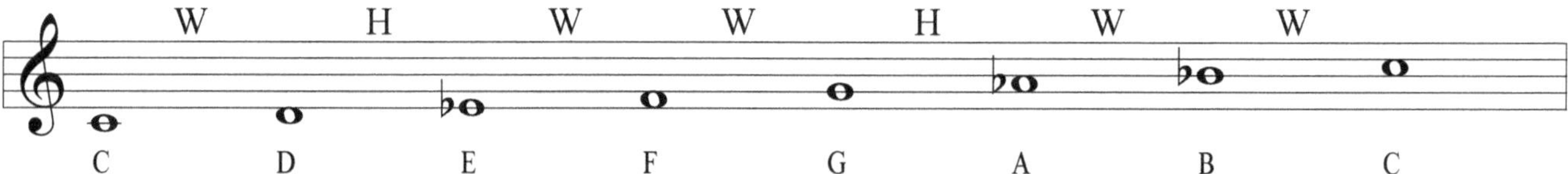

Here is what a c natural minor scale looks like on a piano keyboard.

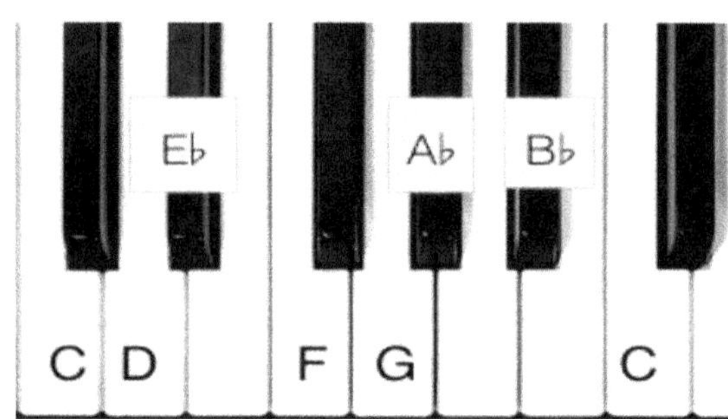

-C to D is a whole step
-D to E♭ is a half step
-E♭ to F is a whole step
-F to G is a whole step
-G to A♭ is a half step
-A♭ to B♭ is a whole step
-B♭ to C is a whole step

*Remember the "natural half steps" between B-C and E-F. These pitches are right next to each other. Look at the keyboard above to see how close they are on a piano!

Every Major key is related to a minor key because they share the same key signature (sharps/flats). For instance, E♭ and c minor are related because they both have a B♭, E♭ & A♭ in the key signature. If you sing a scale starting on E♭ (as Do) E♭ - F - G - A♭ - B♭ - C - D - E♭, it will sound happy (Major). If you sing the same scale starting on C (as Do) C - D - E♭ - F - G - A♭ - B♭ - C, it will sound sad (minor).

There are two ways to find a Major key's relative minor key.

1. The relative minor key (Do) is the 6th note of a Major key's scale. In solfege, this is the "La."

2. The relative minor key is a minor 3rd (3 half steps) lower than the Major Key's Do.

Look at the following example. C (La) is the 6th note of the E♭ Major Scale. It is the relative minor key.

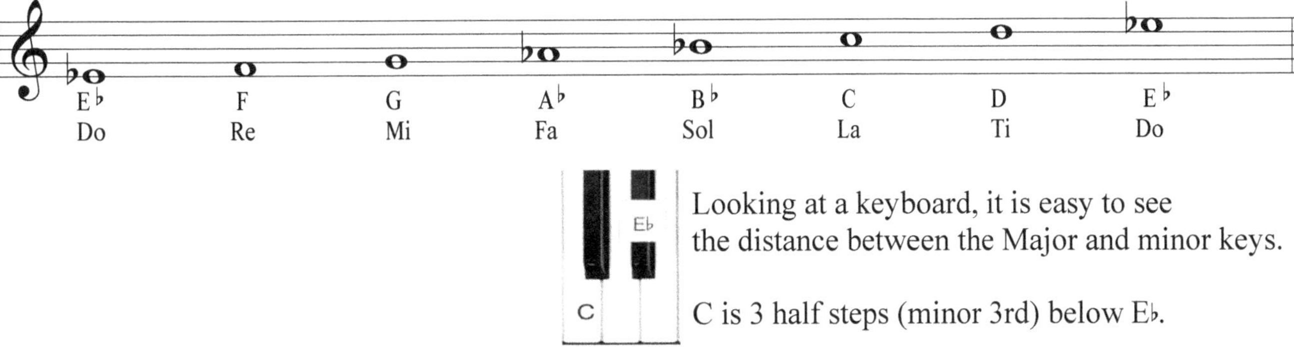

E♭

C

Looking at a keyboard, it is easy to see the distance between the Major and minor keys.

C is 3 half steps (minor 3rd) below E♭.

There are three forms of a minor scale: Natural, Harmonic & Melodic. In this level, you will be introduced to the **Melodic minor scale**. A minor scale in it's "Melodic" state is a **Natural minor scale with a raised 6th & 7th as it ascends & a Natural minor scale (6th/7th lowered as it descends).**

When singing a Melodic minor scale, the solfege is slightly different. The 3rd is lowered while ascending, and the 3rd, 6th & 7th are lowered while descending (Natural minor scale) so the solfege changes. The altered solfege represents the different notes and sounds that are in a minor scale.

Solfege for an ascending Melodic minor scale is: Do-Re-Me-Fa-Sol-La-Ti-Do.
Solfege for a descending Melodic minor scale is: Do-Te-Le-Sol-Fa-Me-Re-Do.

Another way to sing the solfege is with the relative Major key in mind. The minor scale starts on the La of the relative Major scale. In the ascending scale, the Fa and the Sol have been raised so the new solfege is Fi and Si. On the descending scale, the solfege is not altered.

Here is a **c Melodic minor scale**. Note that the 6th & 7th note have been raised by adding a natural sign.

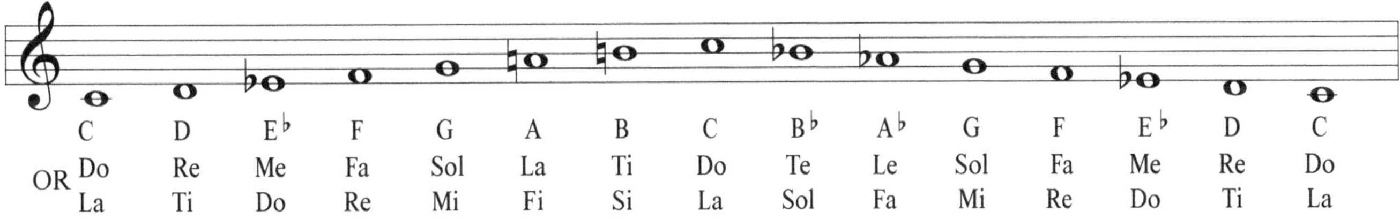

To create Melodic minor scales, you can raise the 6th & 7th note of the ascending natural minor scale in the following ways:

1. If the 6th/7th note is a flatted note according to the key signature, then add a natural sign to raise it.

2. If the 6th/7th note is not a flat or sharp according to the key signature, then add a sharp sign to raise it.

3. If the 6th/7th note is a sharped note according to the key signature, then add a double sharp to raise it.

Here are some examples of the different ways to create a Melodic minor scale.

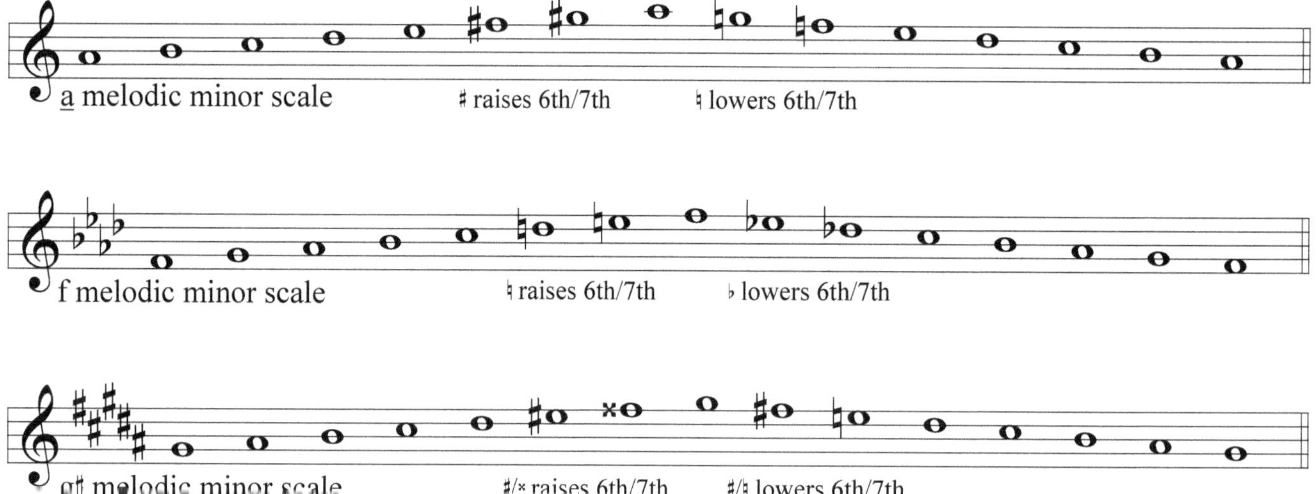

Review of Harmonic minor scales
(a natural minor scale with a raised 7th note, both ascending & descending).

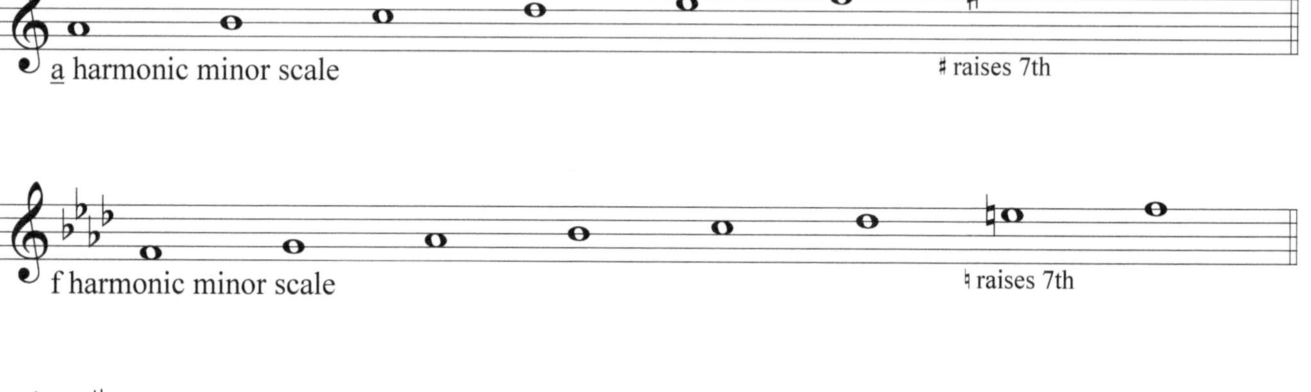

Versions of minor Scales

Below are examples of the three forms of minor scales in the keys of a minor and g♯ minor.

a minor

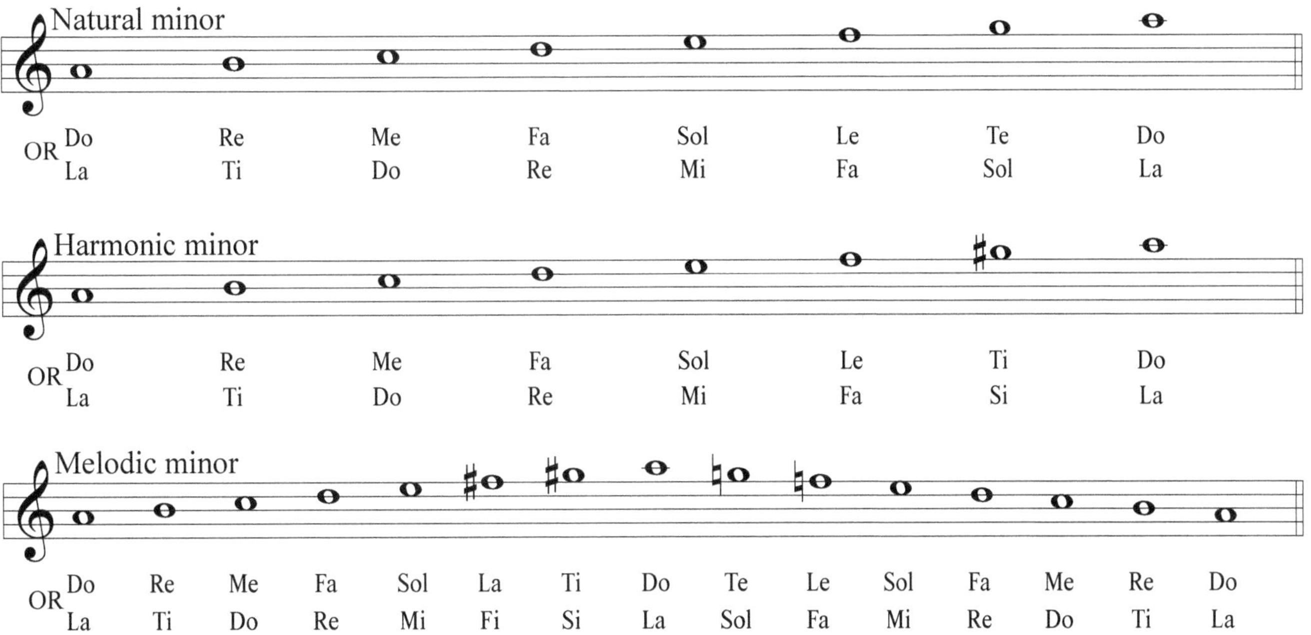

g♯ minor

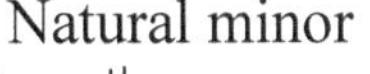

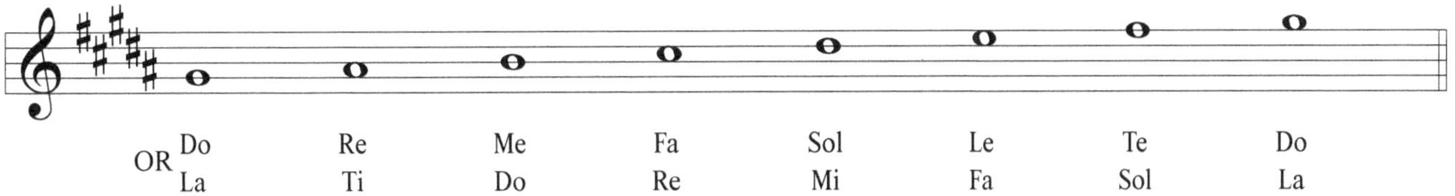

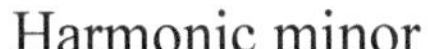

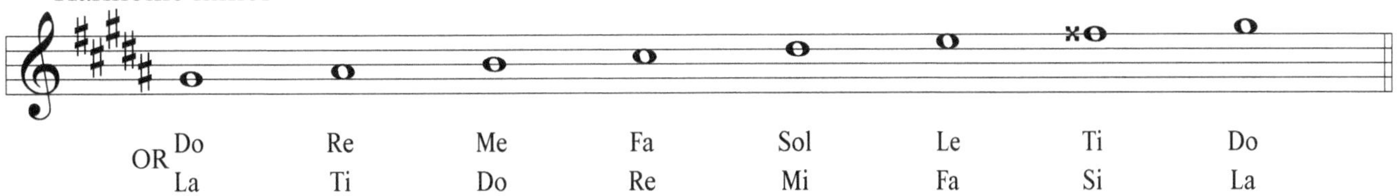

Melodic minor

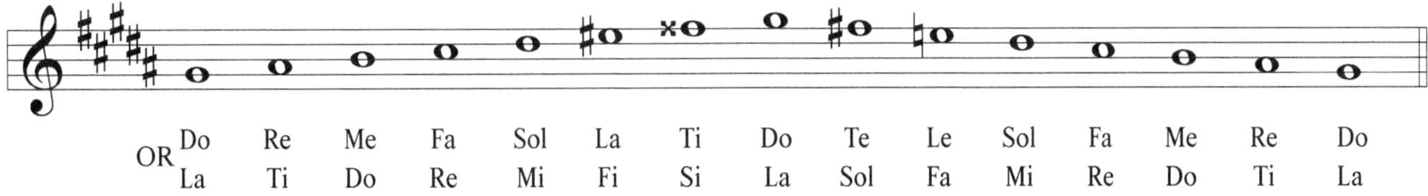

Review: Lesson 1

1. Label these minor scales as either "natural," "harmonic," or "melodic."

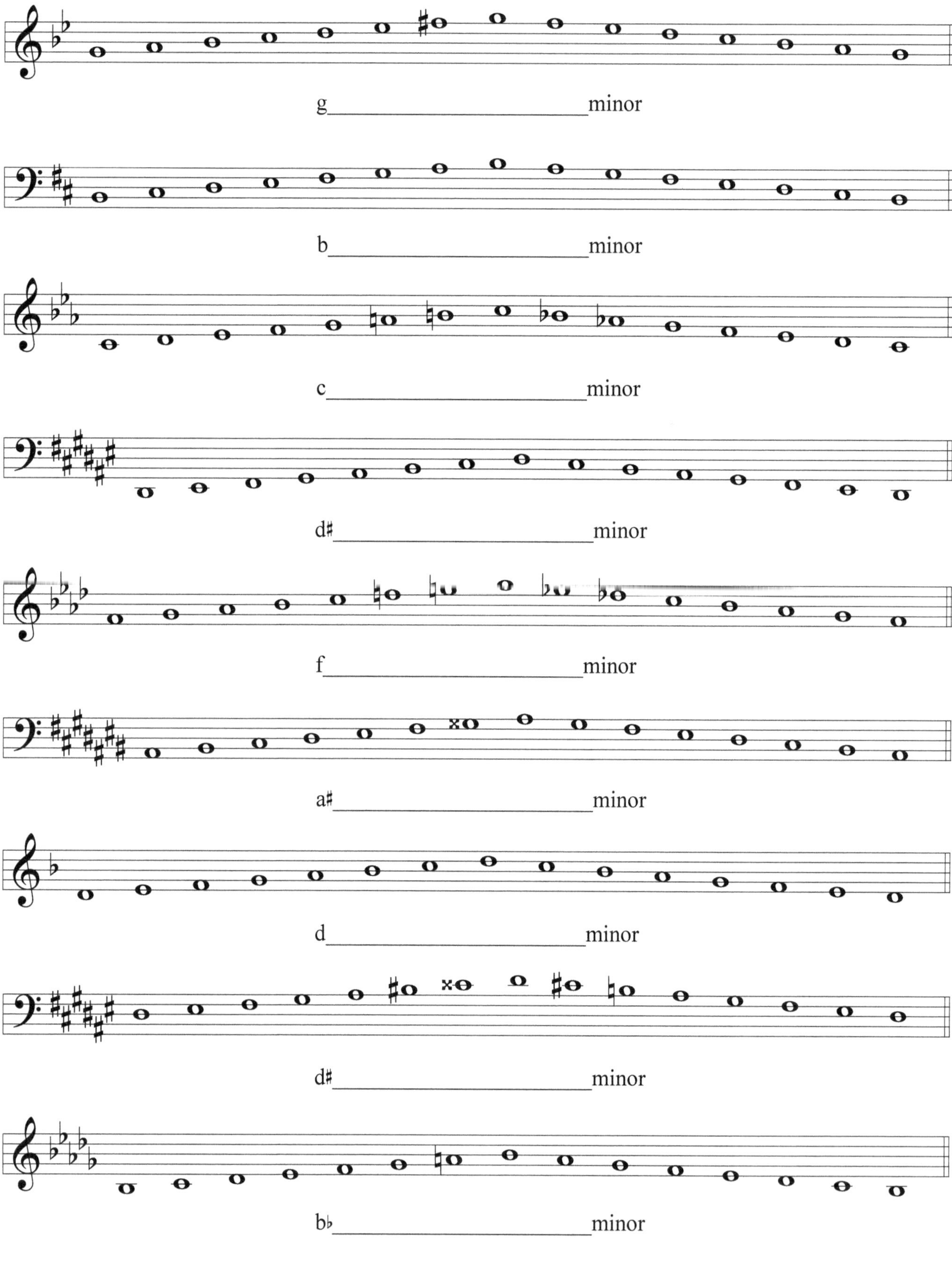

2. Add the necessary accidentals to the following natural minor scales to create melodic minor scales.

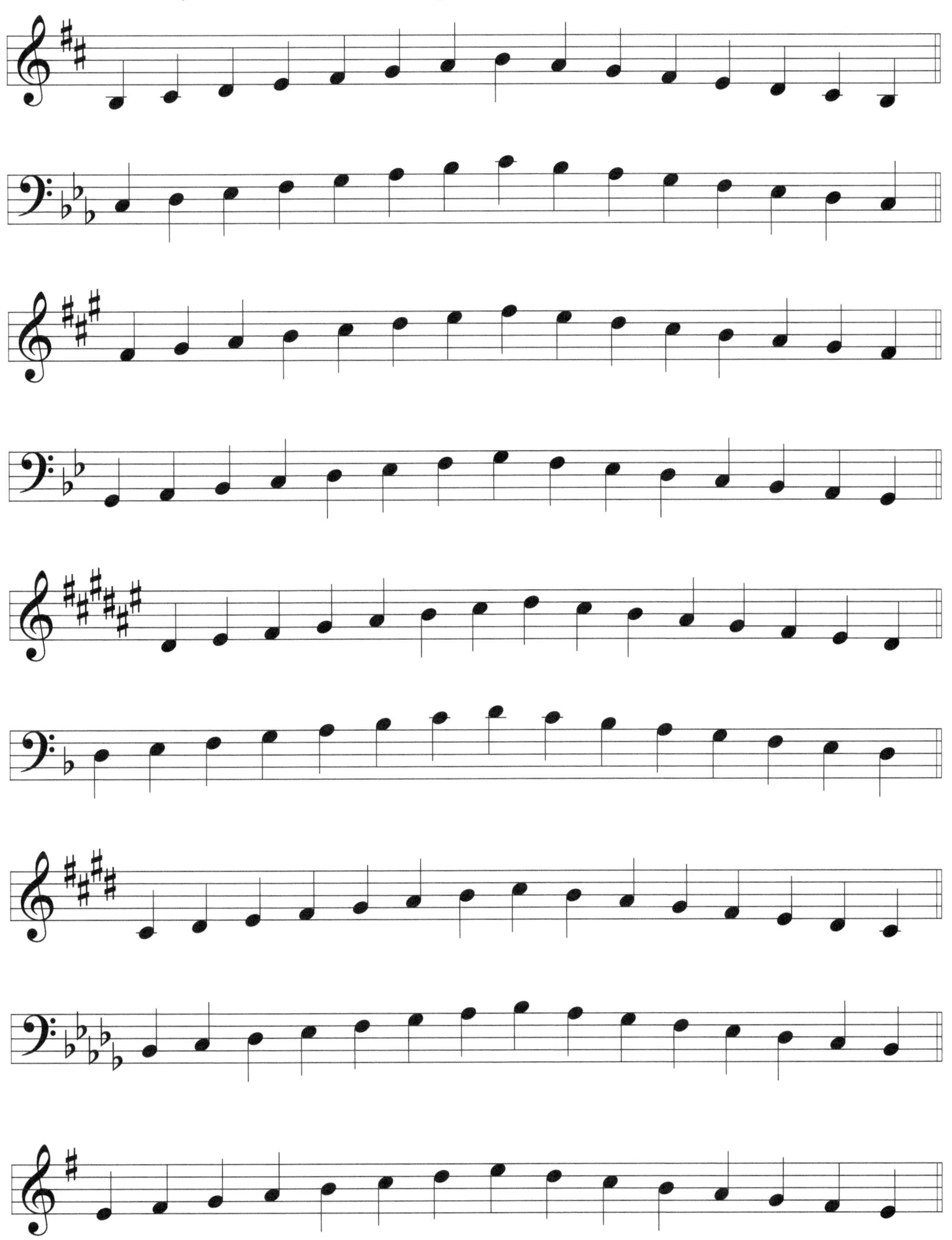

3. Following each given Major scale:
   -Name the relative minor scale
   -Add the key signature for the relative minor scale
   -Draw a melodic minor scale using whole notes. Don't forget to add necessary accidentals to make the scale melodic.

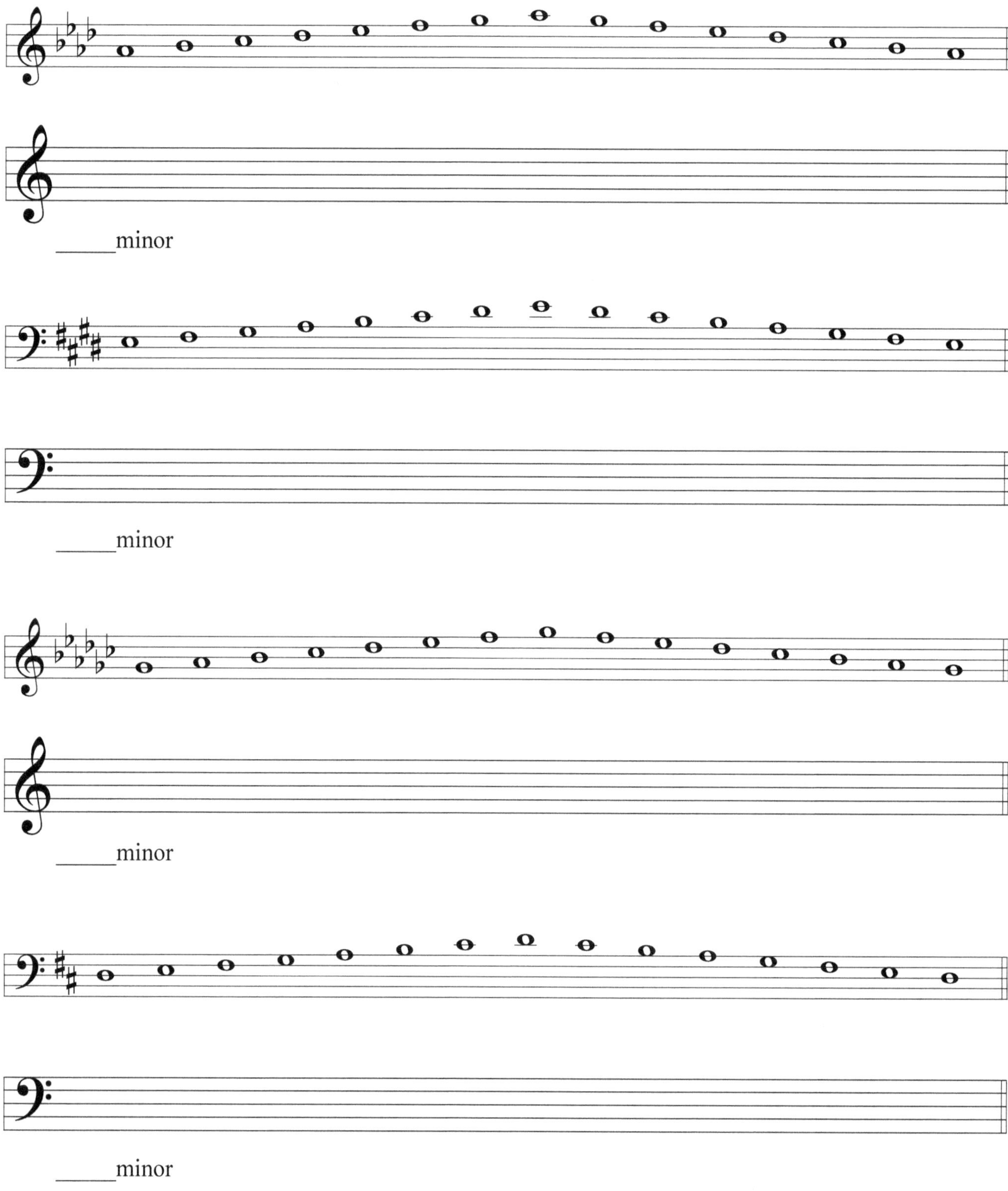

Lesson 2: Major & minor Key Signatures

Every Major key has a "relative" minor key. The Major and relative minor key share the same key signature (sharps/flats). You can find the relative minor key by going to the 6th note of the Major Key's scale (in solfege, this is the "La," or by singing the note that is a minor third (3 half steps) lower than the Major Key's Do).

In the examples below, there are scales in a Major key and in it's relative minor key. You'll notice that both the Major and minor keys have the same key signature (sharps/flats).

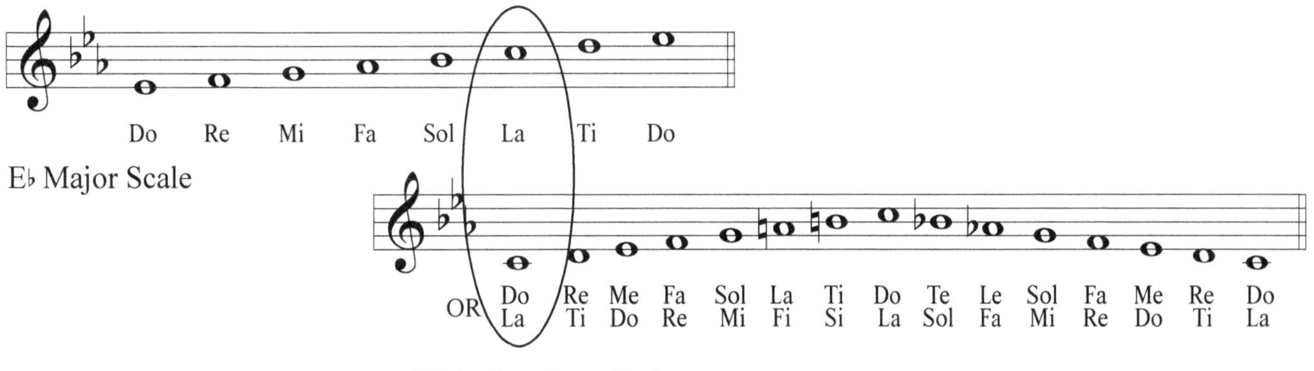

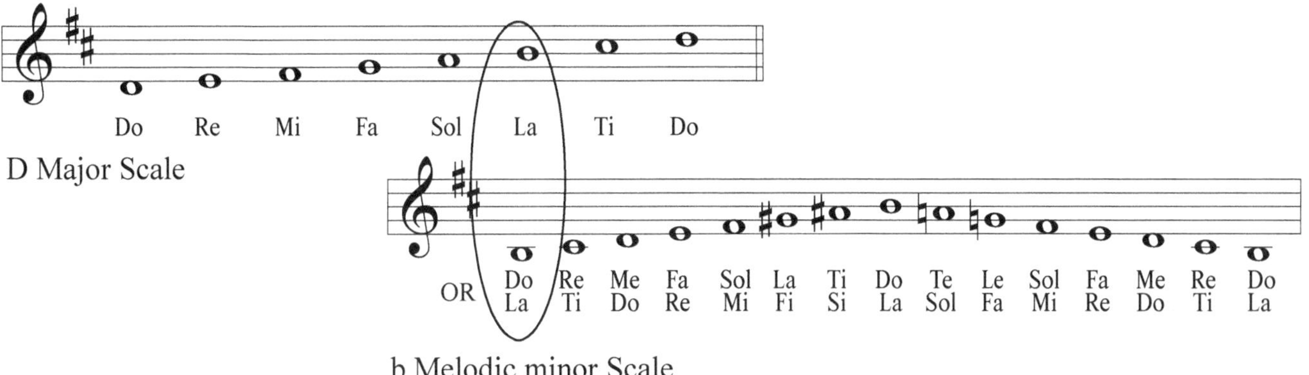

Note that the Do of the Relative Major Scale is the 3rd tone, "Me," of the minor scale.

Look at the following page for a chart of Major keys with their relative minor keys.

Major & minor Key Signatures

This is a chart of all of the Major and relative minor key signatures with Root position triads.

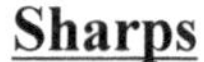

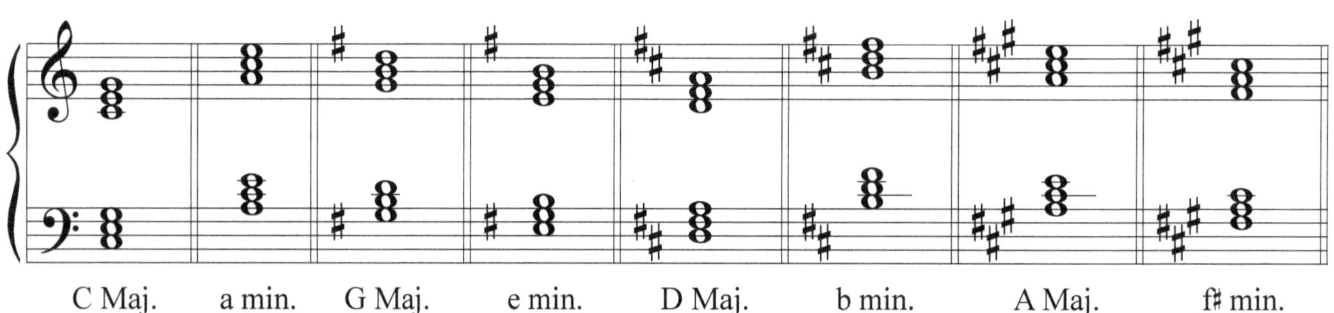

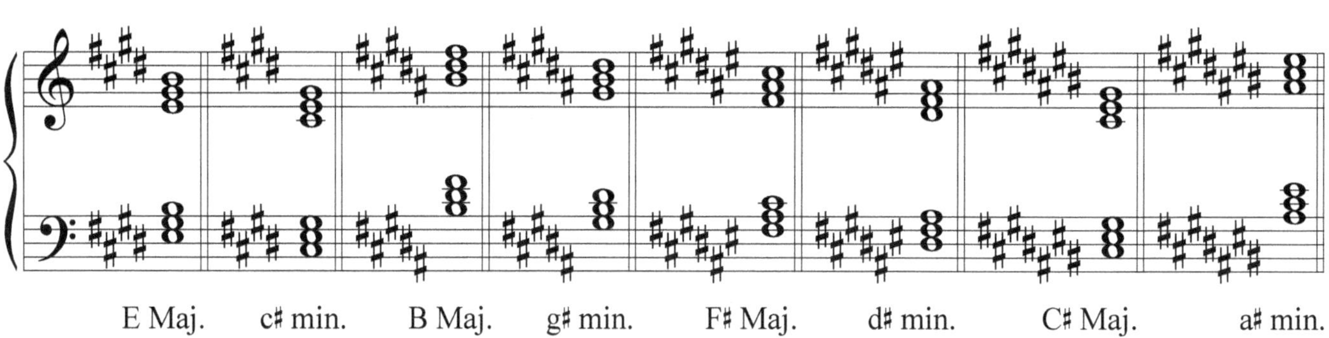

Flats

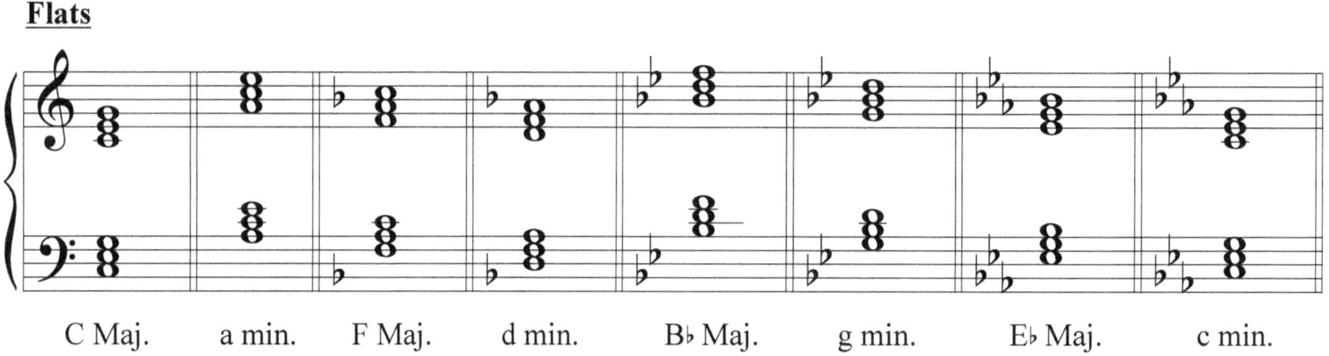

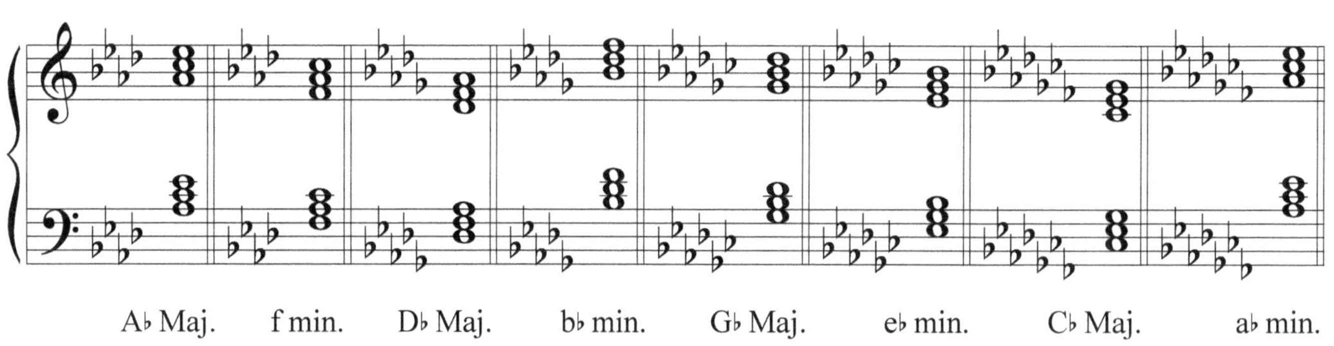

Review: Lesson 2

1. Circle the correct pattern of Whole steps and Half steps that create a natural minor scale.

   a. W W H W W W H

   b. W H W W H W W

2. Check the correct answer for the following:

   a. A relative minor key shares the same__________________as the Major Key.

   b. You can find the relative minor key by looking at the________of the Major scale.

   c. Songs in a minor key sound________while Major keys sound________.

3. Fill in the relative minor key for each of the Major keys listed. Refer to the piano to count down 3 half steps to find the minor key, or go to the La of the scale.

   F Major - ______minor G♭ Major- ______minor

   C♯ Major- ______minor D Major- ______minor

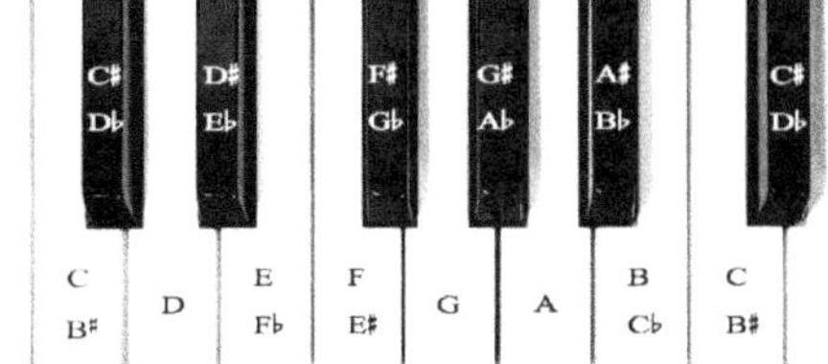

4. Circle the relative minor note (La) in each of these Major scales.

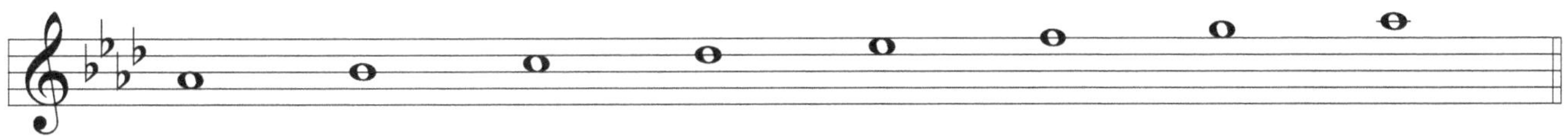

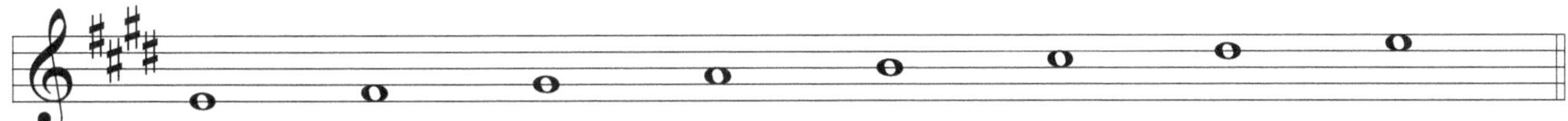

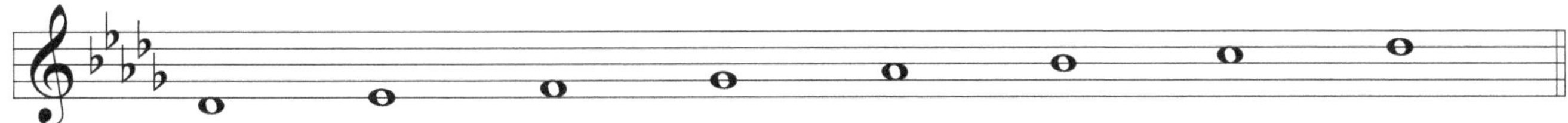

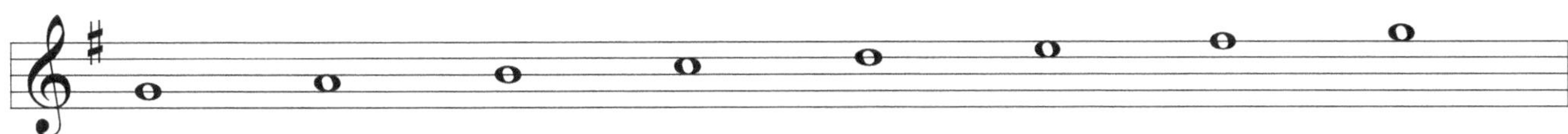

5. What is the order of sharps in a key signature?

_____ _____ _____ _____ _____ _____ _____

6. What saying can be used to remember the order of sharps?

____

7. What is the order of flats in a key signature?

_____ _____ _____ _____ _____ _____ _____

8. What saying can be used to remember the order of flats?

____

9. The order of sharps is in the_______________________________order than the order of flats.

10. Draw the sharps 2 times, in order, on both the treble and bass staves. Be careful that the center part of the sharp is on the correct line or space.

11. Draw the flats 2 times, in order, on both the treble and bass staves. Be careful that the center part of the flat is on the correct line or space.

12. Name the sharps, in order, in the following keys.

____

13. Name the flats, in order, in the following keys.

____

14. For the following examples:
-Determine the key, and if it begins and ends in the Major or minor key.
Hint: If you see added ♯/♮, it is most likely in a minor key.
-Write the note names underneath the notes. Be sure to add the ♯/♭ if the note is affected by the key signature. Watch the clef changes - it may help to circle the Bass clefs so you don't forget!
The first measure is done for you.

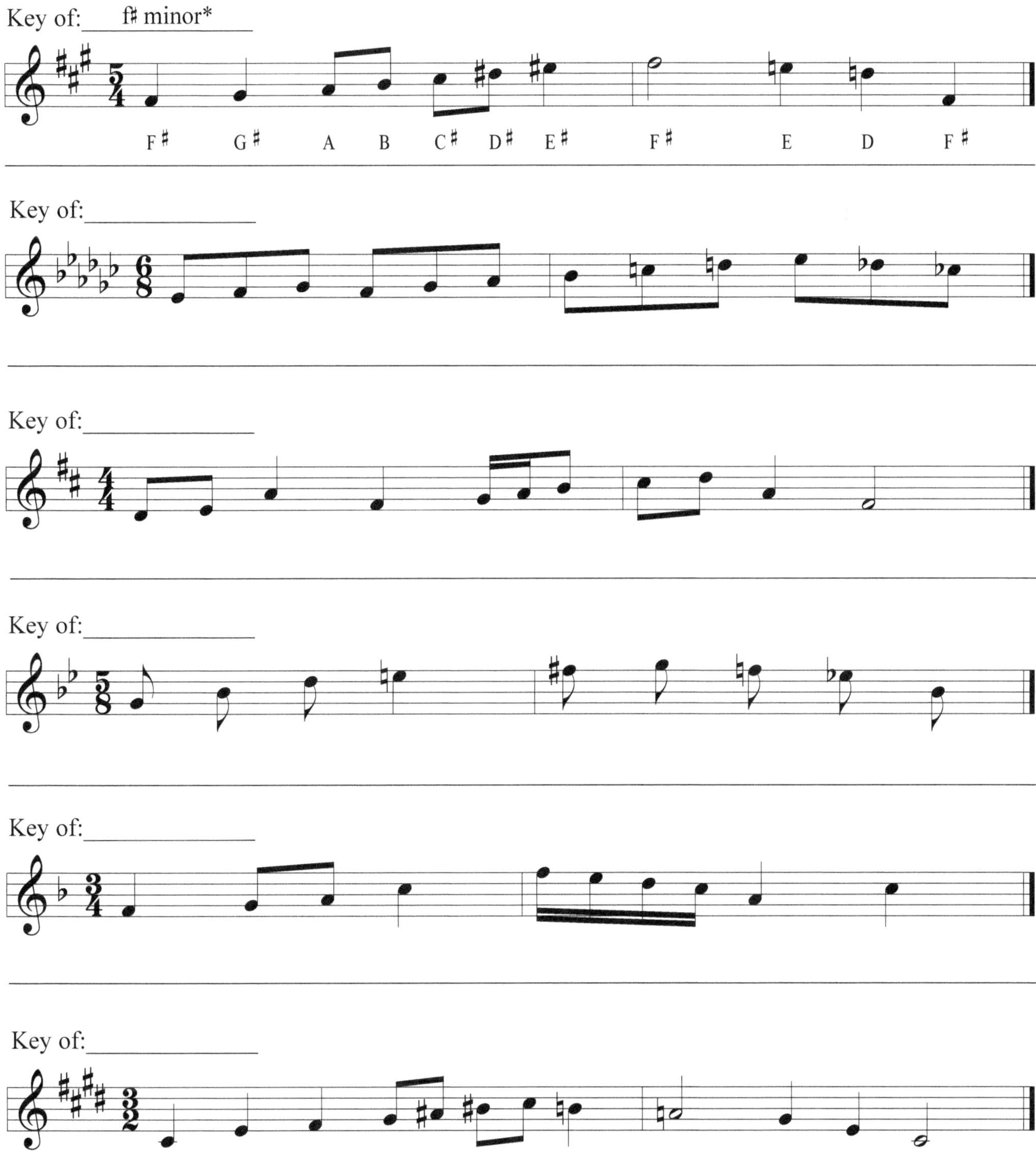

*starts and ends on an f♯, and has a raised 6th & 7th, so in this example, f♯ is "Do."

15. Use whole notes and accidentals to complete each scale. Draw an **ascending** scale in the first measure and a **descending** scale in the 2nd measure. Do not use a key signature.

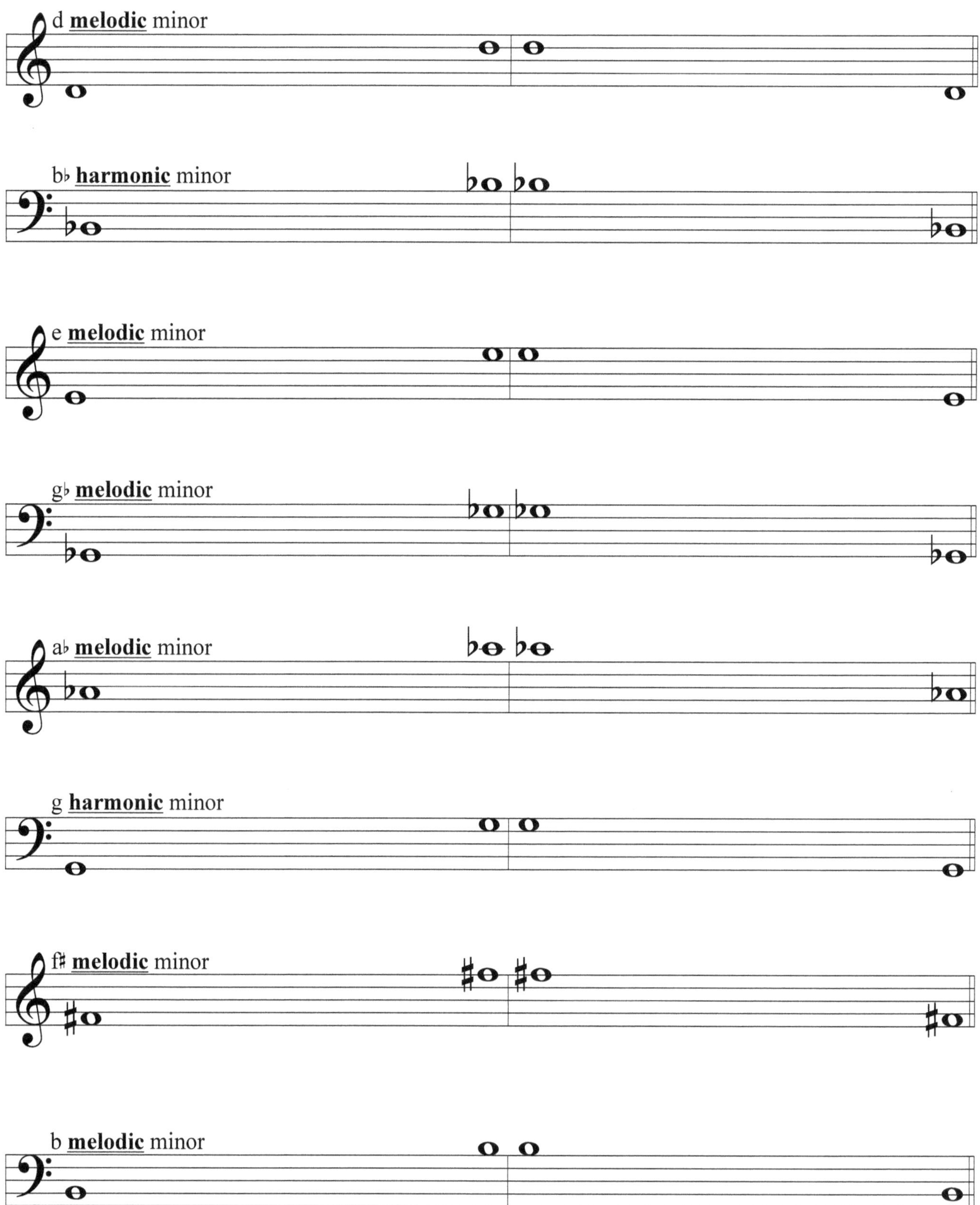

16. Add the necessary accidentals to the natural minor scales below to create **melodic minor** scales.

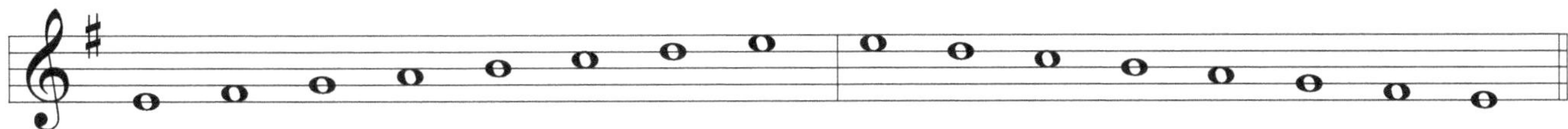

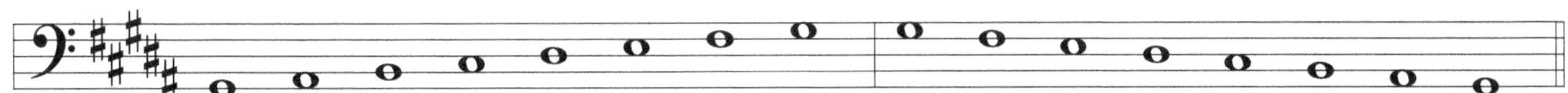

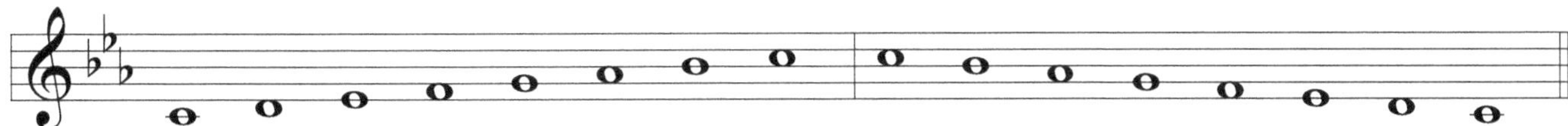

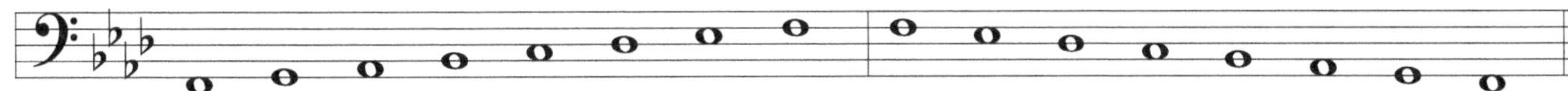

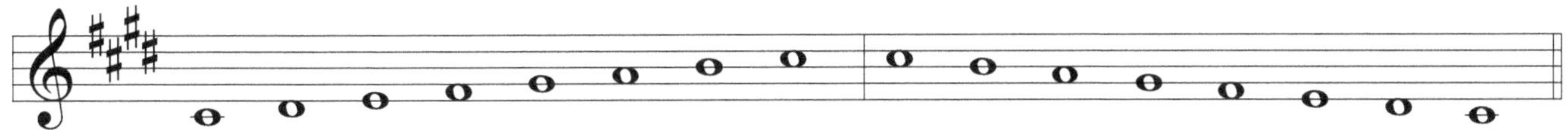

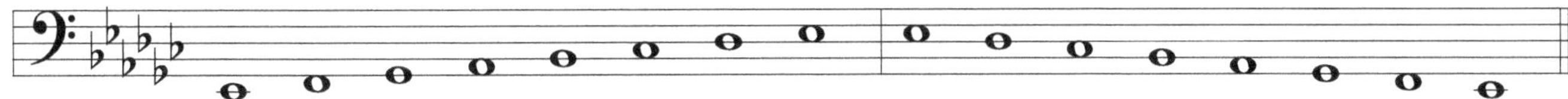

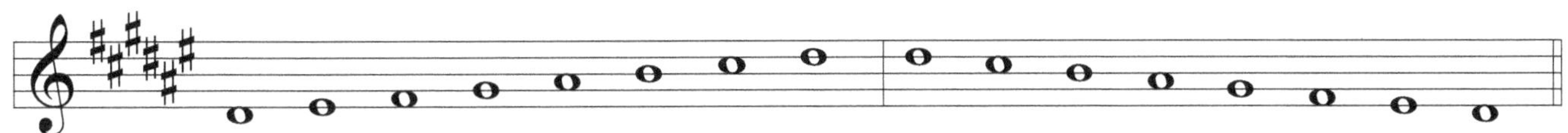

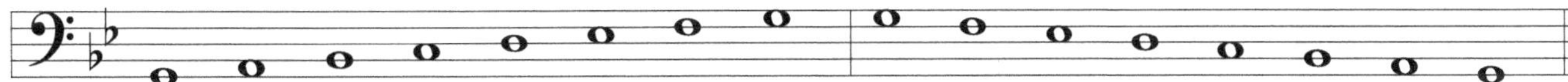

17. Fill in the missing solfege for the following **melodic minor** examples. **Choose either the fixed or moveable Do line.**

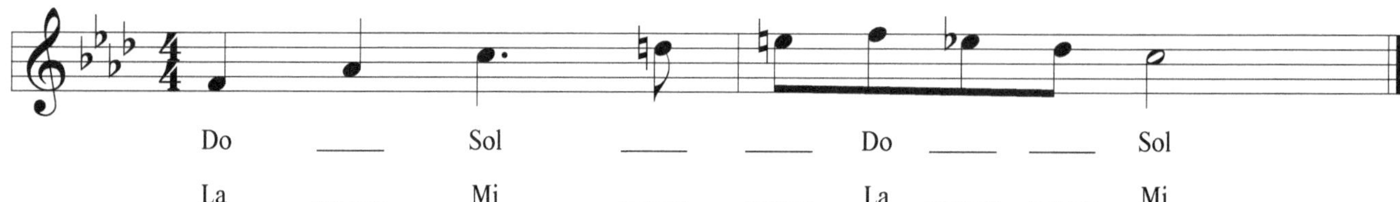

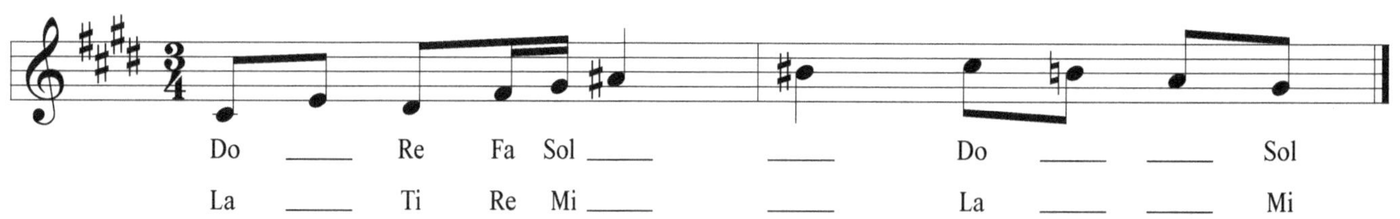

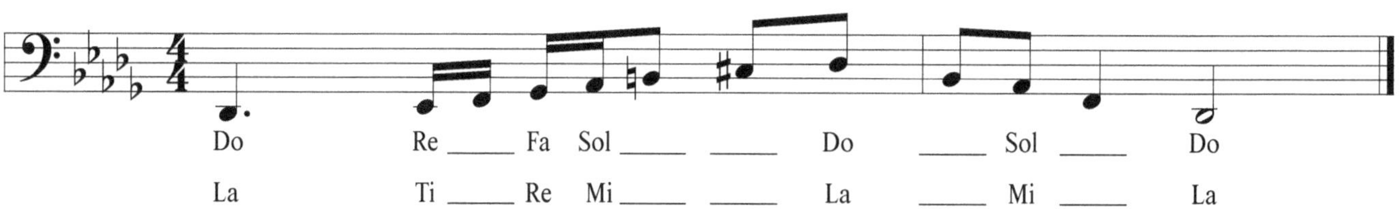

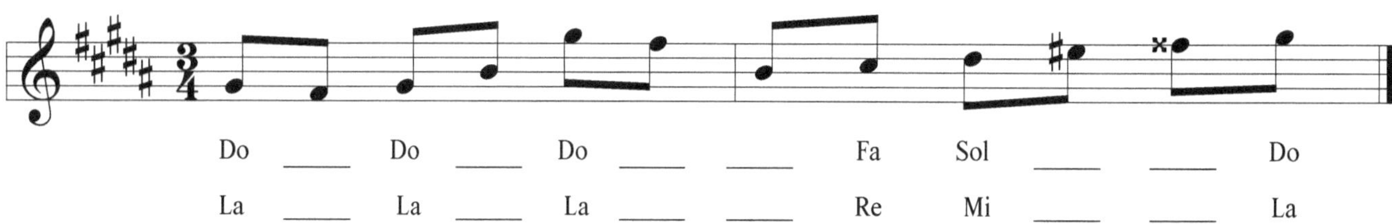

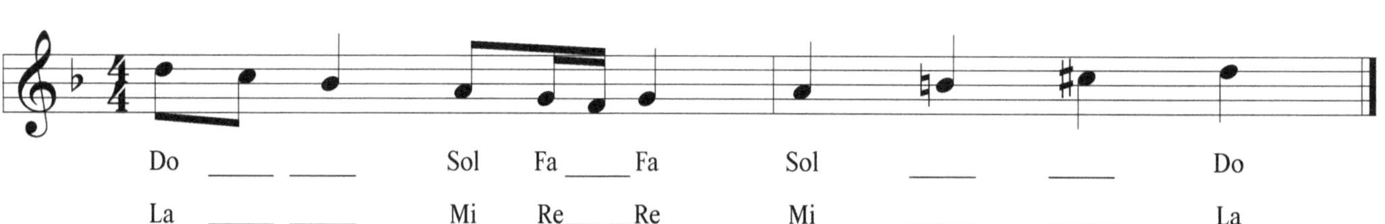

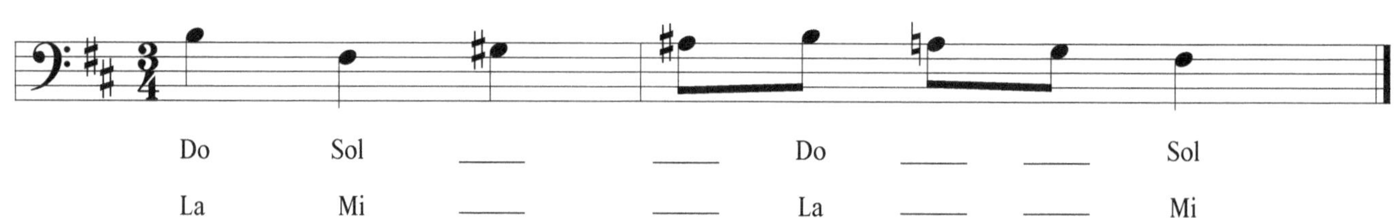

18. Name the following **Major** key signatures. Don't forget to add a ♯/♭ in the key signature name, if necessary.

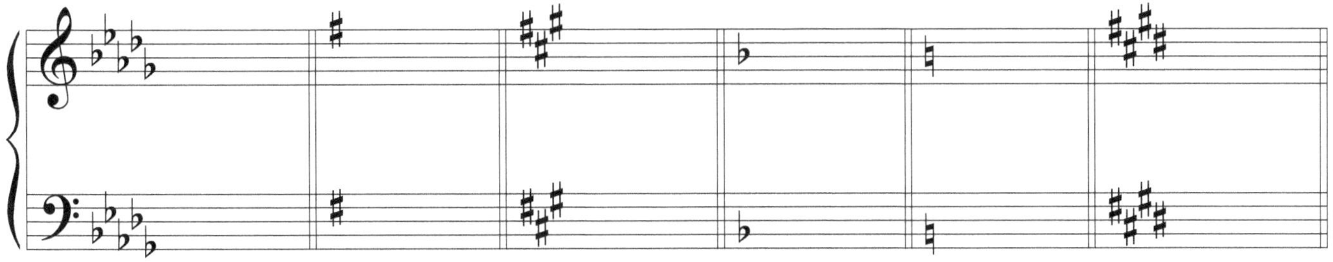

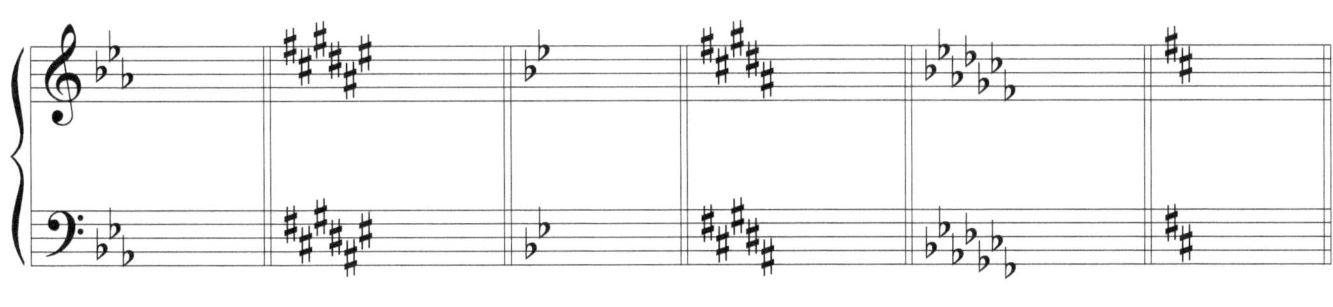

19. Name the following **minor** key signatures. Don't forget to add a ♯/♭ if necessary.

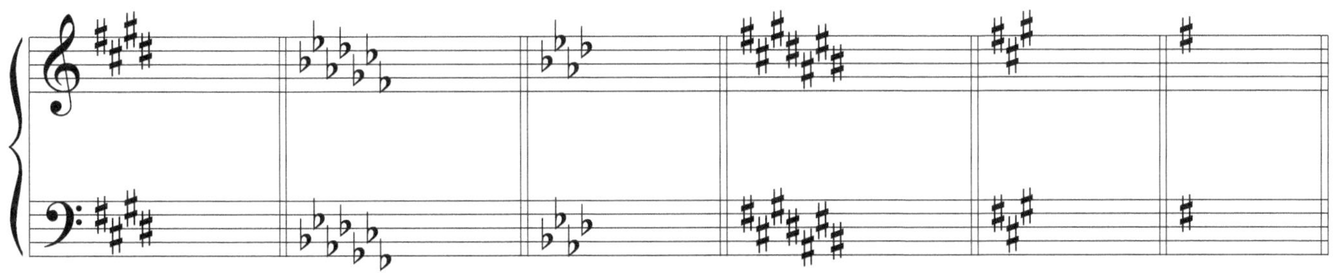

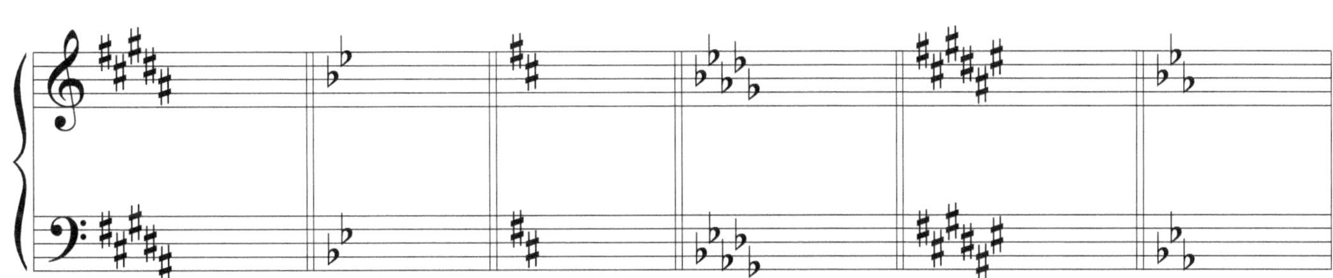

Lesson 3: Rhythm Review

A Time Signature tells us how many beats are in each measure of music, (top number) and what type of note gets one beat (bottom number).

In Levels 1-5, you learned about 2/4, 3/4, & 4/4 time signatures where a 4 was the bottom number. In these time signatures, a quarter note received one beat.

Levels 6 & 7 introduced 3/8, 6/8, 9/8 & 12/8 time signatures where an 8 was the bottom number. In these time signatures, an eighth note received one beat.

Level 8 introduced 3/2, 5/4, 7/4, 5/8 and 7/8 time signatures. Look at the review below.

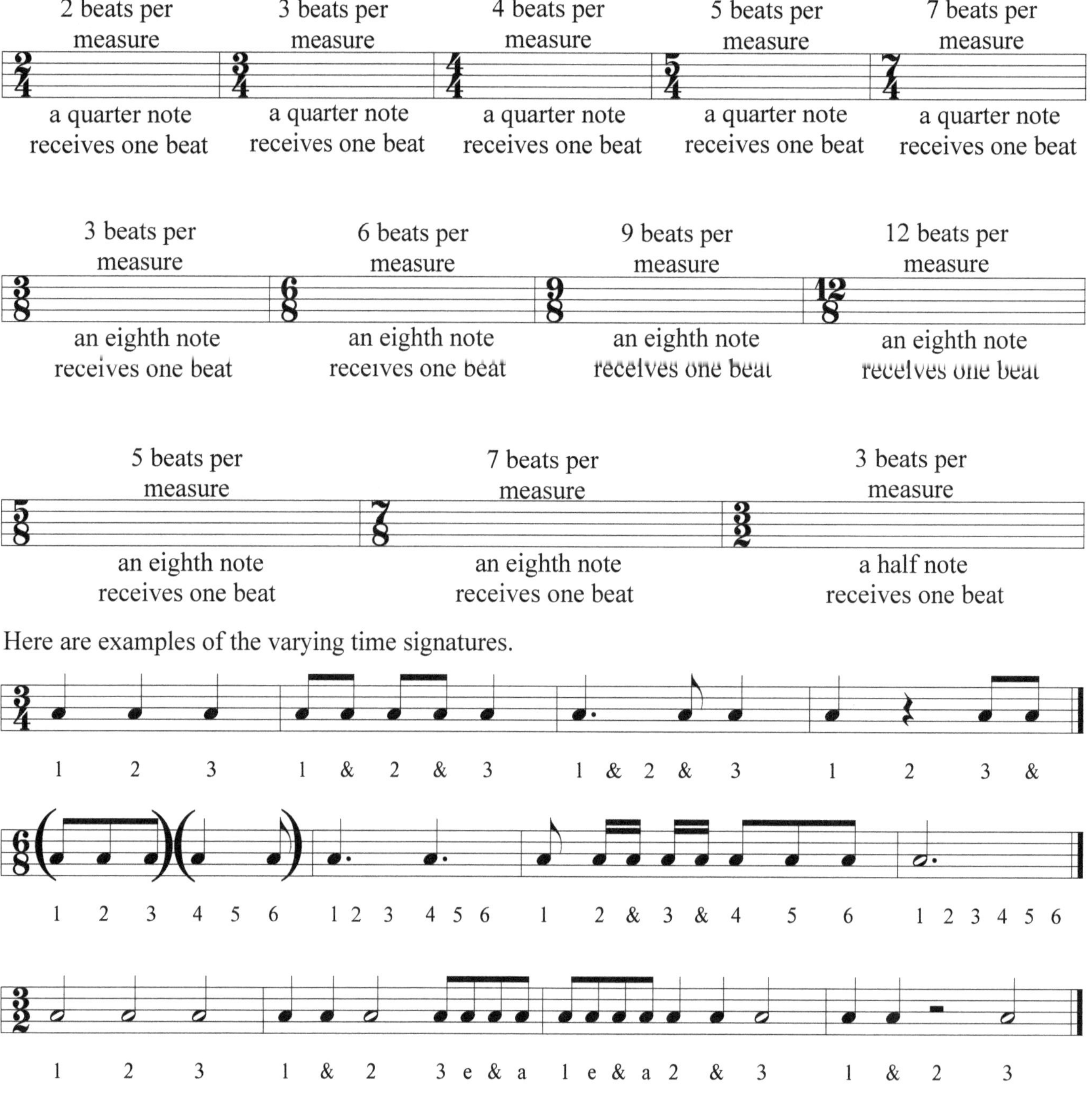

Review: Lesson 3

Hints:

An easy way to think about note & rest values in time signatures with an 8 on the bottom is, all notes are worth twice as much as they are in common time (4/4) and any other time signature with a 4 on the bottom.

In time signatures with a 2 on the bottom, (where a half note is worth 1 beat) an easy way to think of this is every note is worth 1/2 as much as it is in common time. (4/4) A half note = 1, a quarter note = 1/2, an eighth note = 1/4 beat, etc.

1. Write in the missing time signatures in the following examples. Each example is in either 3/4, 3/8 or 3/2.

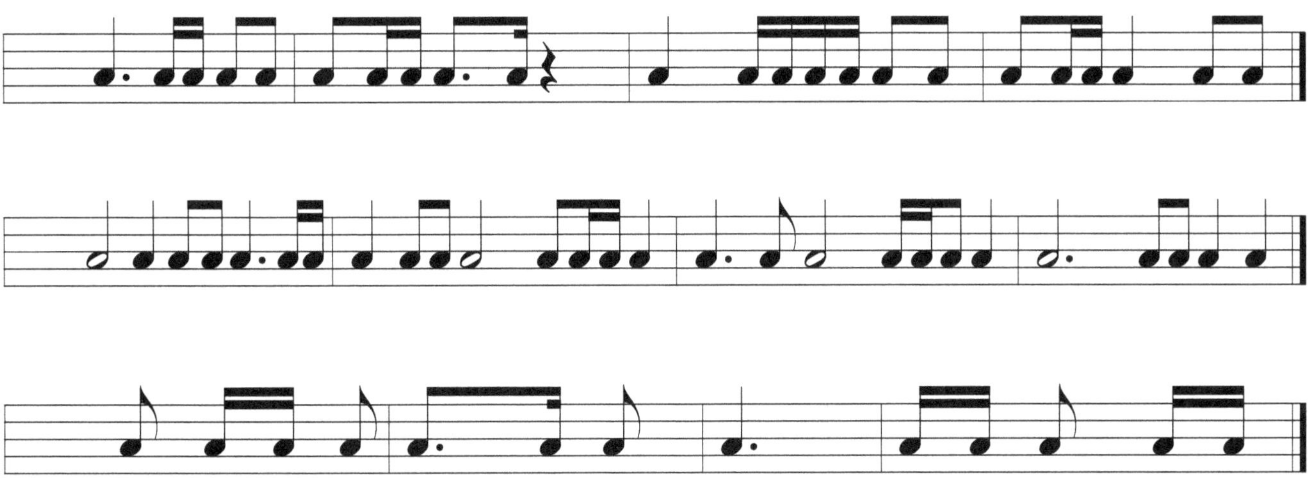

2. Write in the missing time signatures in the following examples. Each example is in either 5/4, 5/8 or 7/8.

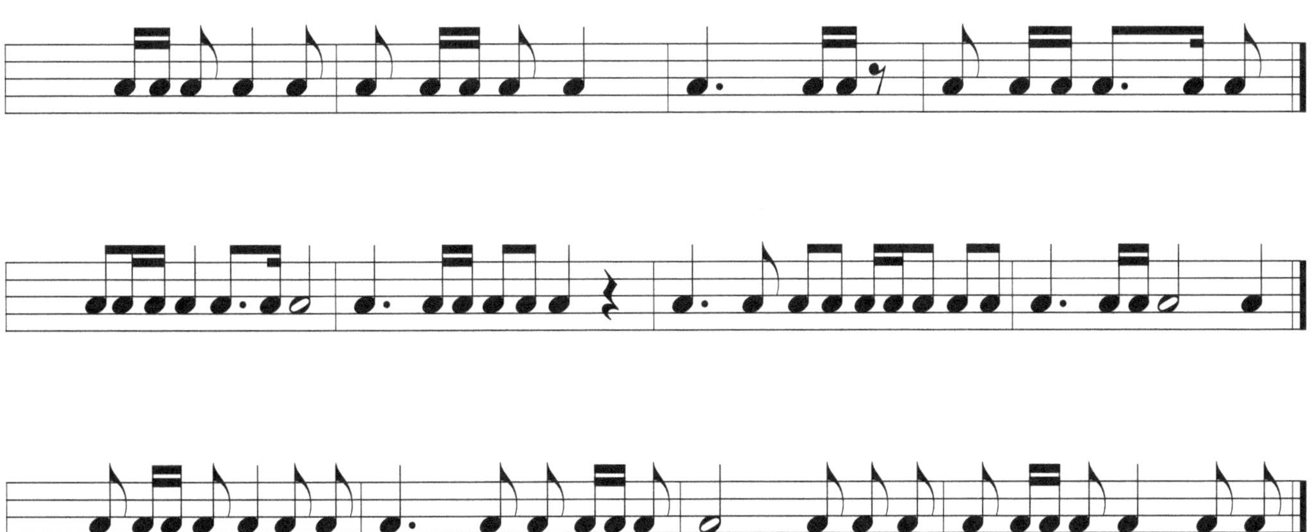

3. Add **one** note to the end of each measure to complete these rhythmic patterns.

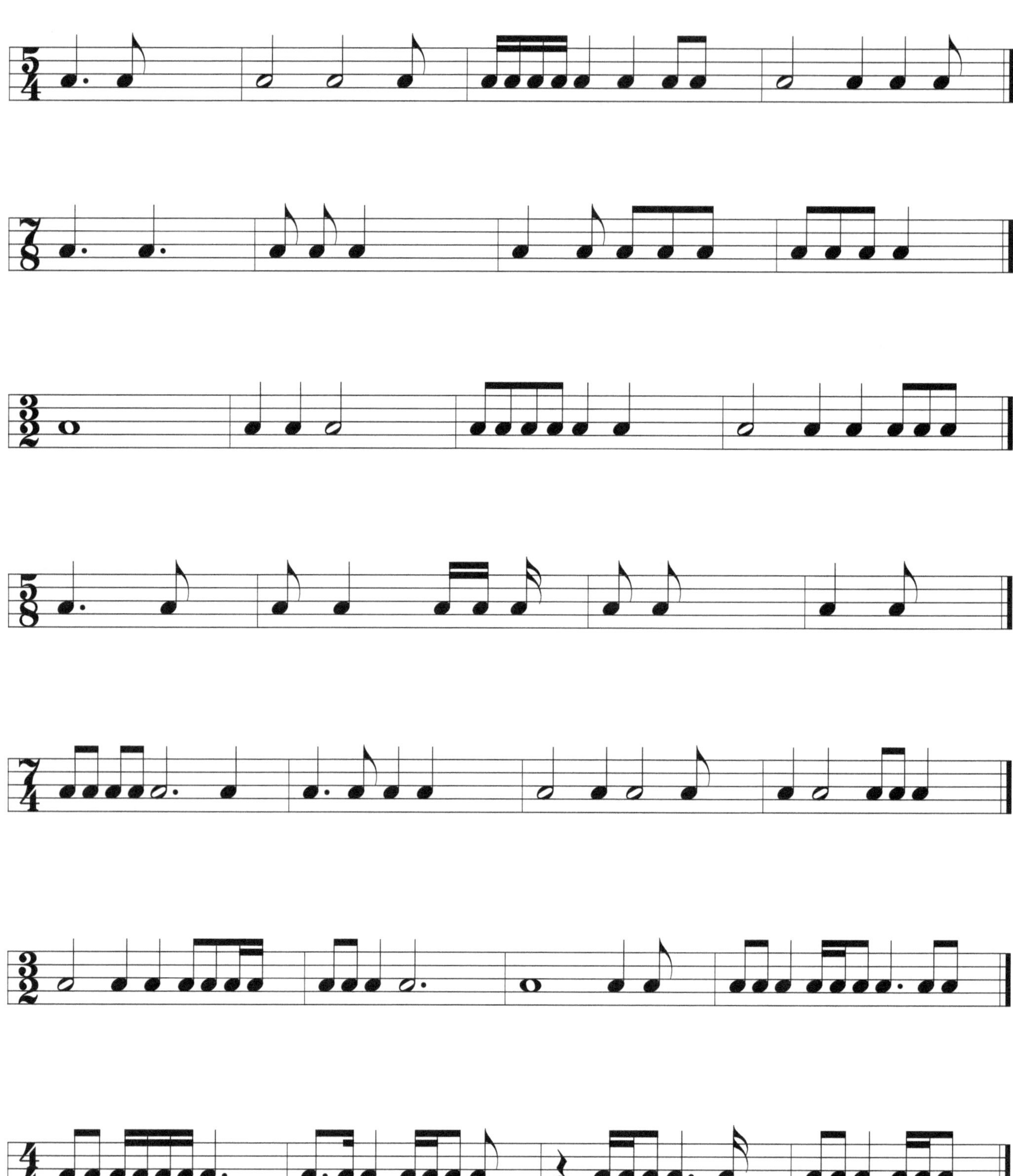

4. Write the beats underneath the notes/rests in each example. Then add the three missing bar lines and a double bar line. Then practice singing each example on "La."

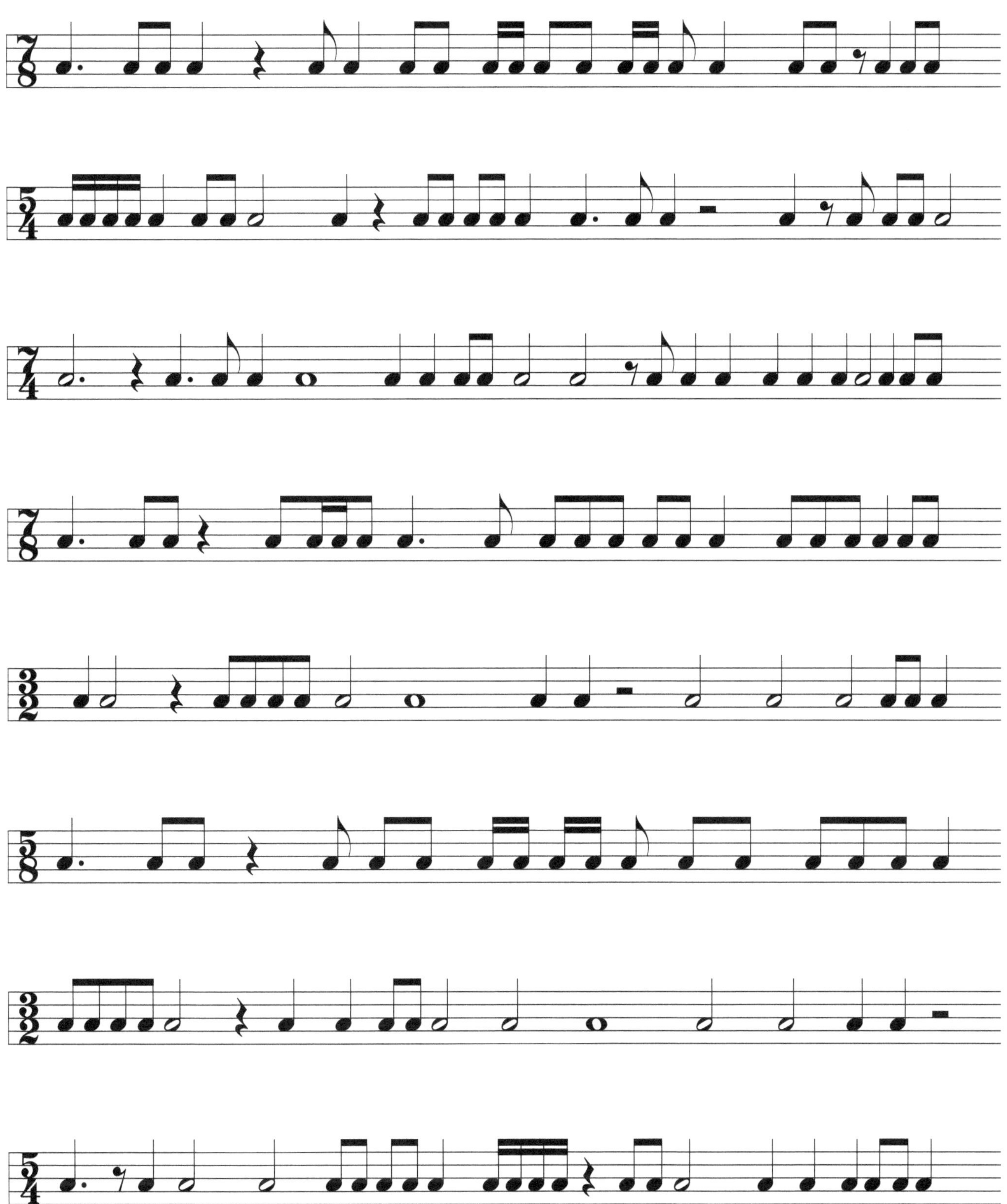

Lesson 4: Triads and Inversions

A **Triad**, or 3-note chord, is formed when the first, third and fifth notes of a scale are sung or played, either consecutively or at the same time. The root, or the lowest note of a triad, determines its letter name.

An **inversion** of a triad/chord is simply rearranging the notes in a different order, much like juggling. The three notes in the triad do not change, but their order does. Look at the example below.

The root (F) has been colored in so you can follow where it goes.

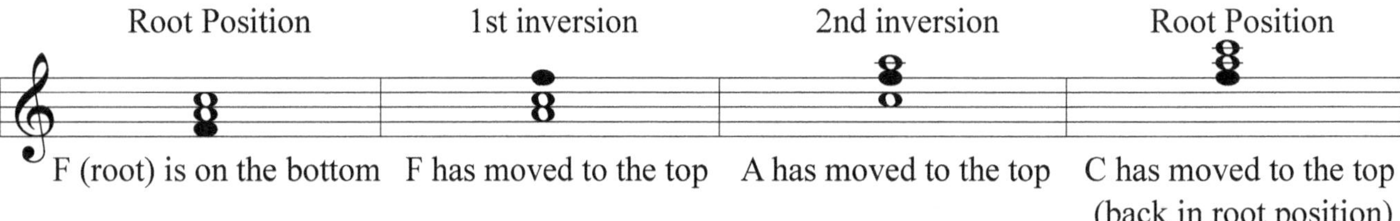

An easy way to remember the inversions is to say:

"One on the top is 1st inversion."

"Two on the top is 2nd inversion."

Inversions of triads/chords are used not only in the piano accompaniment of the songs we sing, but also in choral arrangements. As a singer, it's always important to know where the root of the chord is, so we know how to find our notes (while singing in an ensemble, choir, or duet).

Let's look more carefully at the note order in an inversion.

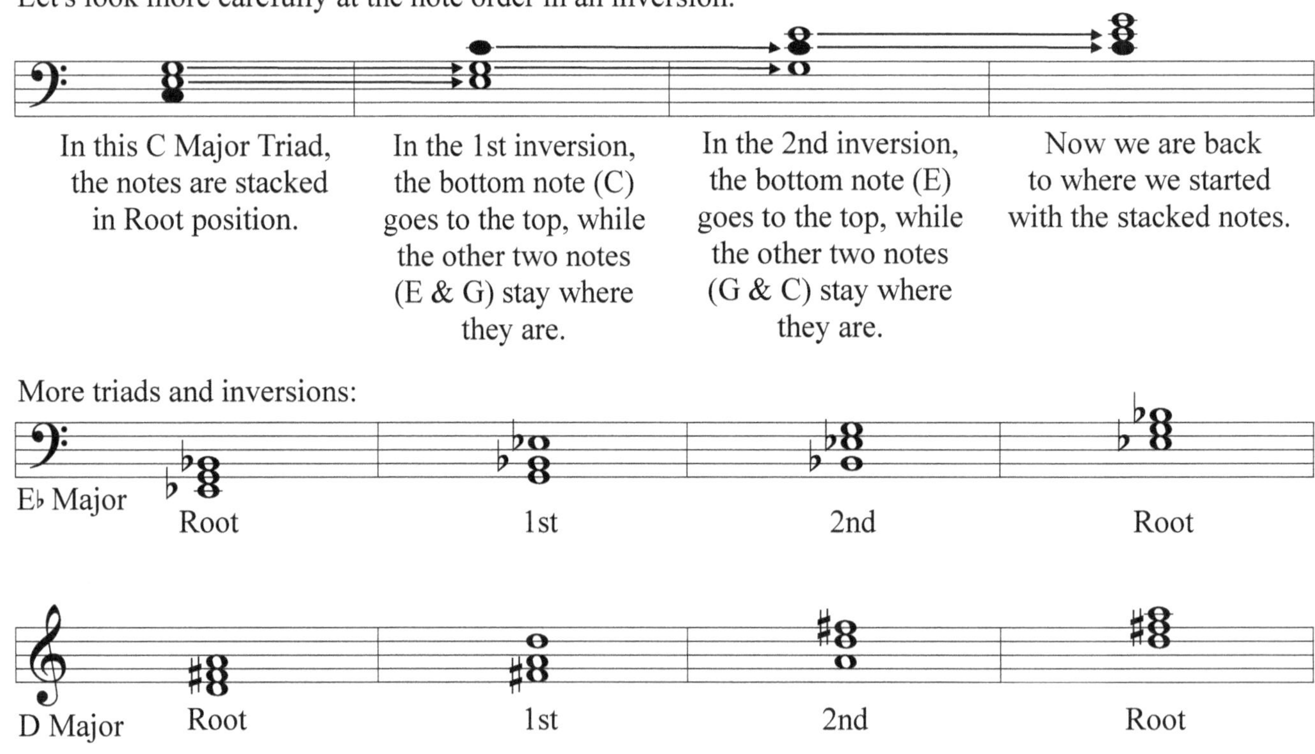

Review: Lesson 4

1. Name the inversion of each triad (Root position, 1st or 2nd inversion). The first one is done for you.

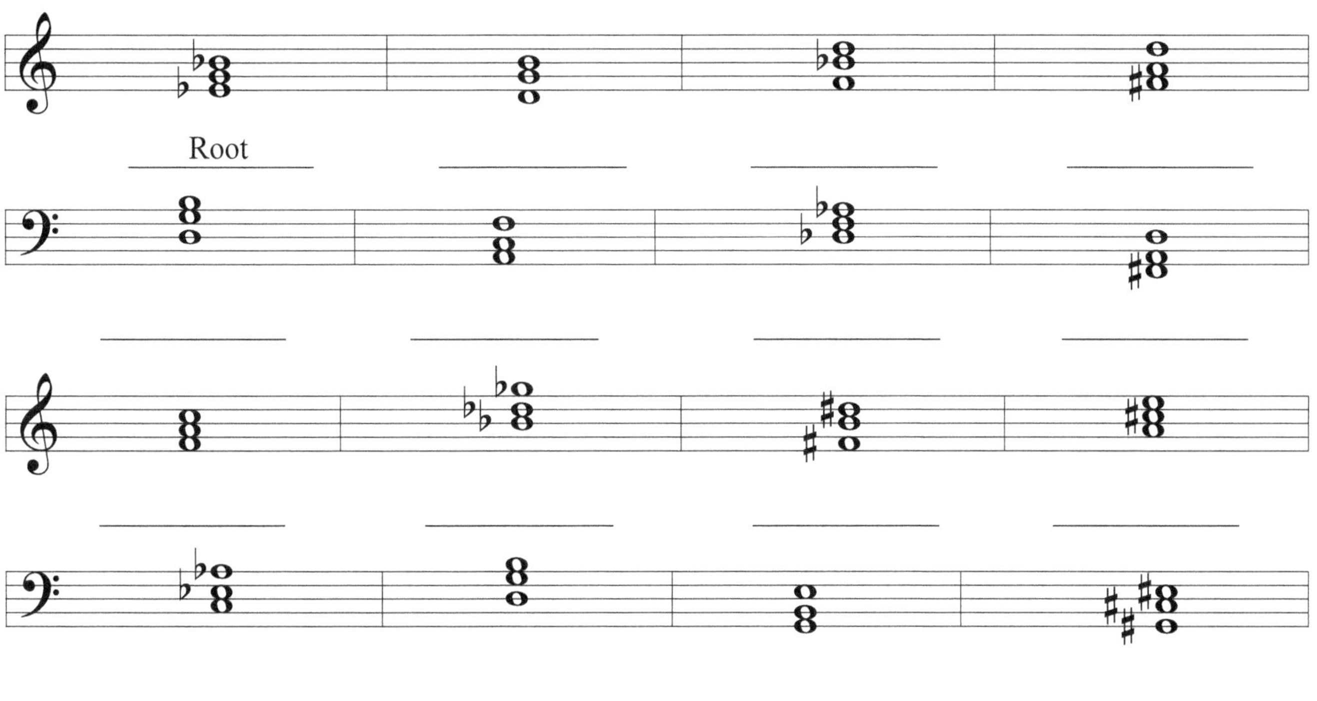

2. Write each triad in the requested inversion. Add the necessary accidentals to each triad. Do not use a key signature. The first one is done for you.

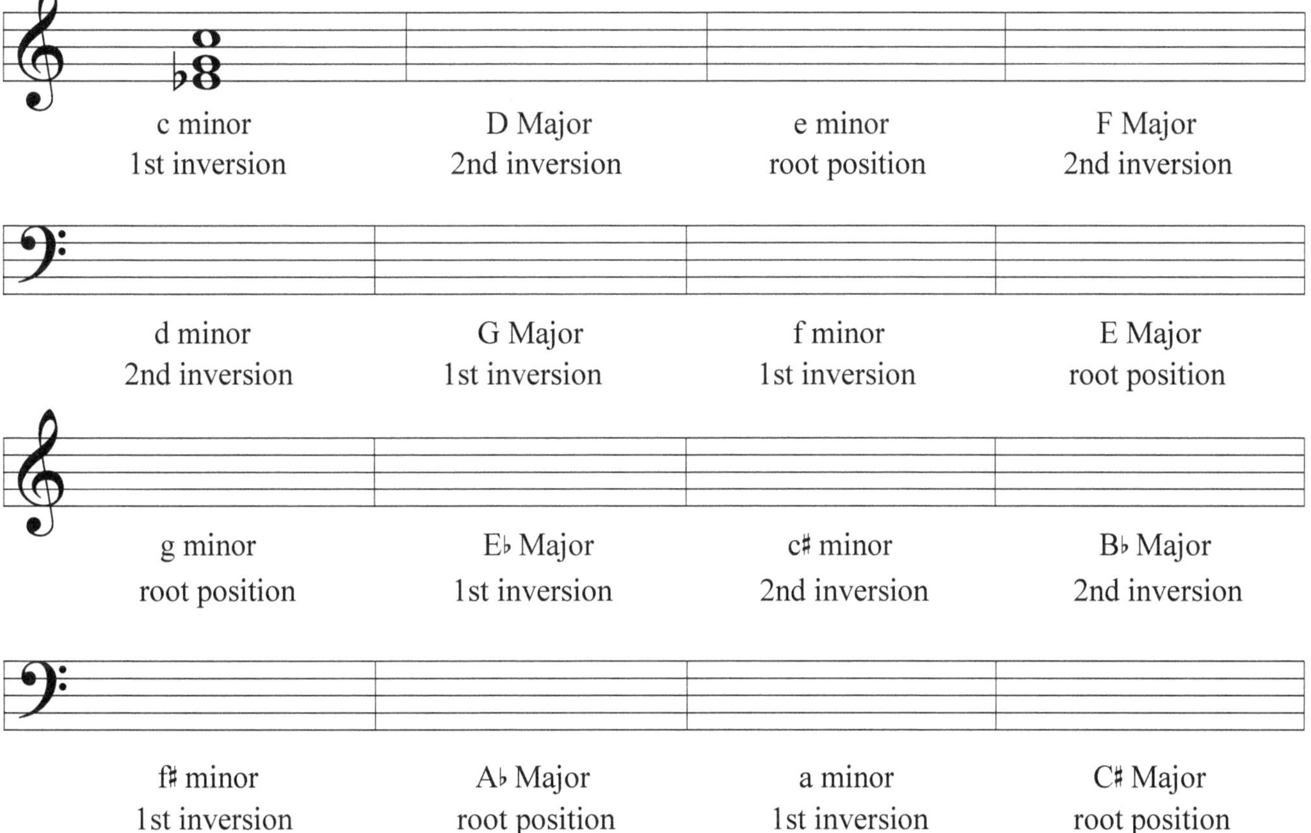

Lesson 5: The Dominant 7th Chord

The Dominant triad (3-note chord) is a Major triad, built on the 5th note of a Major Scale.

A Dominant 7th chord is a chord built on the dominant (5th note of a Major scale) containing a Major triad and an added minor seventh (for example: G-B-D-F in C Major).

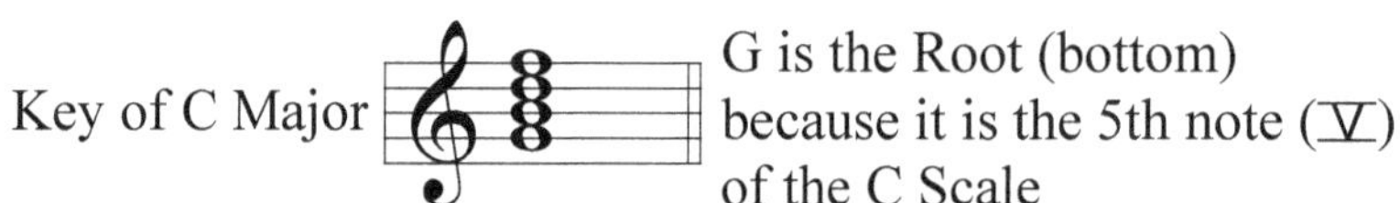

The Dominant 7th chord or V 7 is the most commonly heard version of a V chord in music. It is usually written in an inversion, but both the root and inversion are notated below.

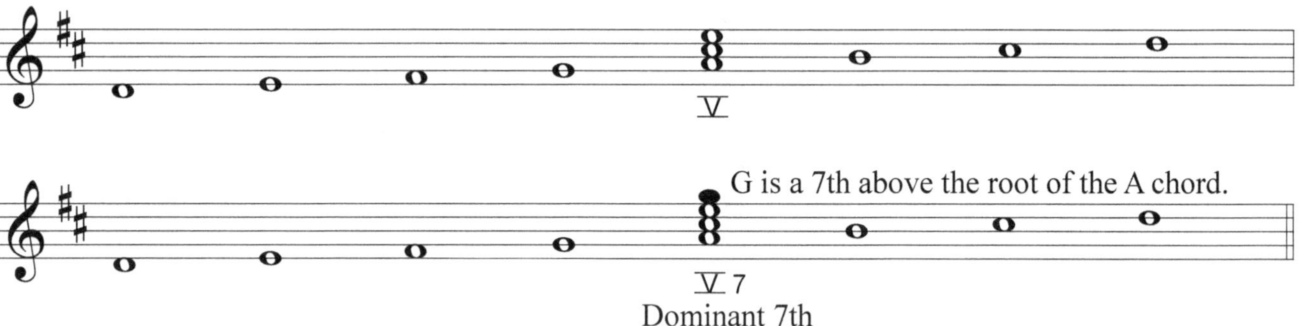

Here is a Root position Dominant and Dominant 7th chord in the key of A♭ Major.

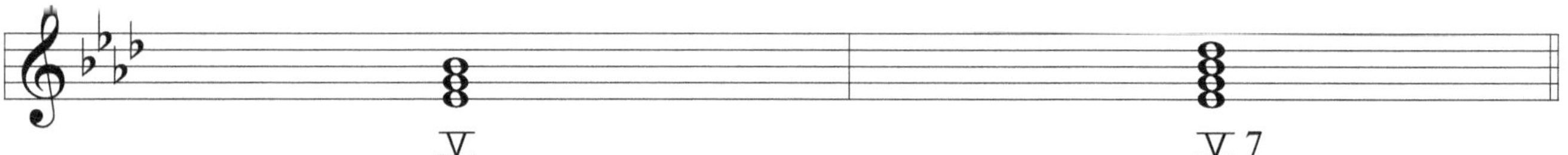

Inversions of Dominant 7th Chords

Dominant 7th chords have three inversions because there are 4 notes. Look at the example below. Follow the Root (G) for each of the inversions.

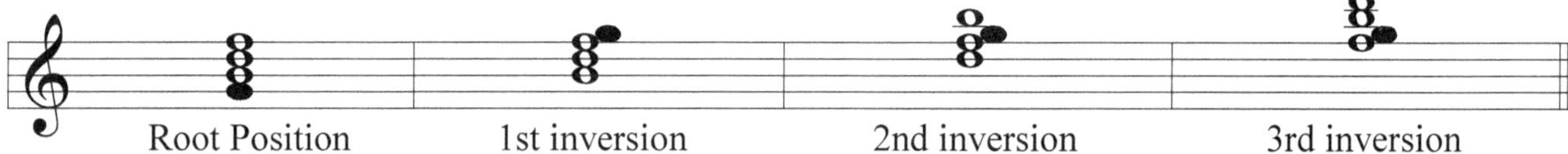

In chord progressions, the 1st inversion of the Dominant 7th chord is typically used and the 5th is often omitted. Since the 5th note is the same in Major and minor keys, removing it doesn't change the quality.

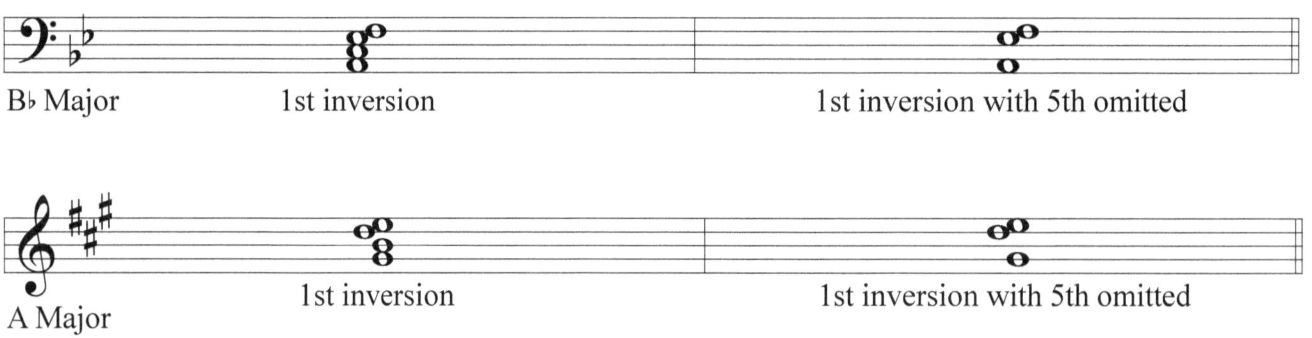

Dominant 7th chords can be tricky. When identifying these chords, remember that "Dominant" means 5; the 5th note of the scale, and the 5 is represented by the Roman Numeral V which identifies the 5th note of the scale.

When you see a Dominant 7th chord, and you are trying to figure out what key it belongs to, look at the bottom note.

For instance, in the following example, there is a D in the Bass, an F♯ stacked on top of it, an A, then an C. Because this is a Root position **Dominant** chord, and the root is a D, D is the 5th note of the Major key. If D is 5 and you count down a 5th to find the Major key, then the Major key is G. This Dominant 7th chord belongs to the key of G Major.

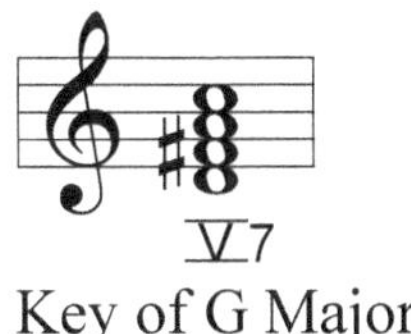

Tip: In order to find out what Major key a Root position Dominant chord belongs to, count down a 5th.

Here are more examples of naming the keys to which each Dominant 7th (V 7) chords belong.

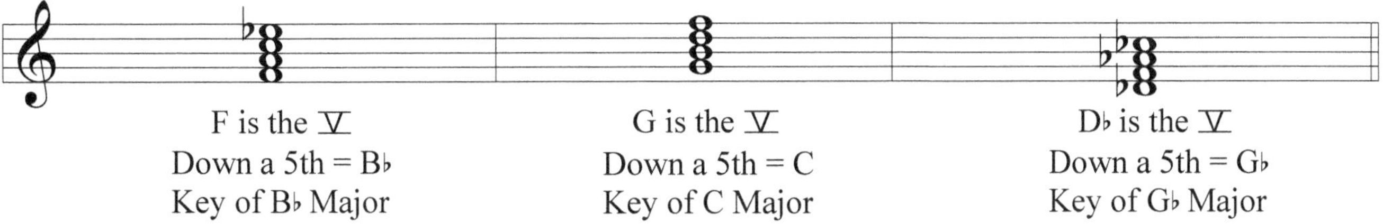

If you are trying to draw a Dominant 7th chord in a Major key:
1. Draw the 5th note of the Major scale (as the root)
2. Stack thirds. It's that easy! Follow the steps below:

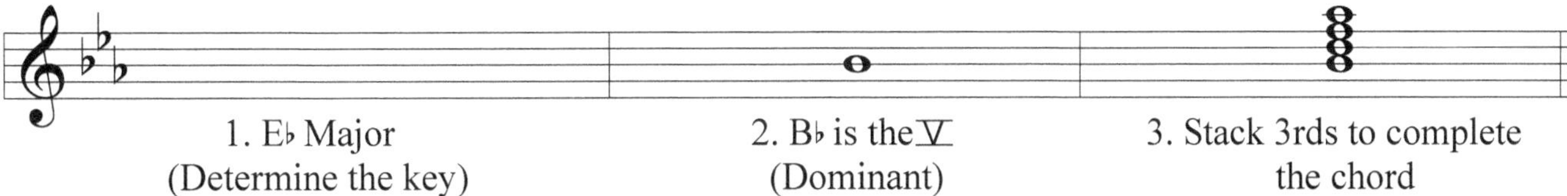

Here are more examples of the steps to draw a Dominant 7th chord when given the Major key.

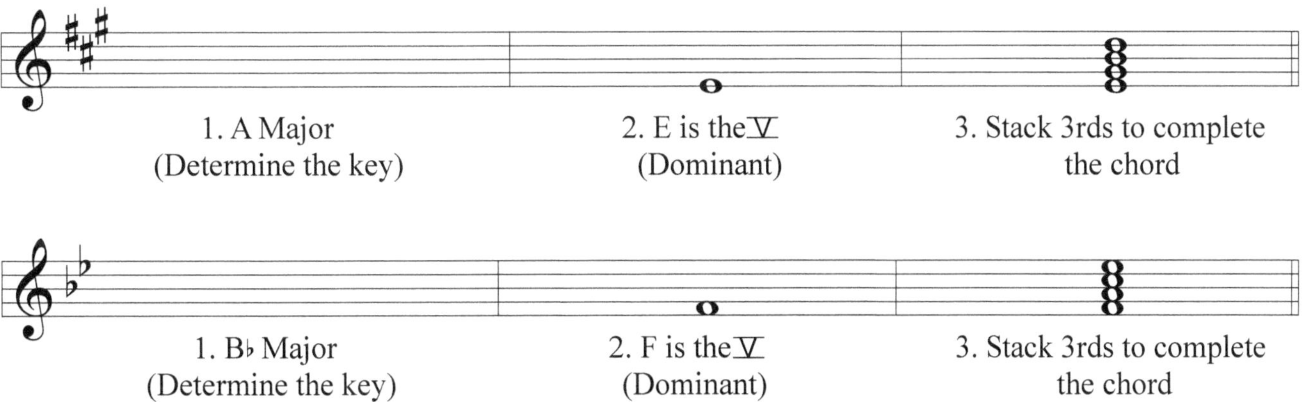

Review: Lesson 5

1. Name the Major key to which each of these Dominant 7th (V7) belongs. Remember to count down a 5th to find the answer.

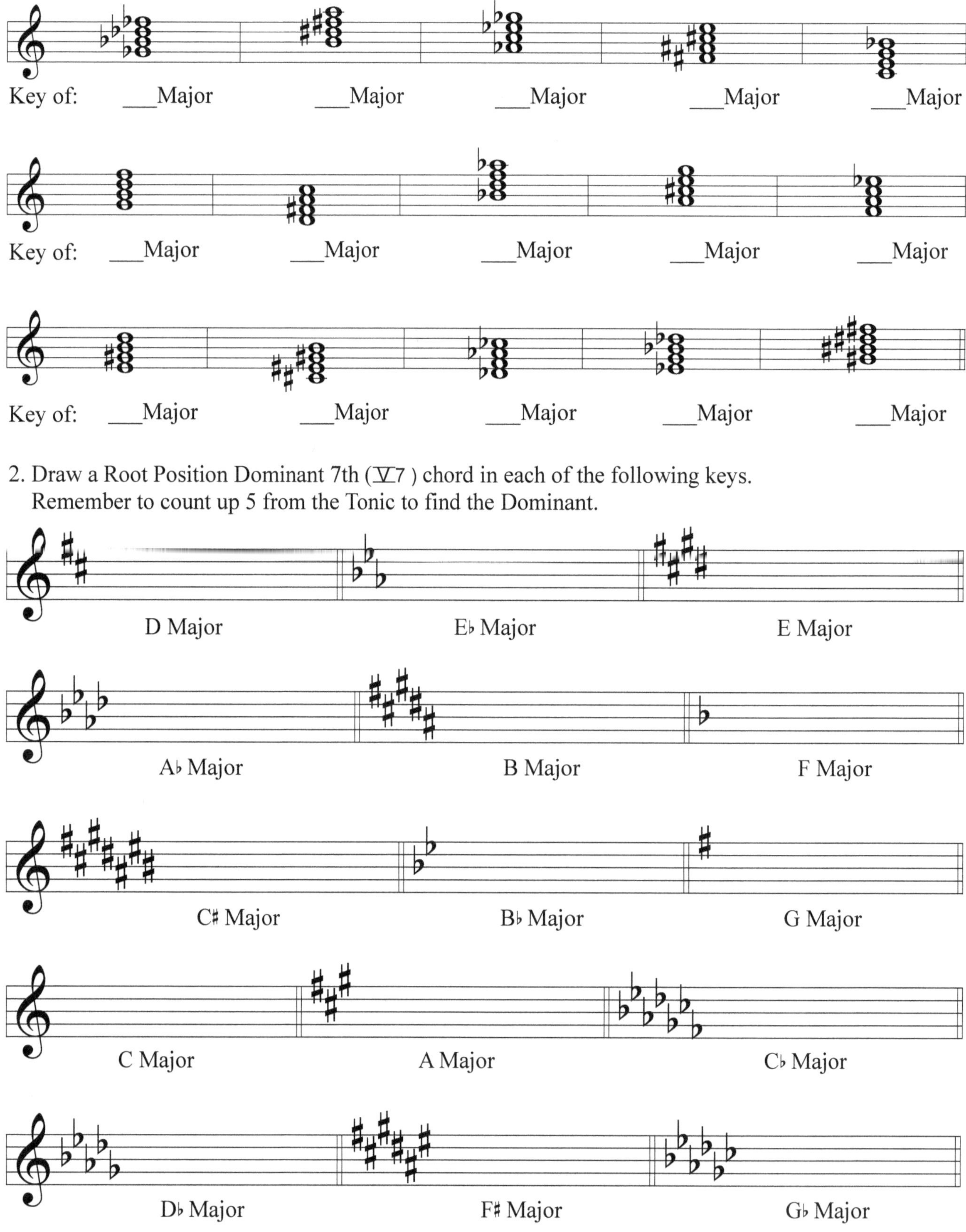

2. Draw a Root Position Dominant 7th (V7) chord in each of the following keys. Remember to count up 5 from the Tonic to find the Dominant.

D Major E♭ Major E Major

A♭ Major B Major F Major

C♯ Major B♭ Major G Major

C Major A Major C♭ Major

D♭ Major F♯ Major G♭ Major

3. Draw a 1st, 2nd & 3rd inversion after the given Dominant 7th chord. The first one is done for you.

Key of B♭ Maj.

Root Position 1st inversion 2nd inversion 3rd inversion

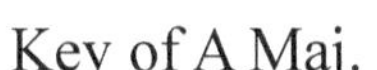

Key of A Maj.

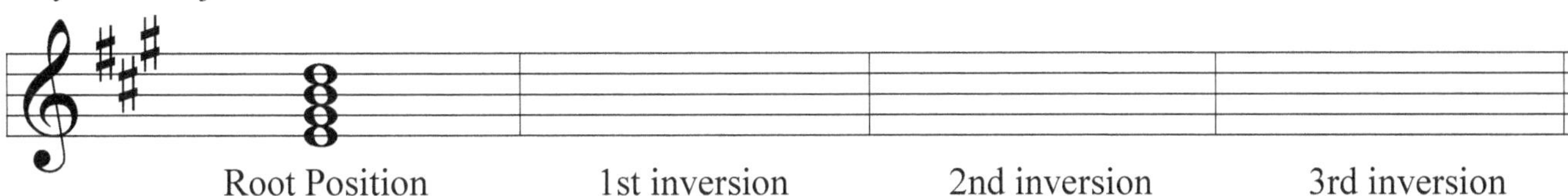

Root Position 1st inversion 2nd inversion 3rd inversion

Key of E♭ Maj.

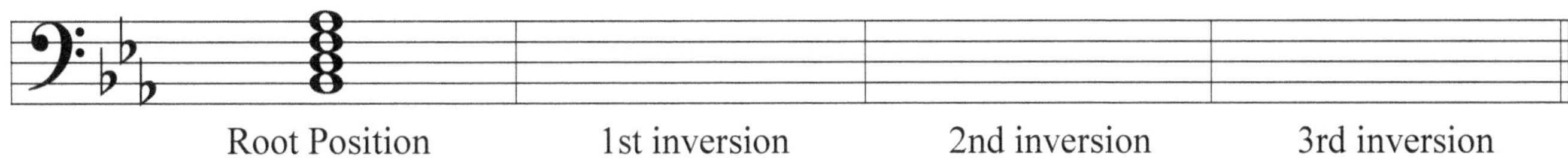

Root Position 1st inversion 2nd inversion 3rd inversion

Key of F♯ Maj.

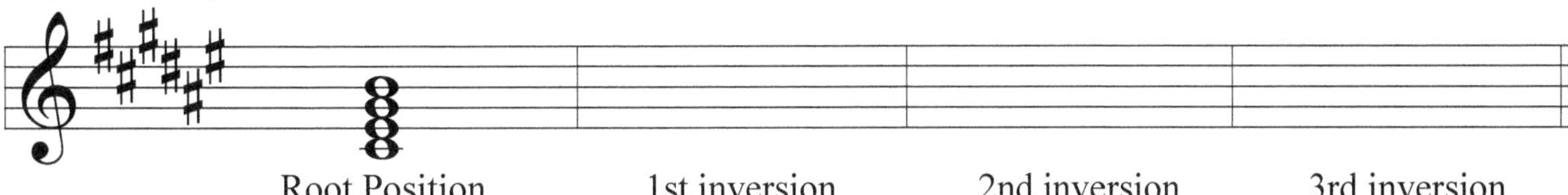

Root Position 1st inversion 2nd inversion 3rd inversion

Key of G♭ Maj.

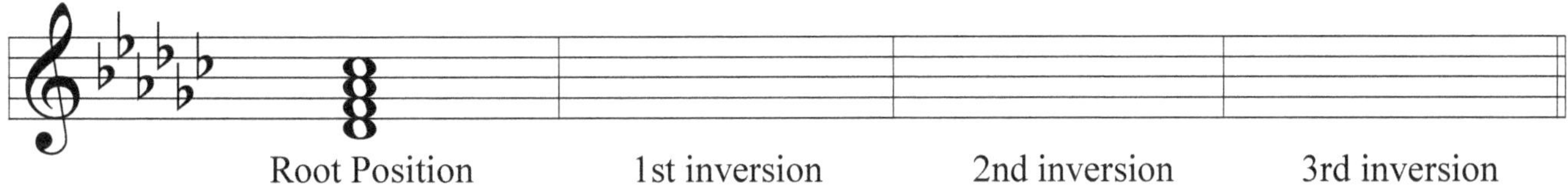

Root Position 1st inversion 2nd inversion 3rd inversion

Key of D Maj.

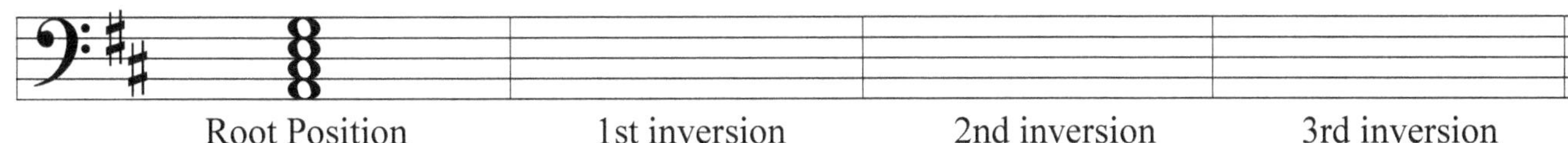

Root Position 1st inversion 2nd inversion 3rd inversion

Key of A♭ Maj.

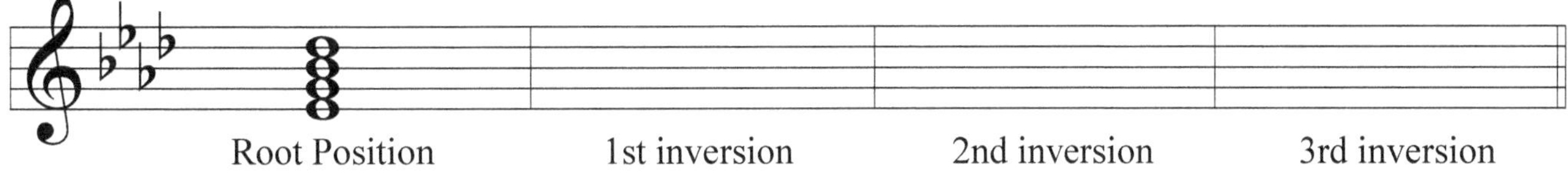

Root Position 1st inversion 2nd inversion 3rd inversion

4. Check the correct inversion for the following Dominant 7th chords.

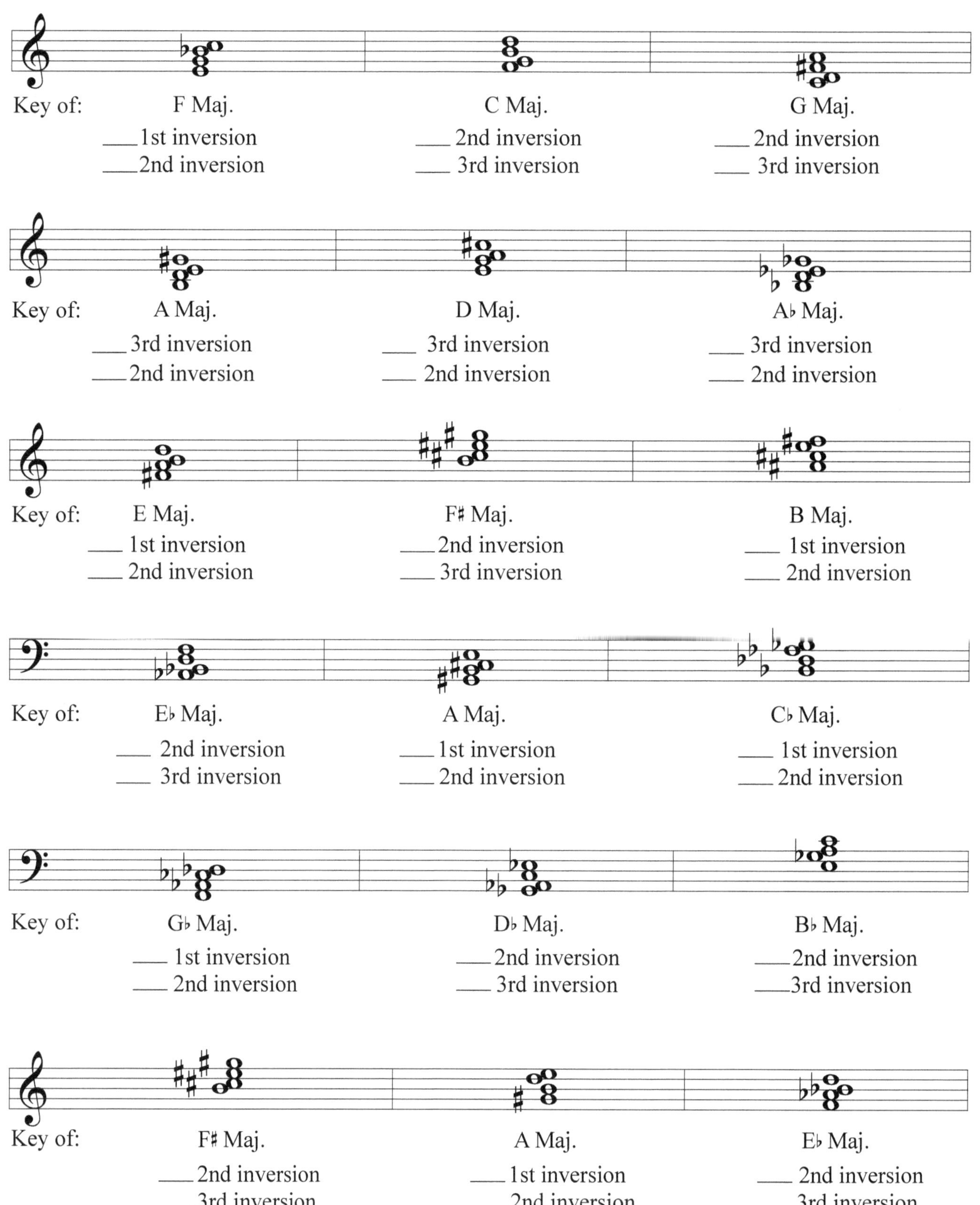

Review: Lessons 1-5

1. Use whole notes and accidentals to complete each scale. Draw an **ascending** scale in the first measure and a **descending** scale in the 2nd measure. Do not use a key signature.

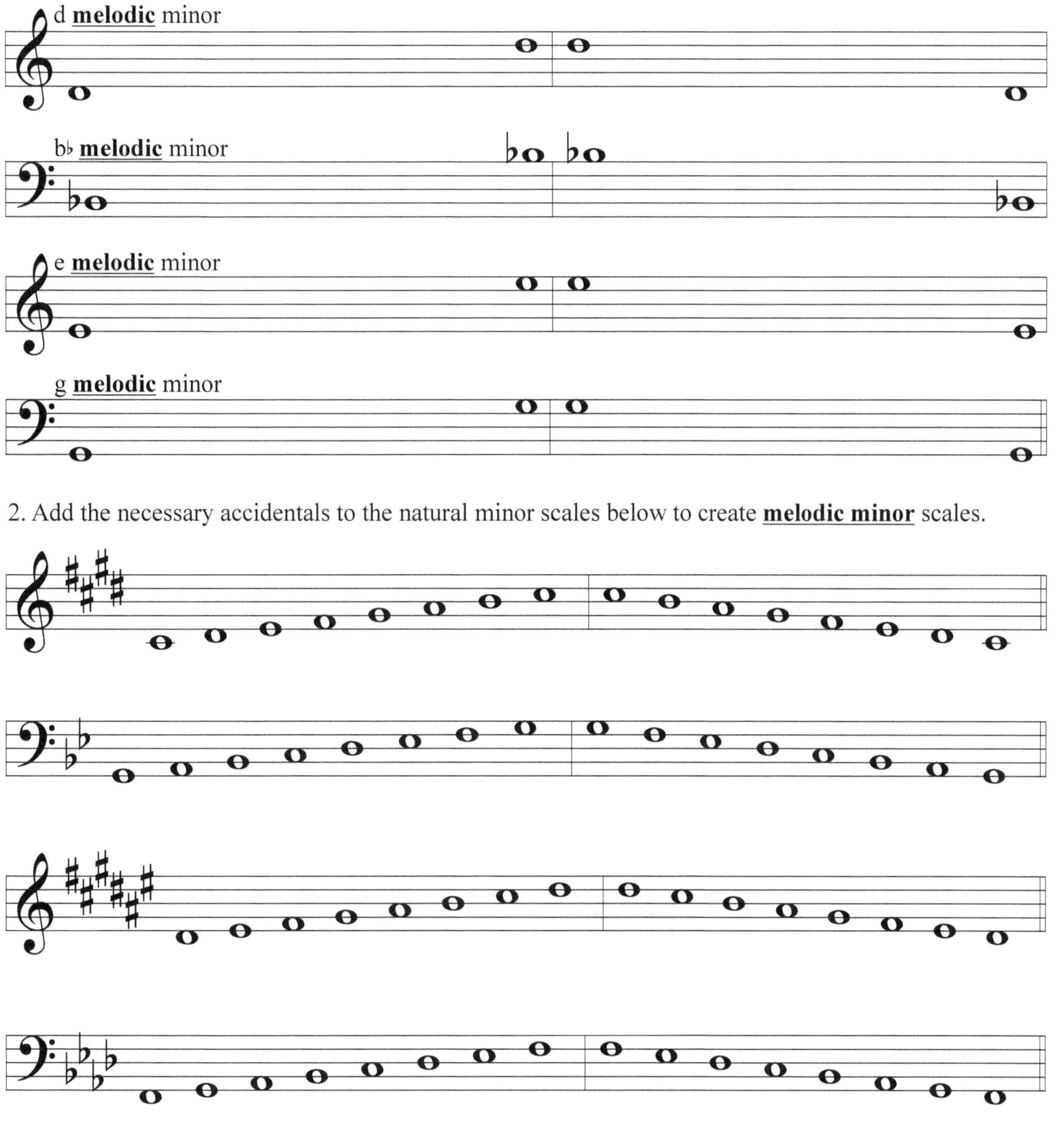

2. Add the necessary accidentals to the natural minor scales below to create **melodic minor** scales.

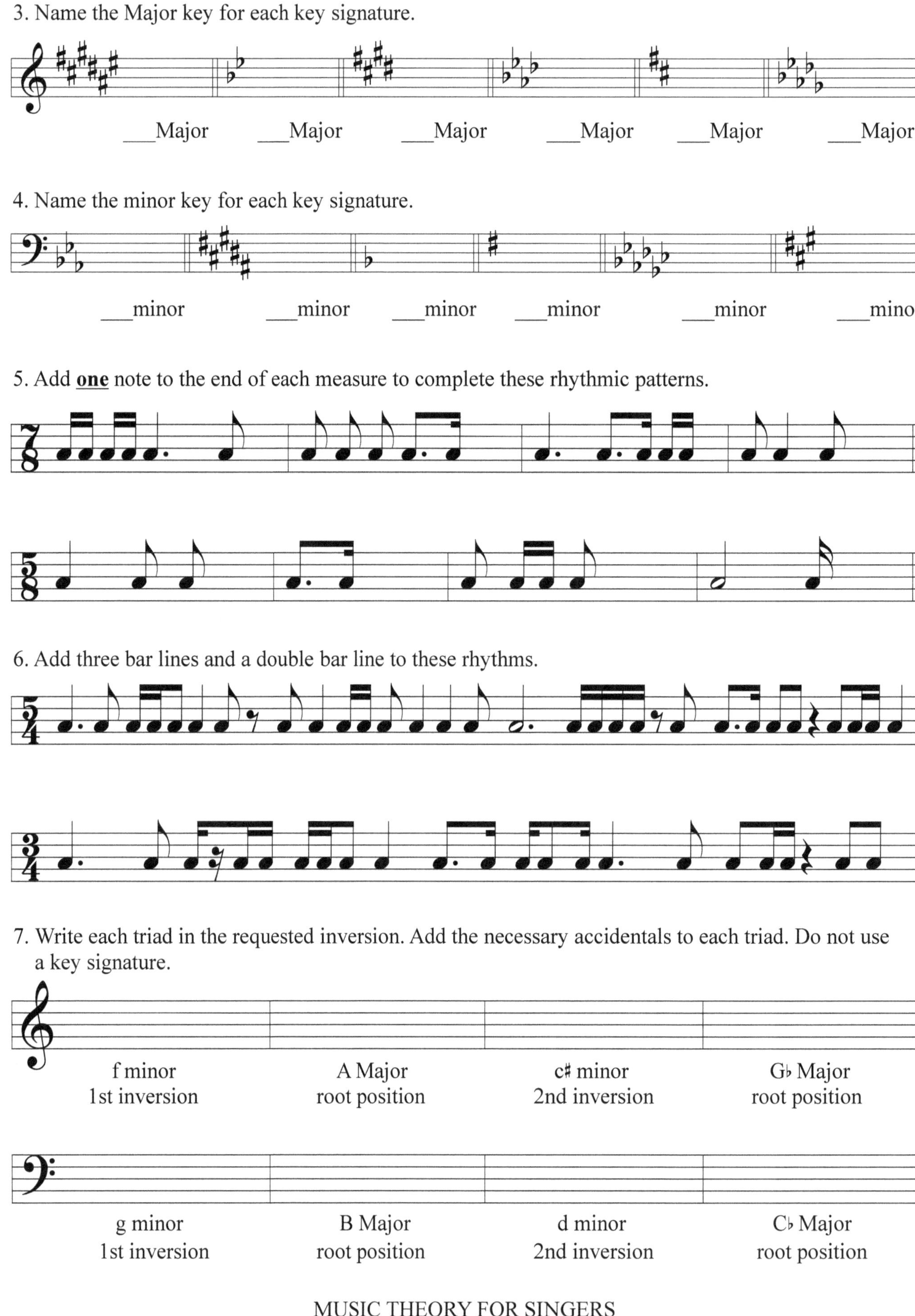
3. Name the Major key for each key signature.
___Major
___Major
___Major
___Major
___Major
___Major
4. Name the minor key for each key signature.
___minor
___minor
___minor
___minor
___minor
___minor
5. Add one note to the end of each measure to complete these rhythmic patterns.
6. Add three bar lines and a double bar line to these rhythms.
7. Write each triad in the requested inversion. Add the necessary accidentals to each triad. Do not use a key signature.
f minor
1st inversion
A Major
root position
c♯ minor
2nd inversion
G♭ Major
root position
g minor
1st inversion
B Major
root position
d minor
2nd inversion
C♭ Major
root position

8. Name the Major key to which each of these Dominant 7ths (V7) belongs.

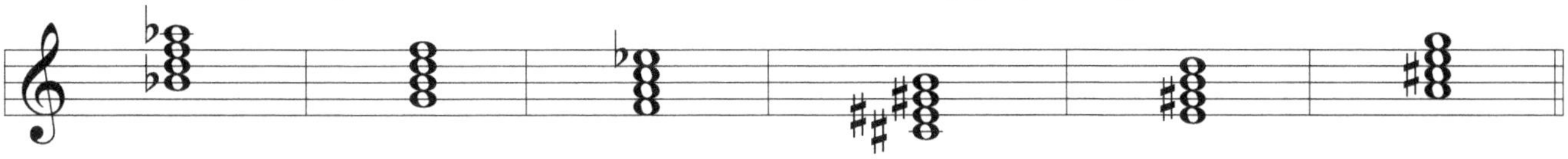

Key: ______ ______ ______ ______ ______ ______

9. Draw a root position **Dominant 7th** chord in each of the following keys.

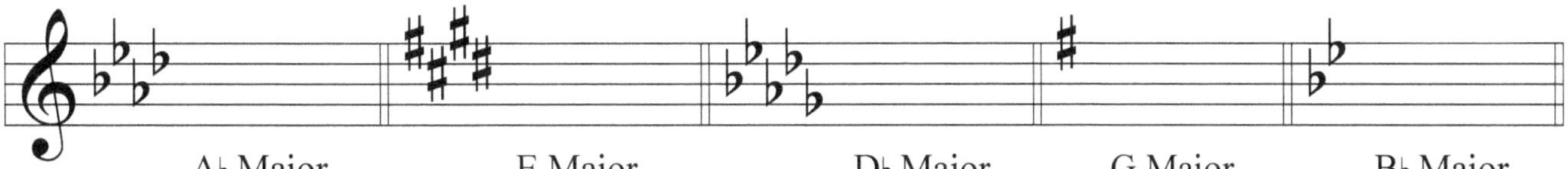

A♭ Major E Major D♭ Major G Major B♭ Major

10. Check the correct inversion for the following Dominant 7th chords.

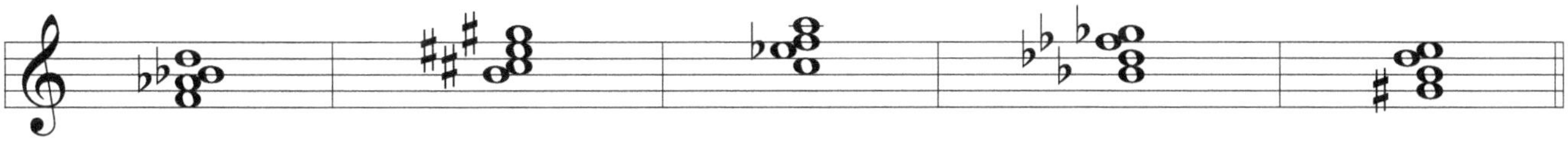

Key of: E♭ Maj.	F♯ Maj.	B♭ Maj.	C♭ Maj.	A Maj.
___ 1st inversion	___ 2nd inversion	___ 1st inversion	___ 1st inversion	___ 2nd inversion
___ 2nd inversion	___ 3rd inversion	___ 2nd inversion	___ 2nd inversion	___ 1st inversion

11. Draw the 1st, 2nd and 3rd inversions of the given **Dominant 7th** chords.

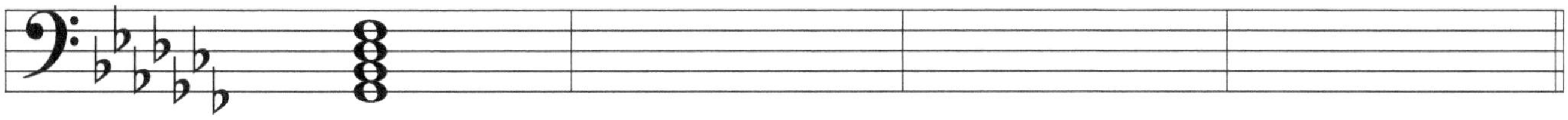

C♭ Maj. Root 1st inversion 2nd inversion 3rd inversion

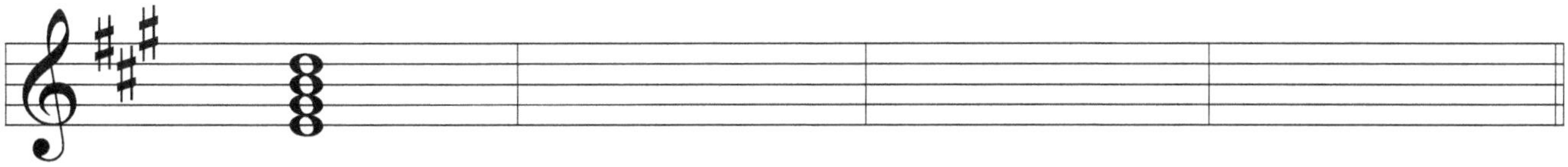

A Maj. Root 1st inversion 2nd inversion 3rd inversion

Lesson 6: The diminished 7th Chord

A diminished 7th chord is a four note chord that consists of a diminished triad plus the interval of a diminished 7th. Another way to think of a diminished 7th chord is "stacked minor 3rds." That is, there are three minor 3rds stacked on top of each other.

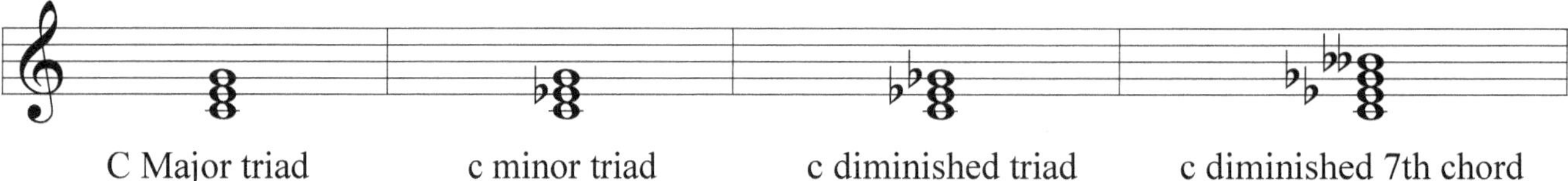

Here are the 3 minor triads that make up the diminished 7th chord.

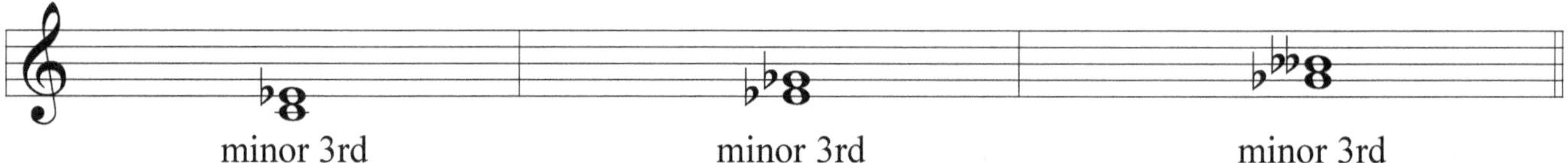

In Jazz music, the diminished 7th chord is usually based on the lowered third scale degree, serving as a passing chord between the tonic triad and the supertonic triad: in G Major, this would be the progression b minor - b♭ diminished 7th - a minor.

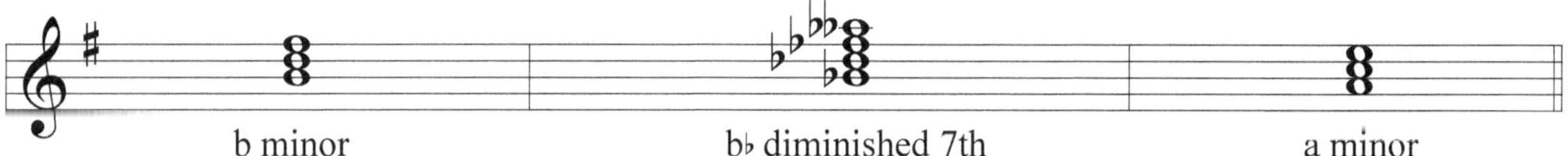

The diminished 7th chord can also function in chord progressions, much like the Dominant 7th chord. It is often used in modulations, especially in 19th century Romantic period music. Because the diminished 7th chord is made up of minor 3rds, the root of the chord is not easy to distinguish. This means, the chord may be enharmonically written in four different ways, (inversions) without changing the sound. Thus, the diminished 7th chord can serve several functions in chord progressions.

Inversions of diminished 7th Chords

Follow the Root (F) for each of the inversions.

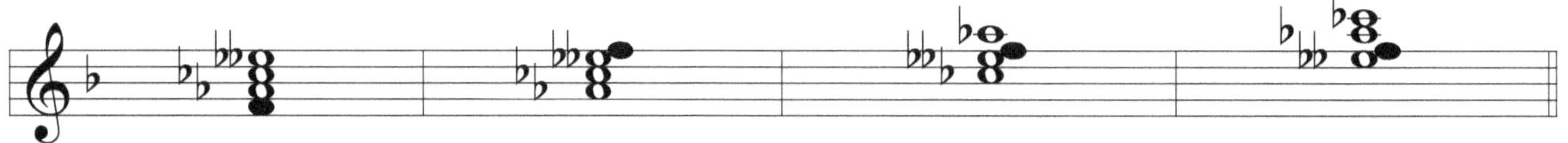

In diminished 7th chords, all four notes are used. Taking out one note of the chord changes the quality of the chord. This is different in the case of dominant 7th chords, where removing the 5th doesn't change its quality.

Dominant 7th Chords versus diminished 7th Chords

The big difference between Dominant 7th chords and diminished 7th chords is a Dominant 7th chord begins on the 5th note (Dominant) of the scale, while a diminished 7th chord can begin on any note of the scale.

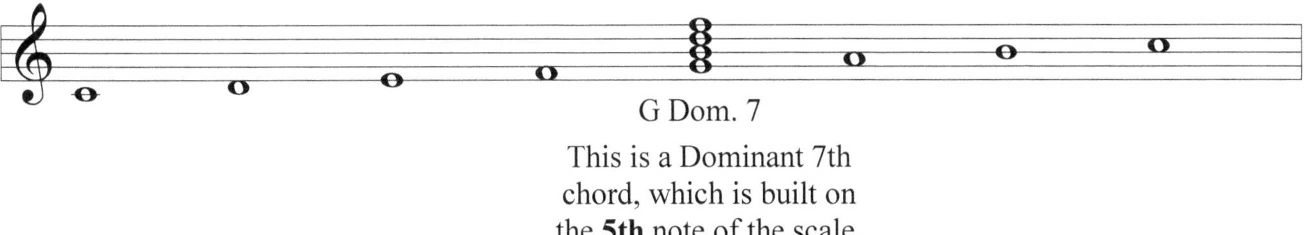

G Dom. 7

This is a Dominant 7th chord, which is built on the **5th** note of the scale.

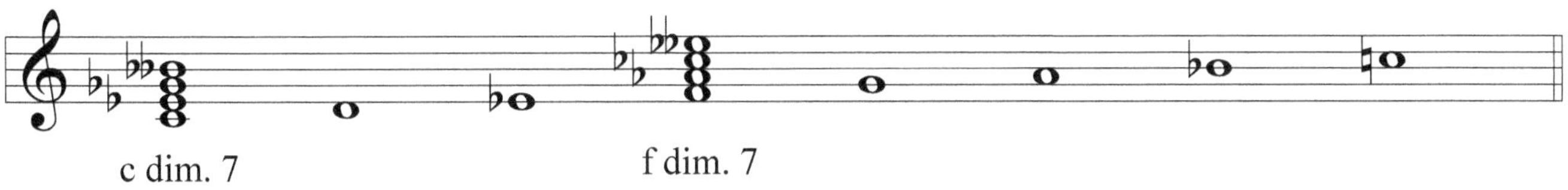

c dim. 7 f dim. 7

These are both diminished 7th chords. Diminished 7th chords can be built on **any** note of the scale.

Below are examples of 7th chords in the keys of G, B♭, D & E♭ Major. The first examples are all Dominant 7th chords, the second examples are all diminished 7th chords.

DOMINANT 7TH CHORDS

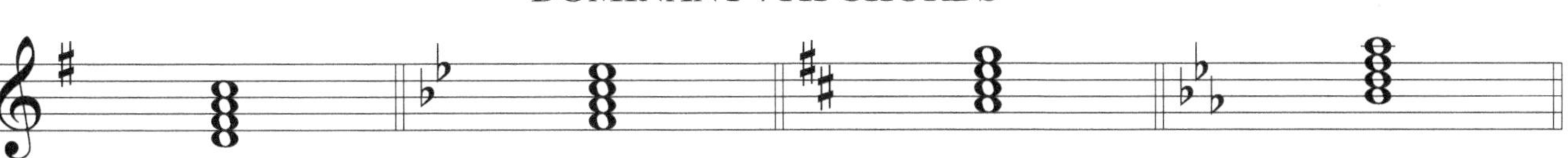

D Dom. 7th F Dom. 7th A Dom. 7th B♭ Dom. 7th

The root of each of the above chords is the 5th note of the Major scale. For example, the first measure is in the key of G Major and D is the 5th note of the G scale.

DIMINISHED 7TH CHORDS

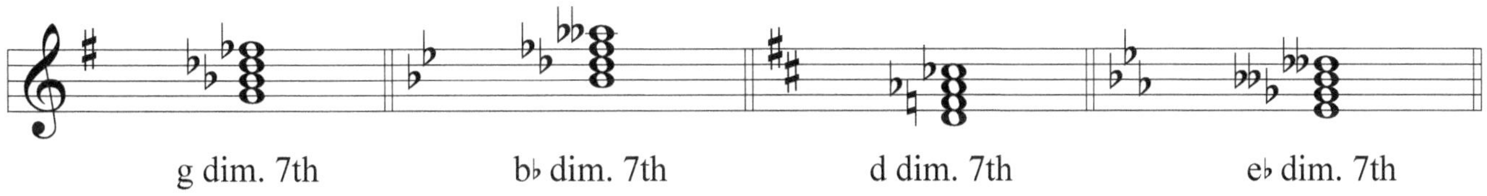

g dim. 7th b♭ dim. 7th d dim. 7th e♭ dim. 7th

The root of each of the above chords is the first note of the Major scale. For example, the first measure is in the key of G major and G is the first note of the G scale.

Review: Lesson 6

1. Add accidentals to create the requested chords. The Major chord is given.
   The first one is done for you.

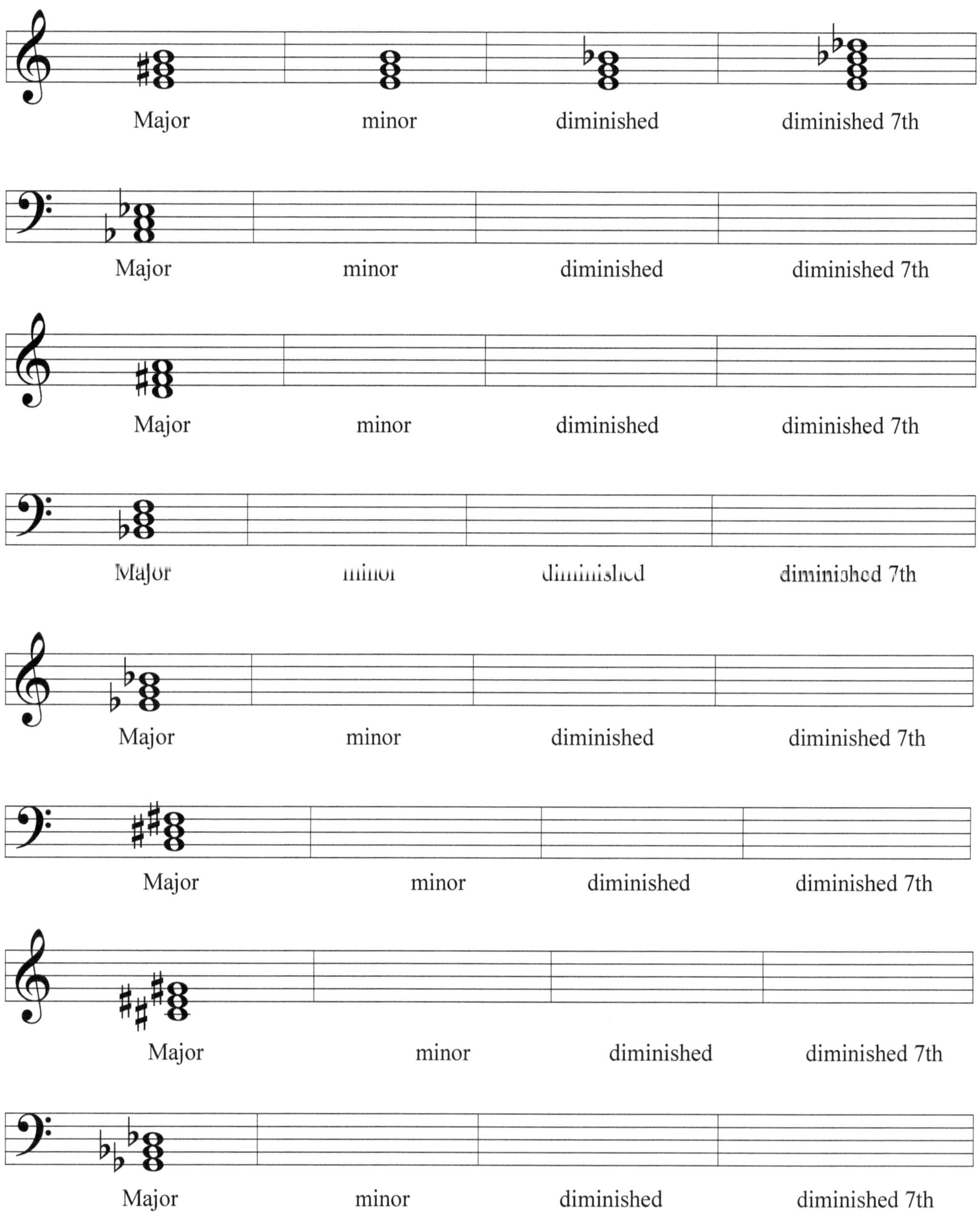

2. Draw the 1st, 2nd and 3rd inversions of the given **diminished 7th** chords. Be sure to add the necessary accidentals.

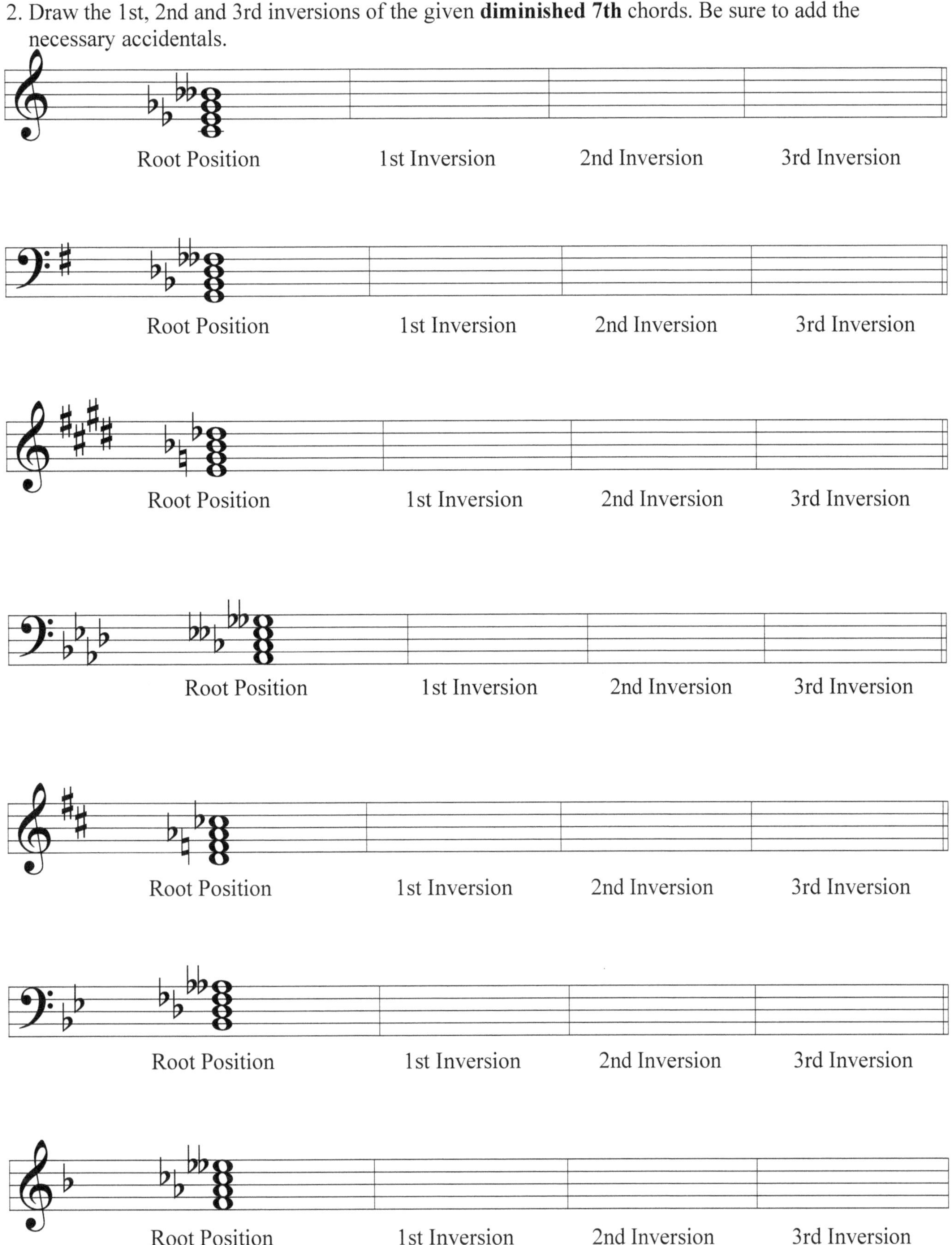

3. For the following examples, name the Major key, name the root of the chord then write its name. All examples are **either** a Dominant 7th or Diminished 7th chord. The first one is done for you.

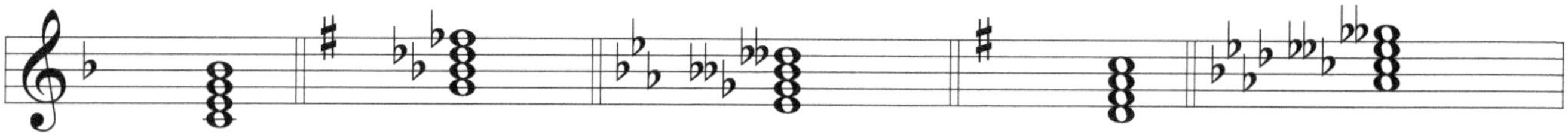

Key: F Maj.

Root: C

Name: C Dom. 7th

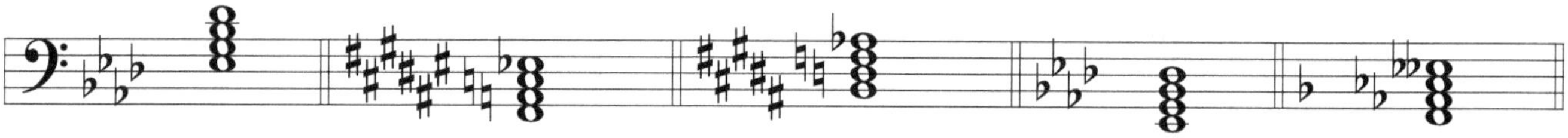

Key:

Root:

Name:

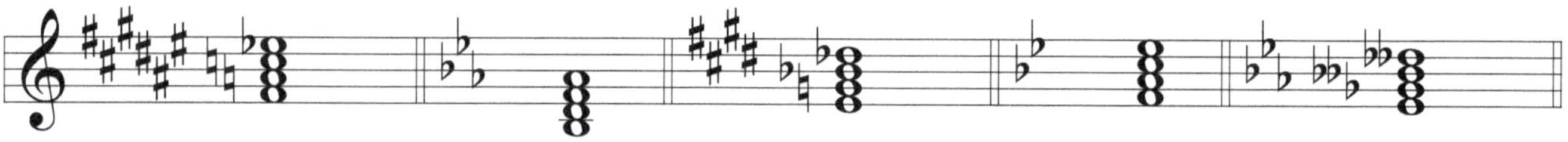

Key:

Root:

Name:

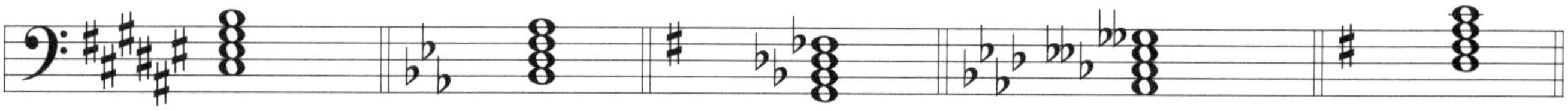

Key:

Root:

Name:

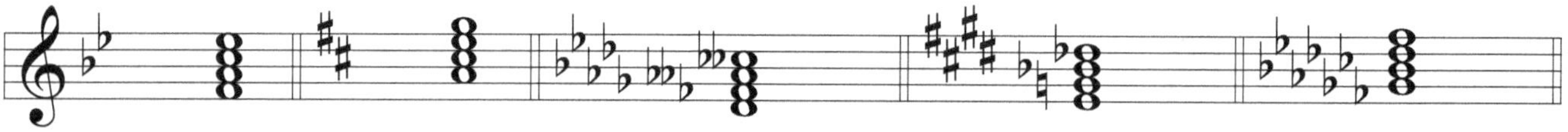

Key:

Root:

Name:

4. Draw the requested chords in Root position. Remember to add all necessary accidentals as well. When drawing Dominant 7th chords, remember to keep the Tonic key signature in mind. For example, in an A Dom. 7th chord, A is the 5th note of the D scale (F♯, C♯), so if there are F's and C's present in an A Dom. 7th chord, they must be sharps. The first ones are done for you.

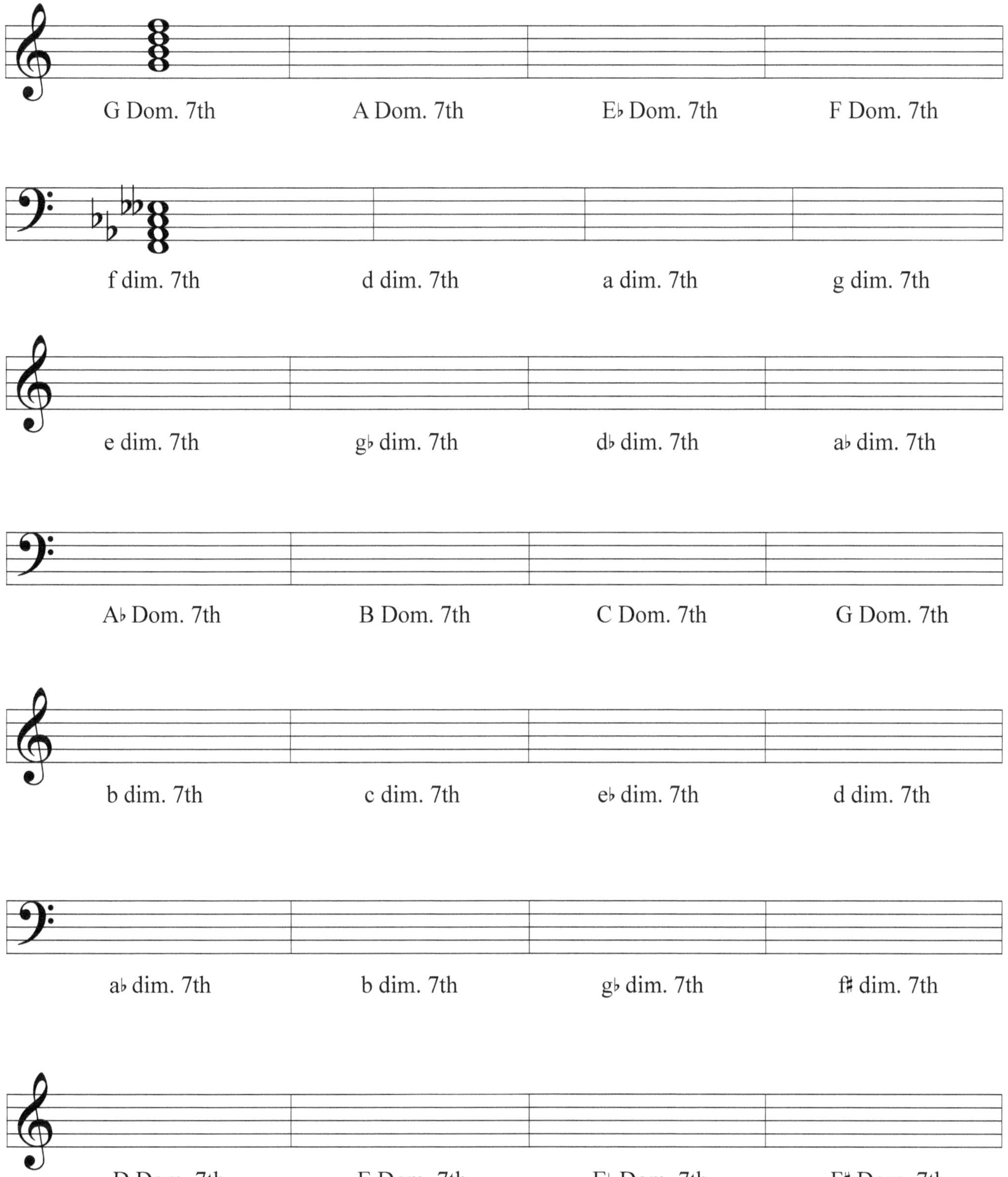

Lesson 7: Vocal Harmony

An important part of singing is being able to sing with others, either in a choir, a cappella group, duet, trio or other settings. Depending on your voice type, you may sing the melody or harmony. Once you are confident with key signatures and triads, you can begin to create your own harmonies or write your own music with ease.

The following examples show a simple melody, then that same melody with a harmony added the interval of a 3rd above.

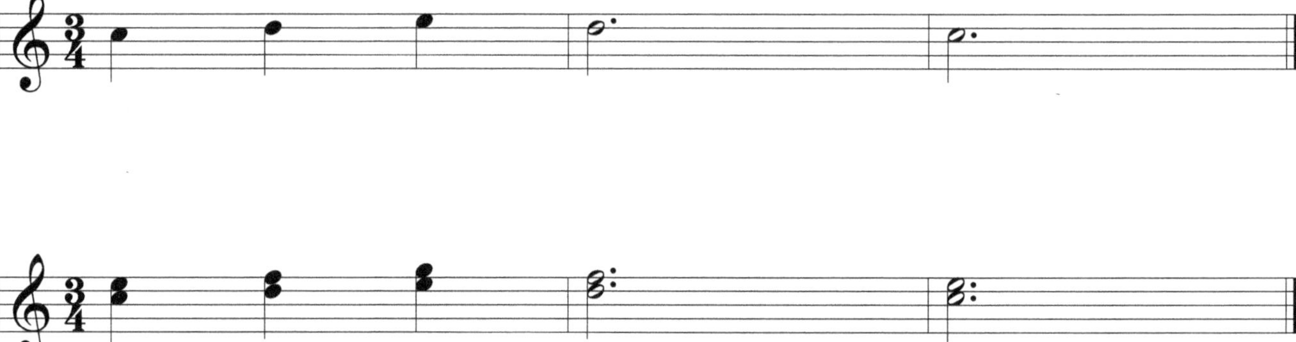

Here's an example with an added 3rd below the melody line. In the first example, the melody alone sounds like it's in D Major. When you add the harmony below, it creates a minor sound, thus would be considered to be in b minor.

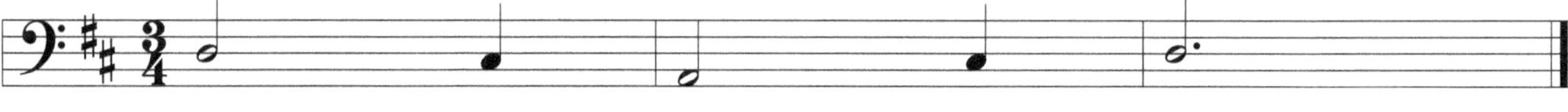

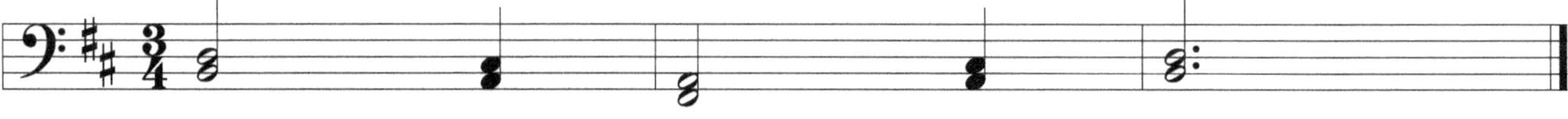

Another interval that leads to beautiful harmonies is the interval of a 6th. Look at the examples below.

This example, in b minor, shows the melody first, then the harmony added a 6th above.

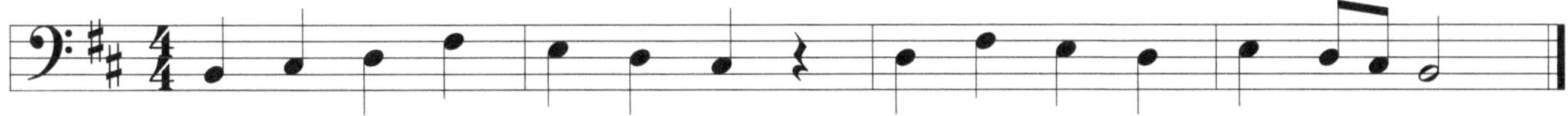

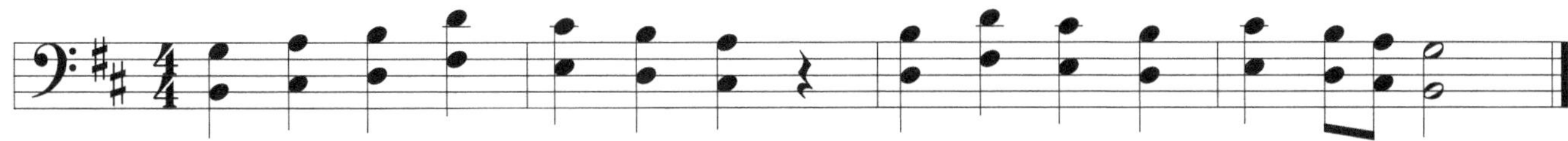

This example shows the melody line, then the same melody with the added harmony of a 6th below the melody line.

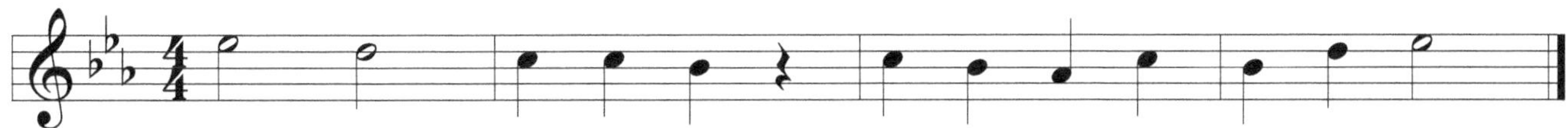

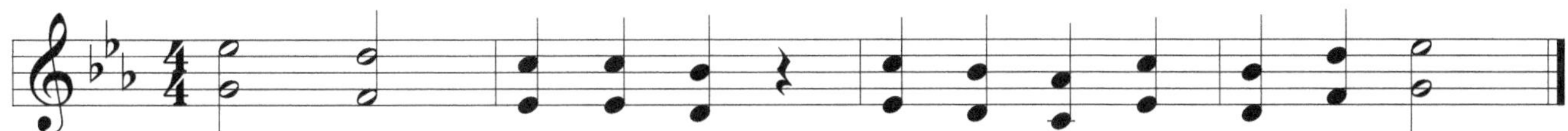

Harmonies can occur between any two notes. They don't have to be a 3rd or 6th apart. In order for a harmony to sound "consonant" (pleasing to the ears), the two notes need to belong together, according to the key signature. For instance, in the key of G Major, you can pair a G with a B or D and it will work well, because those are the notes in the G chord. If you pair a G with a C♯, it will not sound consonant because C♯ doesn't belong to the key of G. Look at the examples below.

The first example is one of Bach's chorales. This is written in four-part harmony (Soprano, Alto, Tenor & Bass). You'll notice that there is a myriad of intervals (2nds, 3rds, 4ths, etc.). In the Baroque period, harmonies were written according to rules called "Counterpoint," which means "note against note." There were certain harmonies that were forbidden, including the tritone (Aug.4th/dim.5th). Notice the F♯'s because the chorale is in g harmonic minor and the 7th tone is raised.

"Erhalt' uns, Herr, bei deinem Wort" - Johann Sebastian Bach

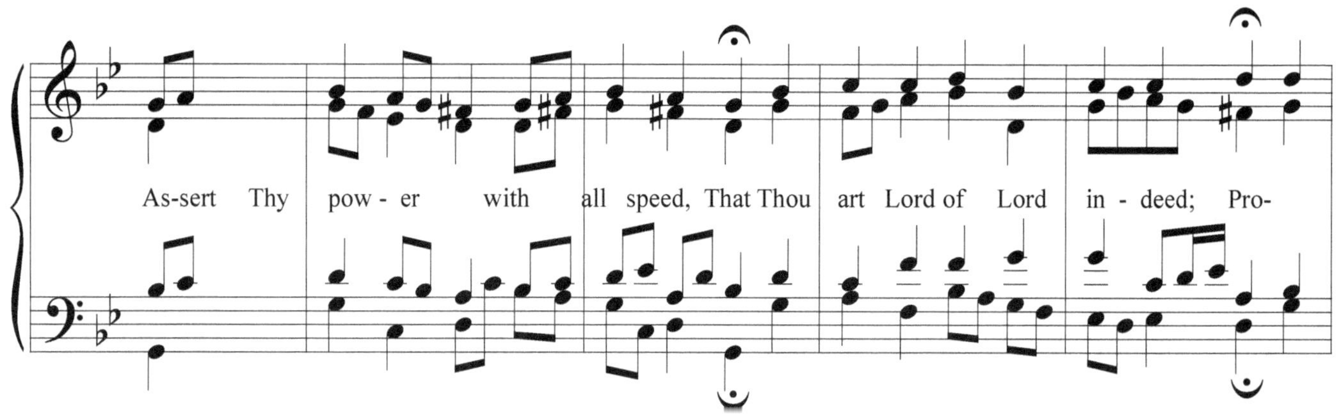

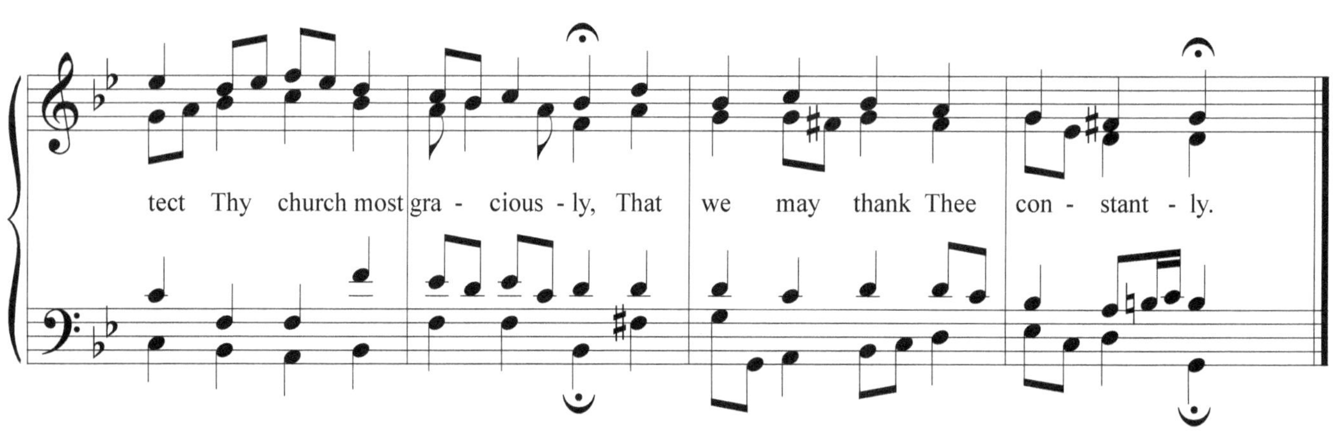

Here is a choral example from the Classical period. Each part is written on its own staff.

Requiem-Mozart
(Excerpt from the "Introitus")

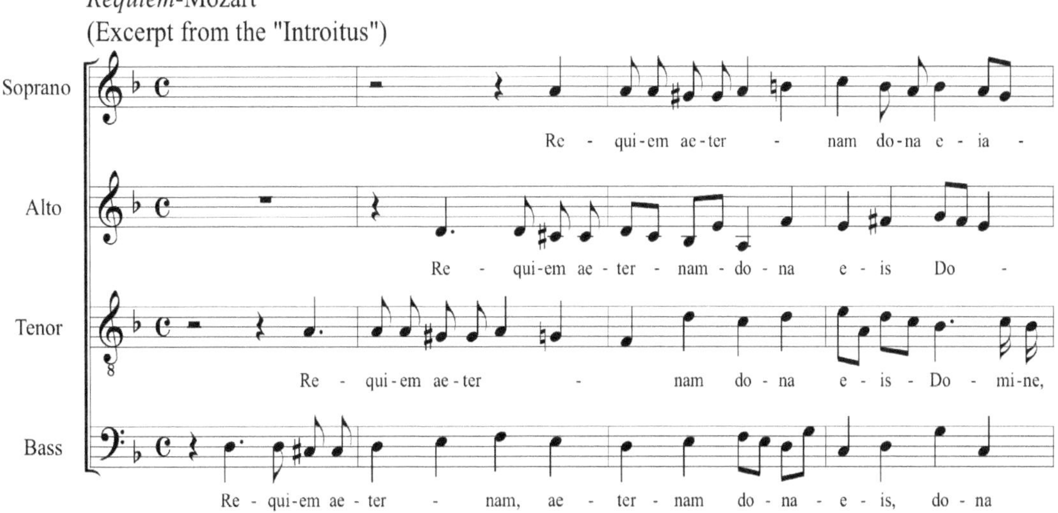

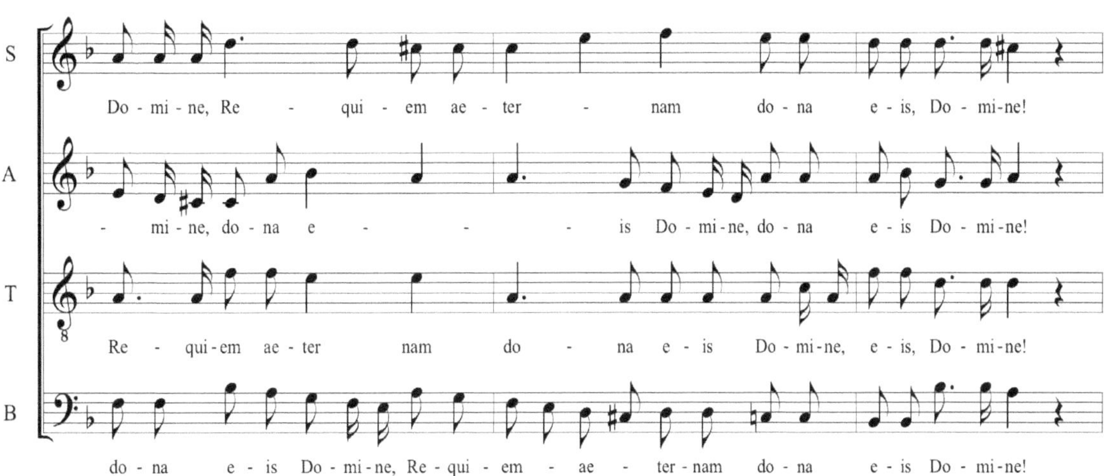

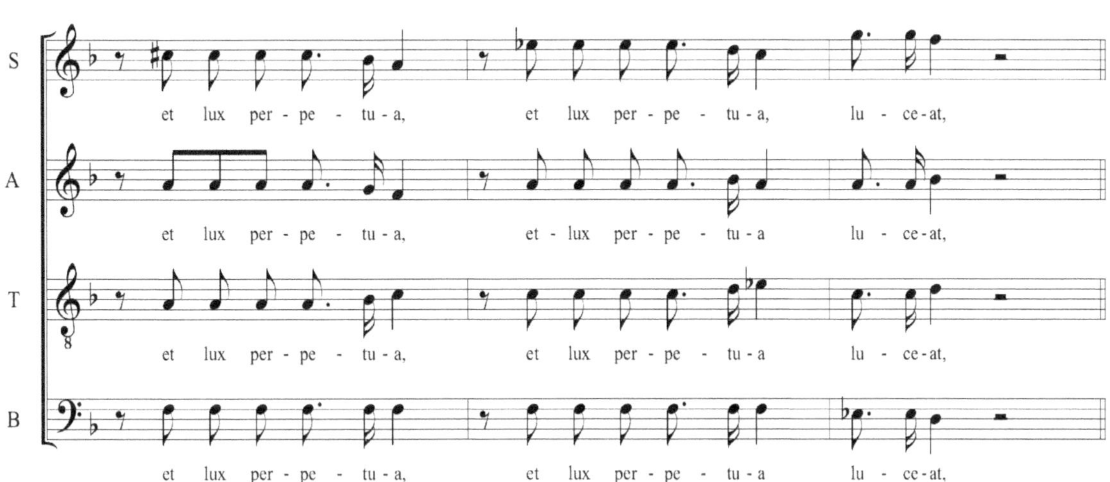

This is a piece from the Romantic period. Each vocal part is written on separate staves, often with harmonies within each voice. The piano accompaniment is also written under the vocal line.

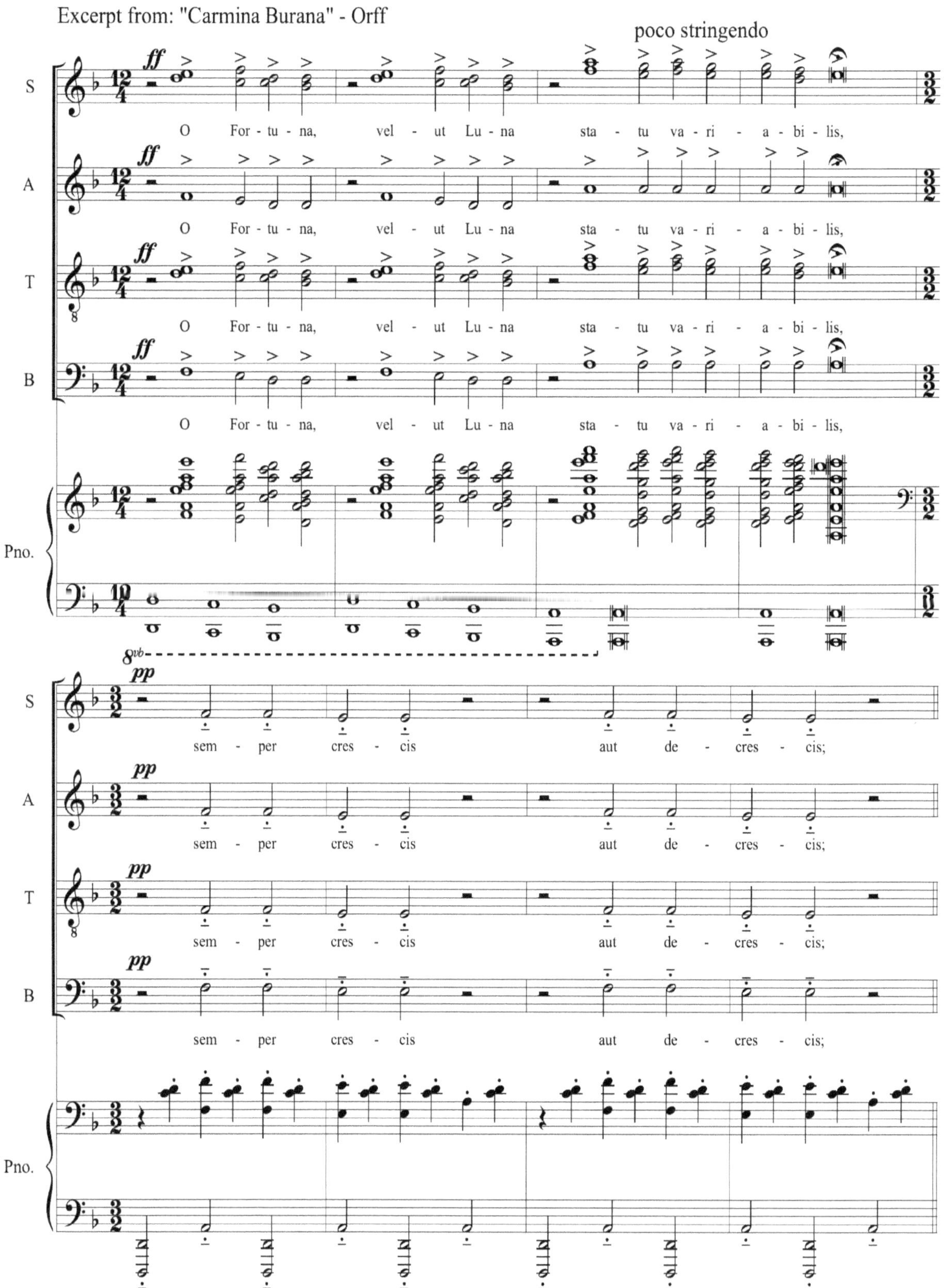

Alternately, music from the Contemporary period often has the harmonies written into the vocal line or directly into the accompaniment. This is especially true of Pop music, Musical Theatre and Jazz. The first example shows the melody and harmonies in the vocal line, while the second example shows the melody and harmonies in the accompaniment only.

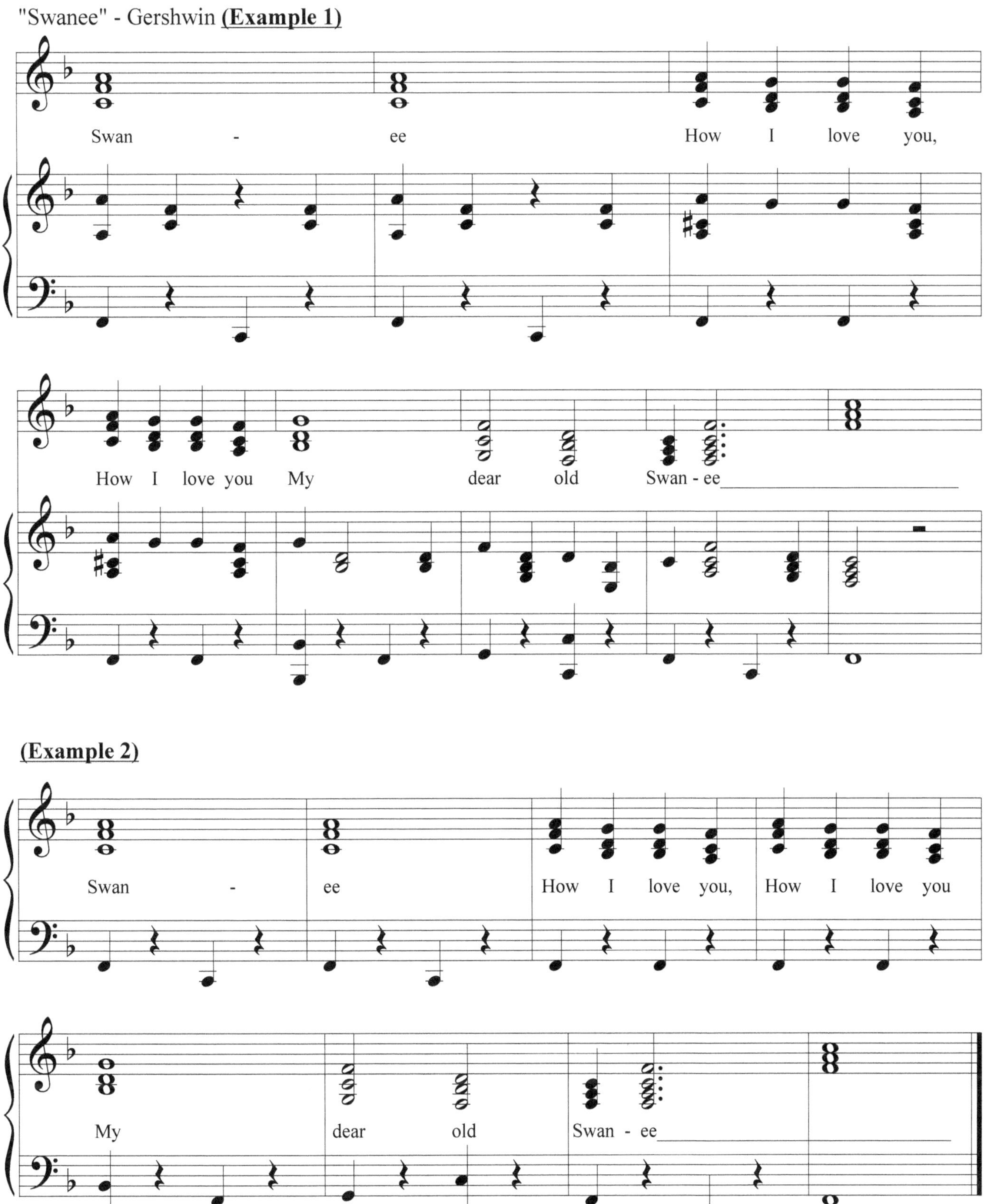

Here is an example of a barbershop quartet arrangement, where the harmonies create unique and interesting sounds. In barbershop, the term "lead" refers to the melody.

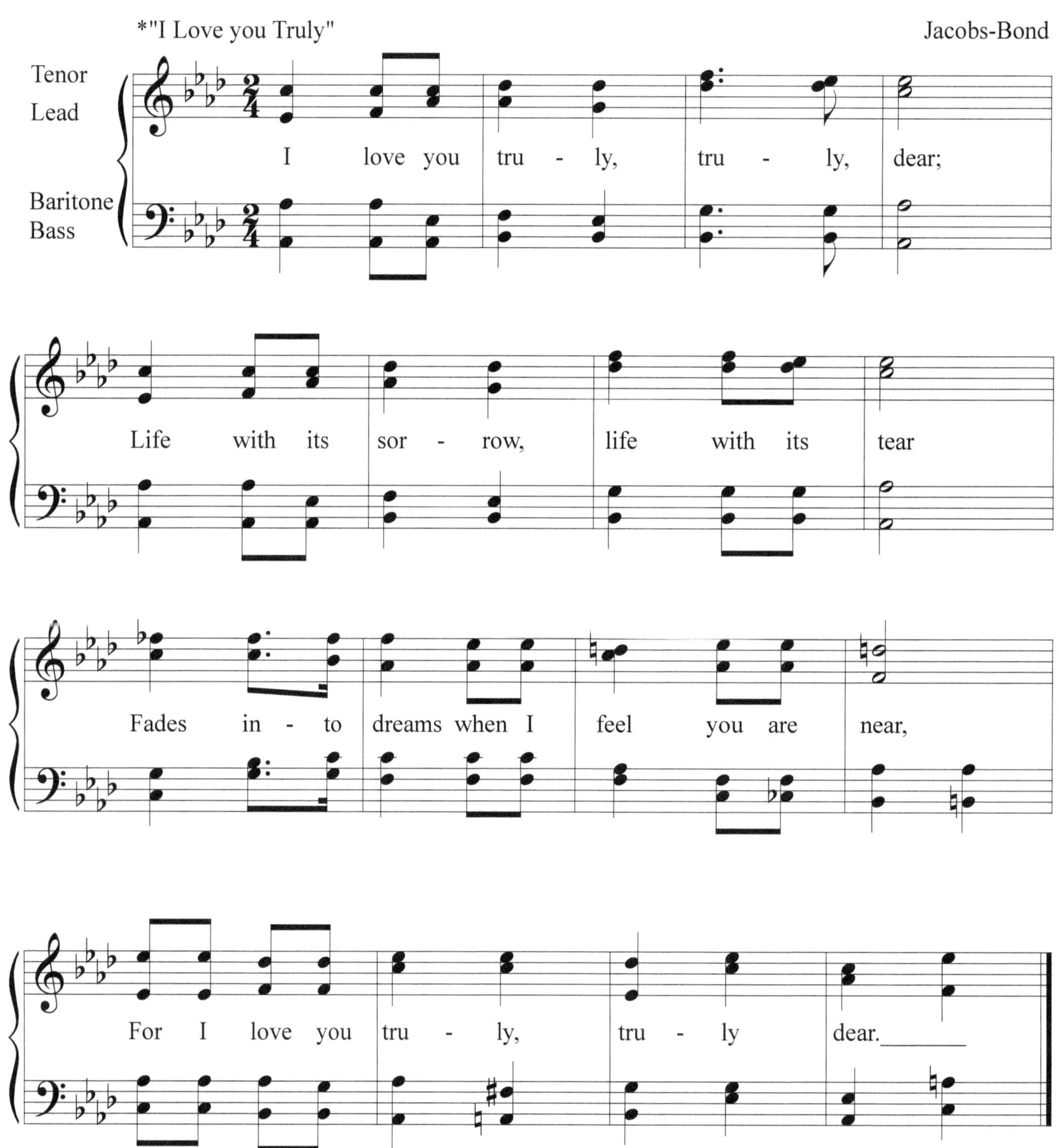

*I picked this song because my grandfather, Burnell Beckham, used to sing it, and he had a beautiful voice!

Review: Lesson 7

1. Add a note, the interval of a 3rd higher, to each of the existing notes in the following melody.

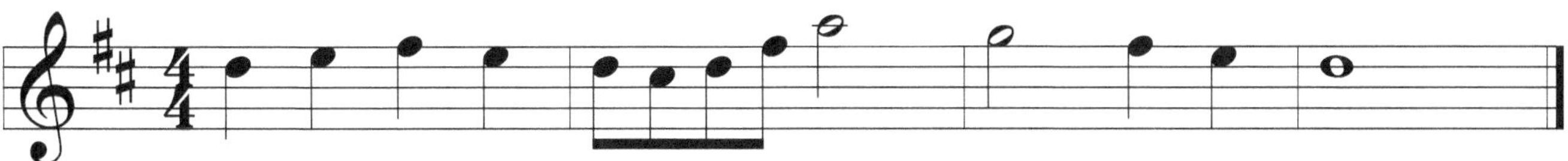

2. Add a note, the interval of a 3rd lower, to each of the existing notes in the following melody.

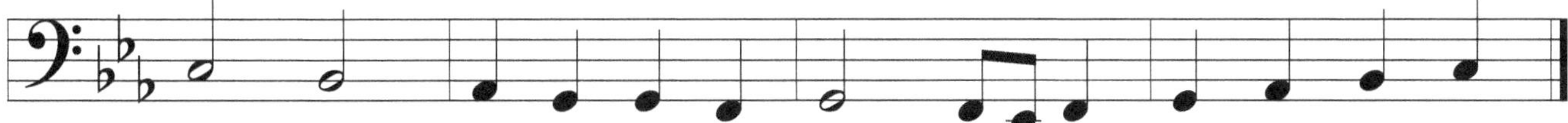

3. Add a note to the vocal line, the interval of a 3rd higher, to each of the existing notes in the vocal line of the following melody.

"Alouette" - French Folk Song

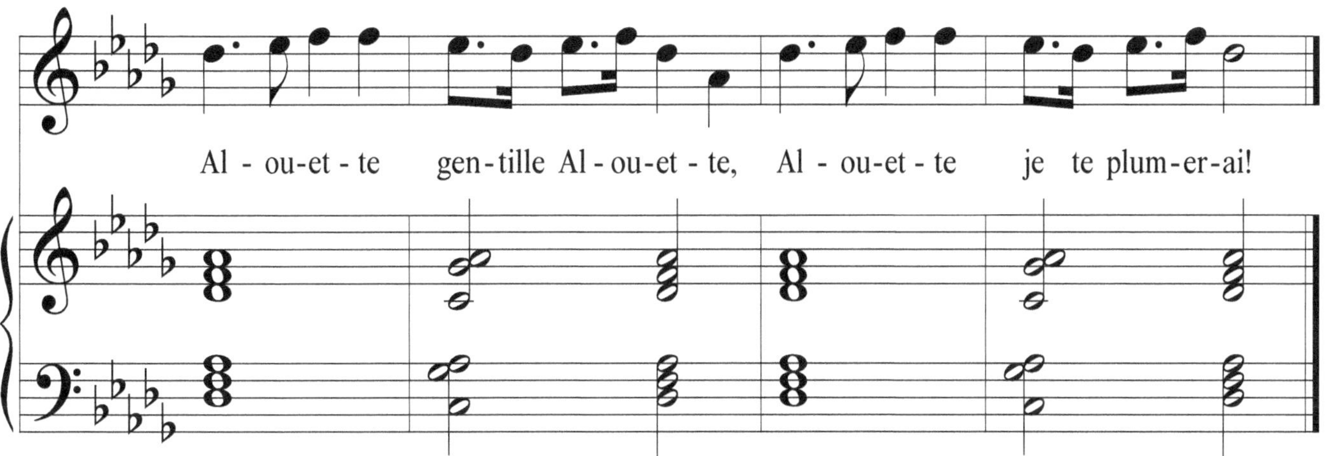

4. Add a note to the top staff, the interval of a 3rd lower, to each of the existing notes in the treble staff of the following melody.

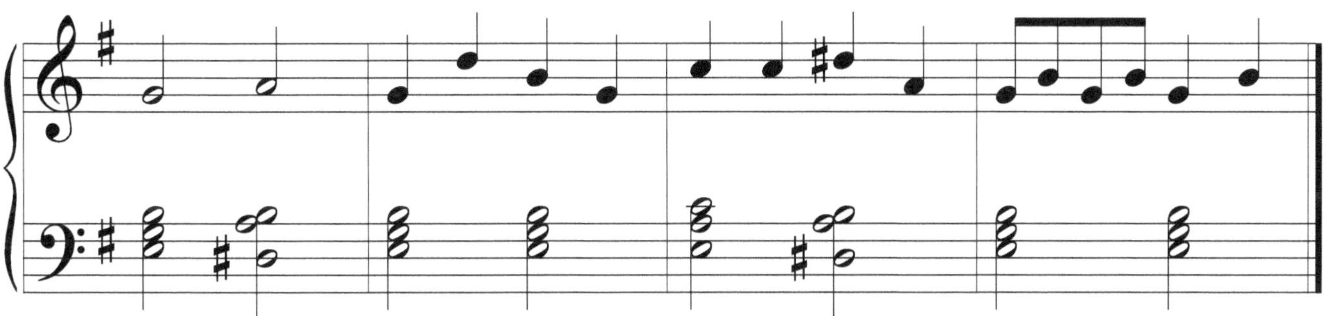

5. Add a note, the interval of a 6th <u>higher</u> to the existing notes in the following melody.

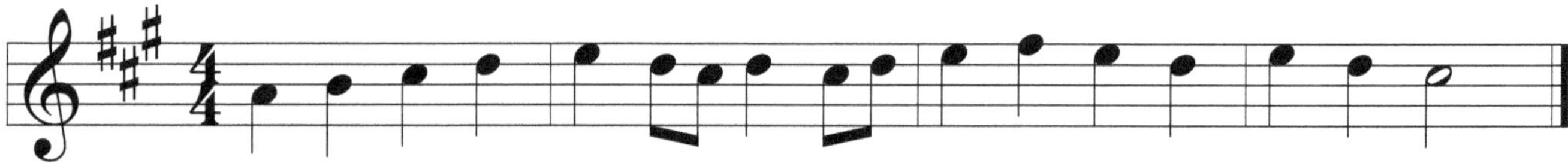

6. Add a note, the interval of a 6th <u>lower</u> to the existing notes in the following melody.

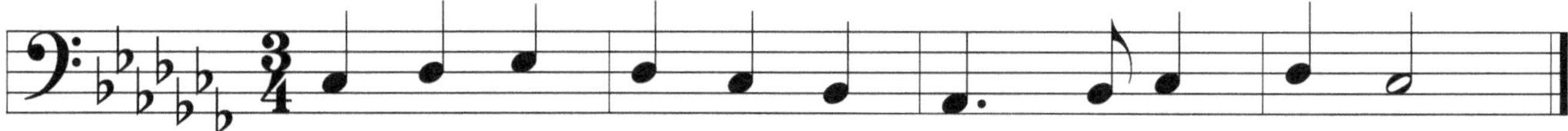

7. Add a note to the vocal line, the interval of a 6th <u>higher</u> to the existing notes in the following melody.

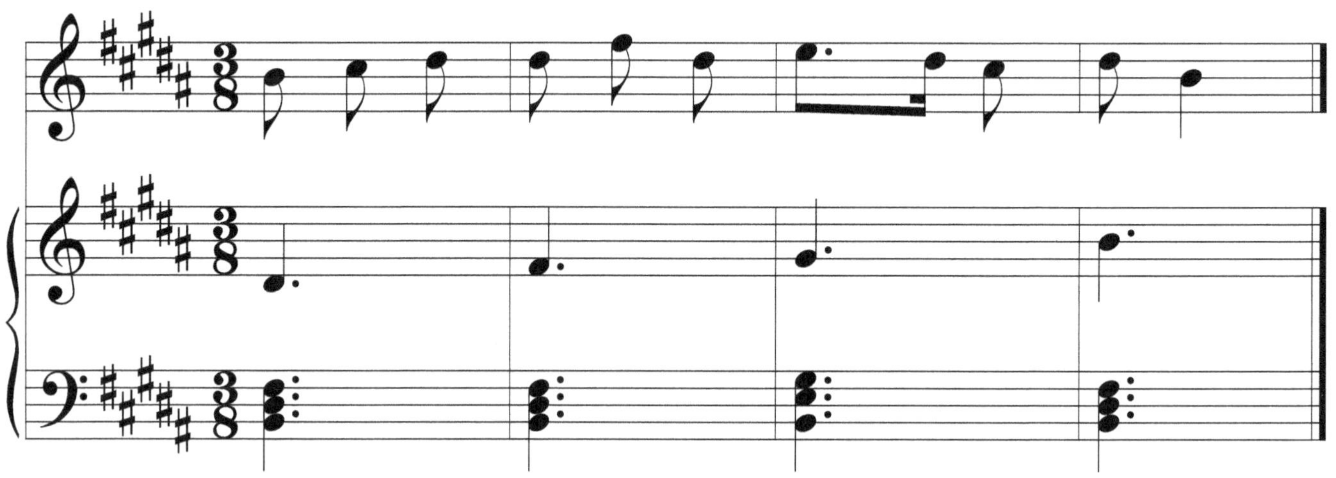

8. Add a note on the top staff, the interval of a 6th <u>lower</u> to the existing notes in the following melody.

"Danny Boy" - Irish Folksong

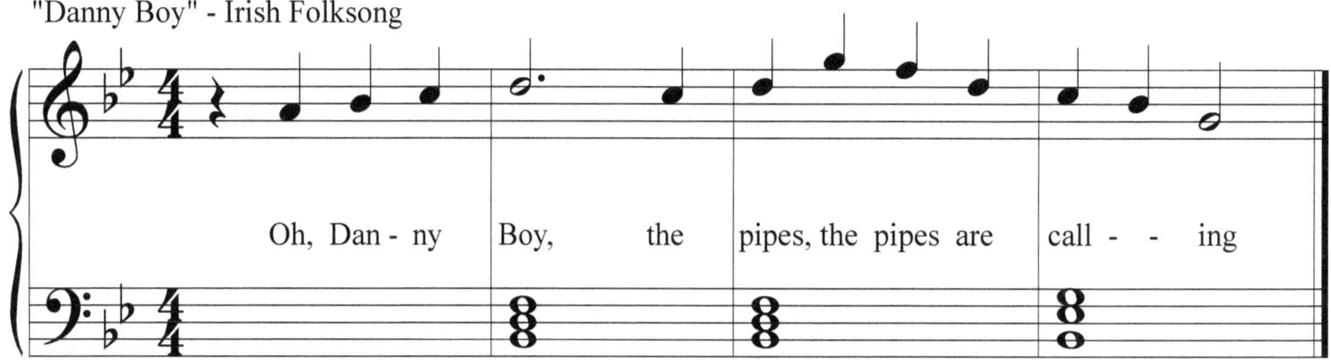

Lesson 8: Transposition

As singers, our instrument and range (tessitura) are constantly changing. The biggest changes take place between the ages of 11-16, but our voice continues to grow and develop as we age. Because of this, we have to be able to sing in appropriate keys for our voice. The process of changing a song from one key to another is called Transposition. Transposing a song is sometimes necessary so we can sing comfortably and sound our best. Most importantly, we need to be able to transpose ourselves, especially if an accompanist or pianist is not available to help.

In order to find out if the key of a song is suitable for your voice, find the highest and lowest notes in the song. If those notes are out of your range, or if the song just feels difficult to sing, then you should transpose the song higher or lower to fit your voice.

Look at this simple melody in the key of C Major. Let's pretend that this is too low for your voice.

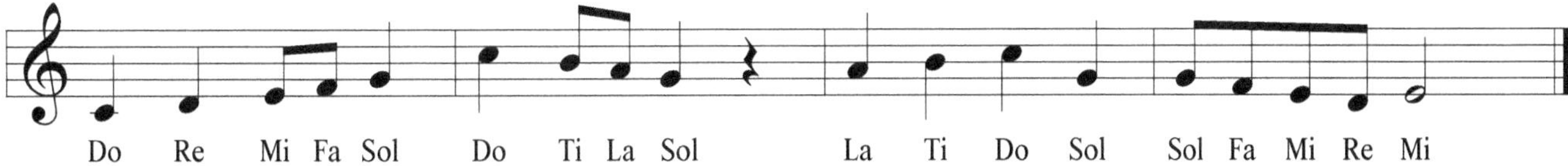

Here is the melody in the key of D Major, a Major 2nd (or 2 half steps) higher.

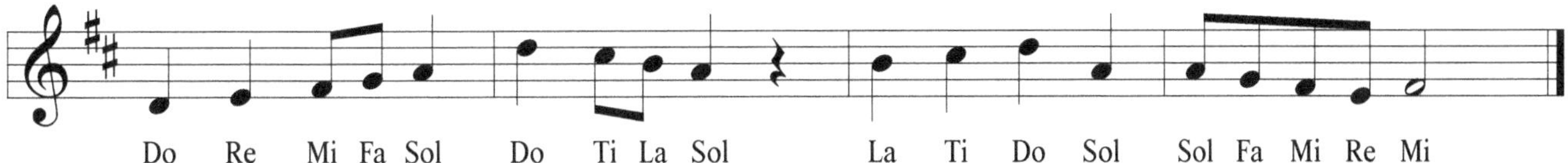

Notice how the solfege is exactly the same in each example. The second example just sounds higher and is a better fit for your voice. In order to transpose a melody, you must look at the intervals between the notes.

Here's the same melody with the intervals written in.

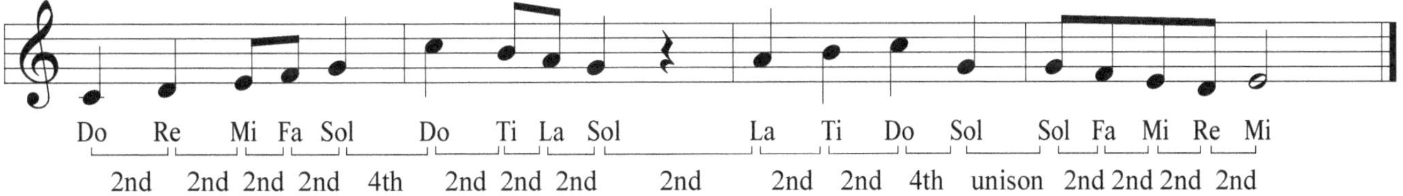

If you wanted to raise the song by a whole step to the key of D Major, where the highest and lowest notes are D's, then you would begin by starting the song with a D instead of a C. Then, follow the interval pattern (above) to see what notes come next. Make sure to add accidentals if necessary.

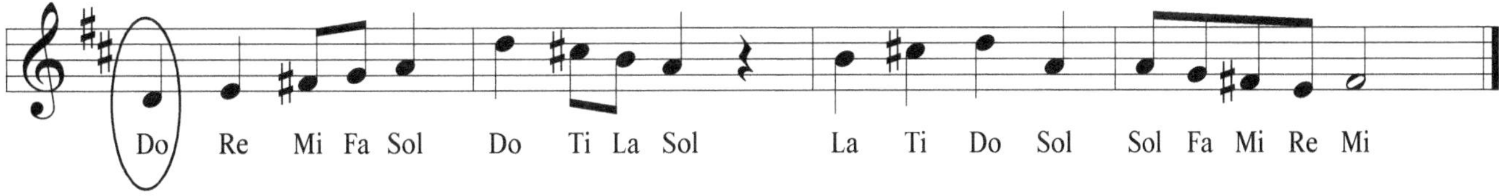

Look at the example of transposition and follow the steps.

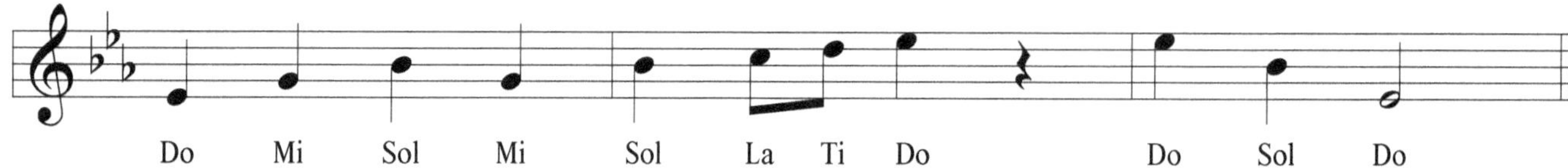

Let's look at the process to transpose this melody down a half step, to the key of D Major.

Step 1: Add the key signature for D Major.

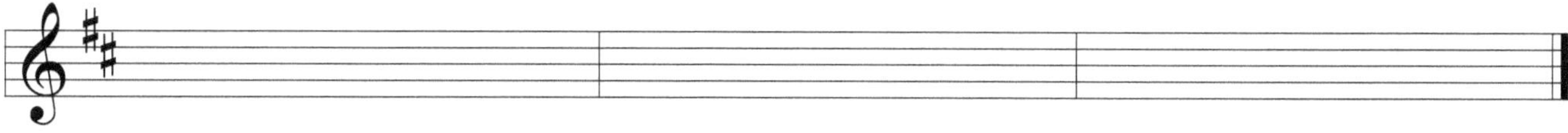

Step 2: Look at the starting note in the original example in the key of E♭ Major. It starts on E♭ which is "Do." For the transposed example, place a quarter note D on the staff (D is "Do" in the key of D Major).

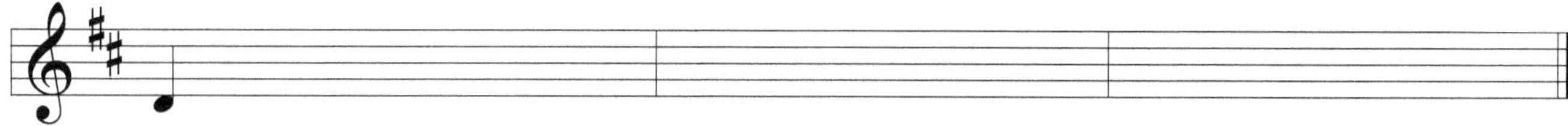

Step 3: Look at the intervals in the original example, and continue to transpose.

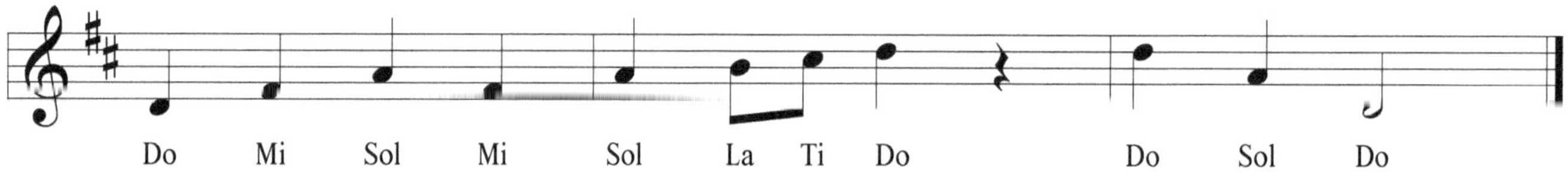

Here's another example in the Bass clef. Let's transpose this up a 4th to the key of C Major.

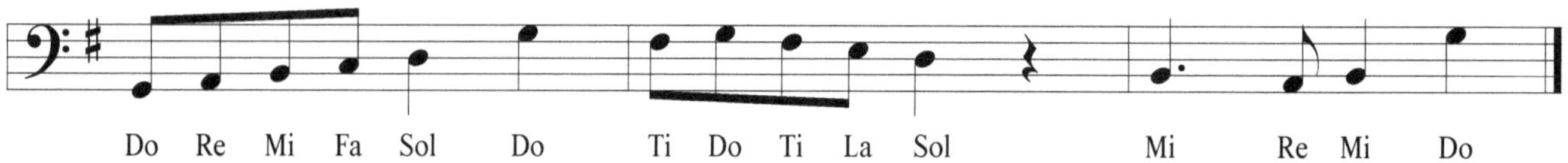

Steps 1 & 2: Add the key signature for C Major, then add the starting note.

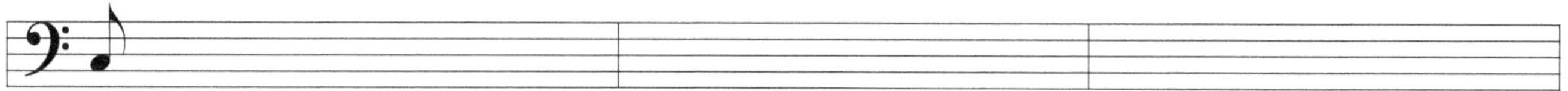

Step 3: Look at the intervals in the original example, and continue to transpose.

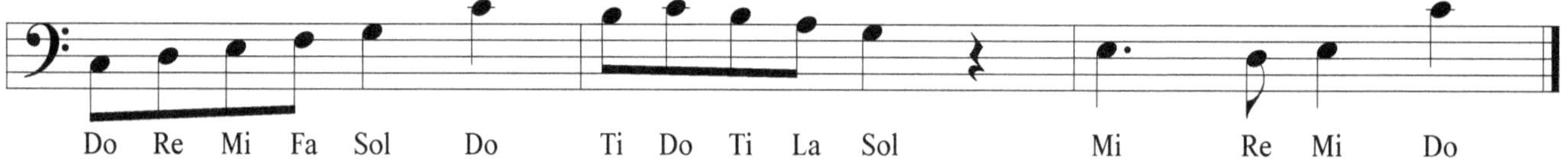

Review: Lesson 8

1. Transpose the following melody up by one whole step. The melody begins on "Do." Use the following steps.
   -Figure out the key signature that is one whole step higher than the given key, then add it to the staff.
   -Add the first note ("Do") according to the new key signature.
   -Continue transposing the melody by following the same intervals in the given example.

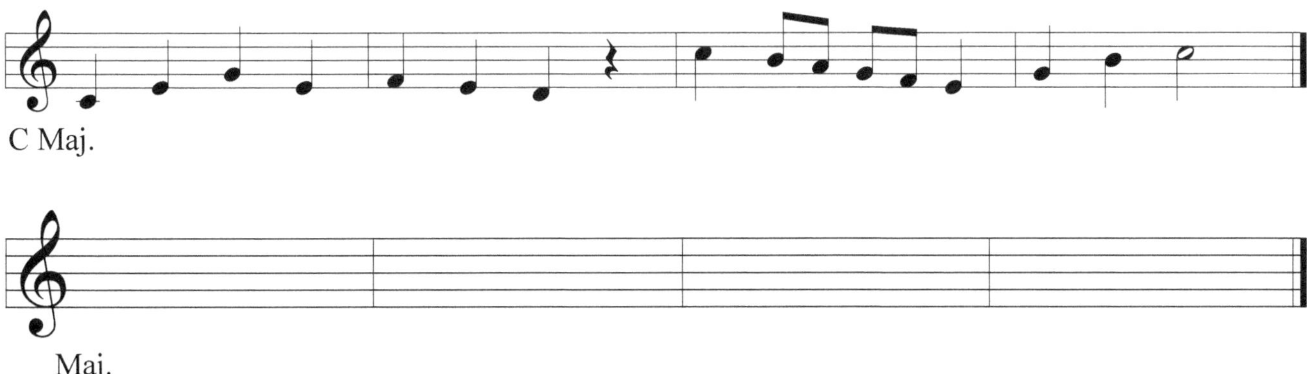

C Maj.

___Maj.

2. Transpose the following melody down by a Major 3rd. Follow the same steps as above.

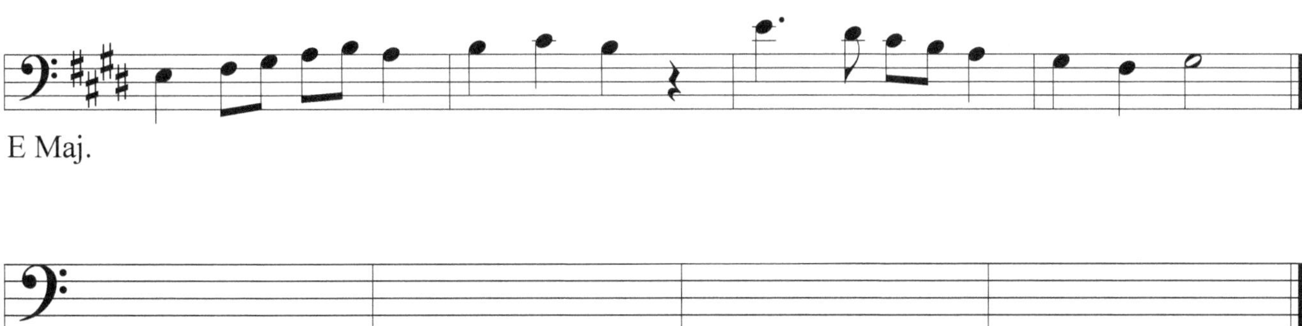

E Maj.

___Maj.

3. Transpose the following melody up by a Perfect 5th. Follow the same steps as above.

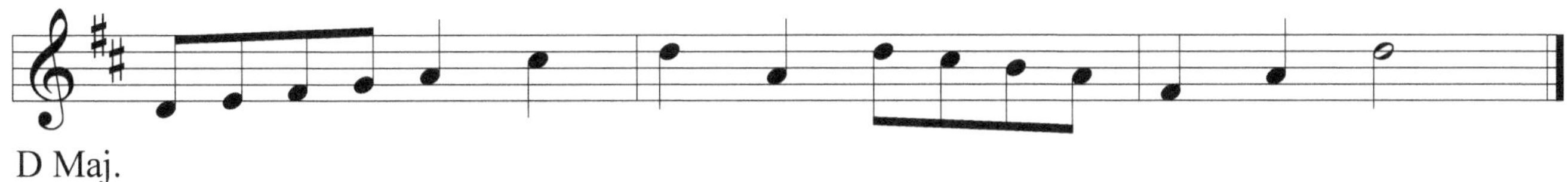

D Maj.

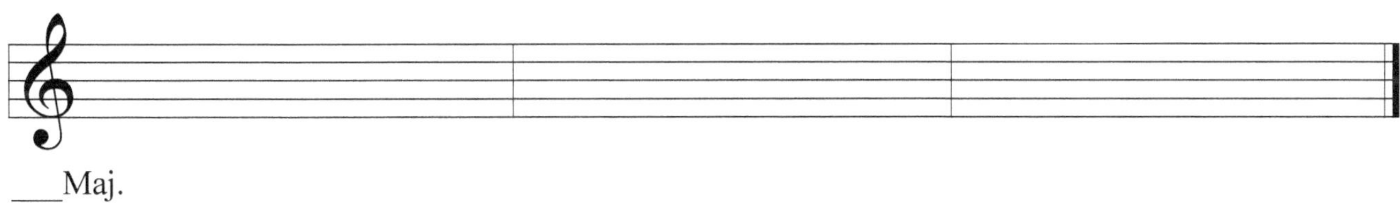

___Maj.

4. Transpose the following melody and/or chords on each staff down a whole step. Remember to add the key signature first, find your starting notes, then continue transposing according to the intervals in the given example. Note that the starting pitch is "Fa" in the given key.

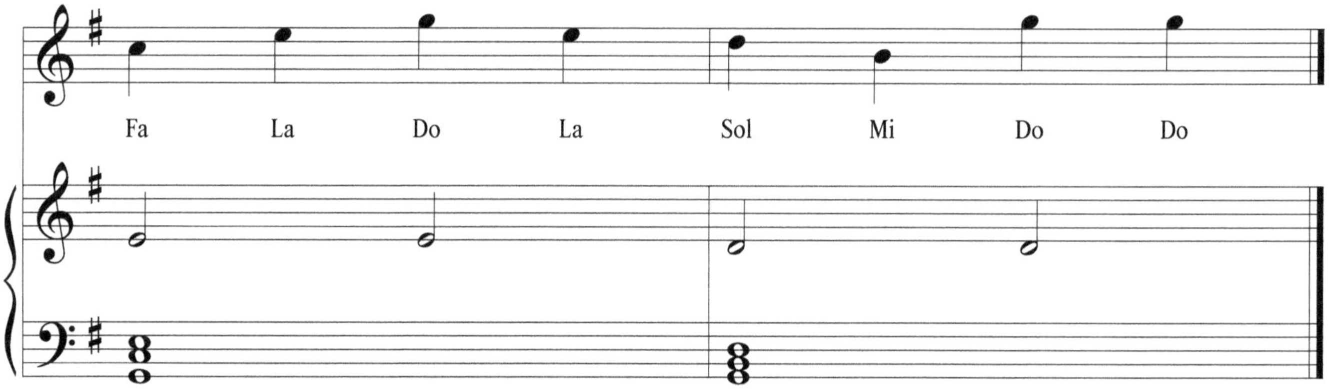

Fa La Do La Sol Mi Do Do

G Maj.

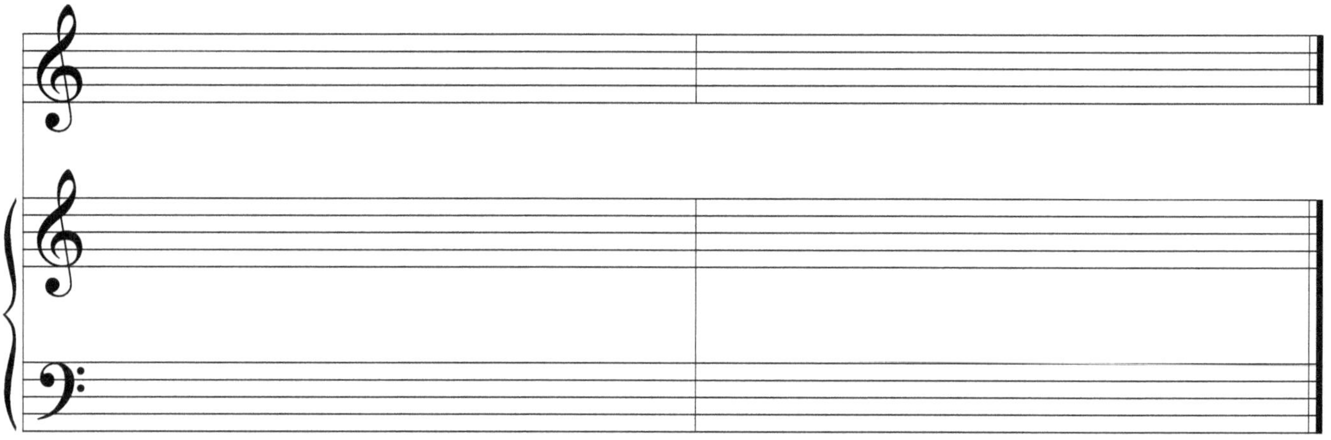

___Maj.

5. Transpose the following melody and/or chords on each staff up a Perfect 4th. Follow the steps above. Note that the starting pitch is "Do" in the given key.

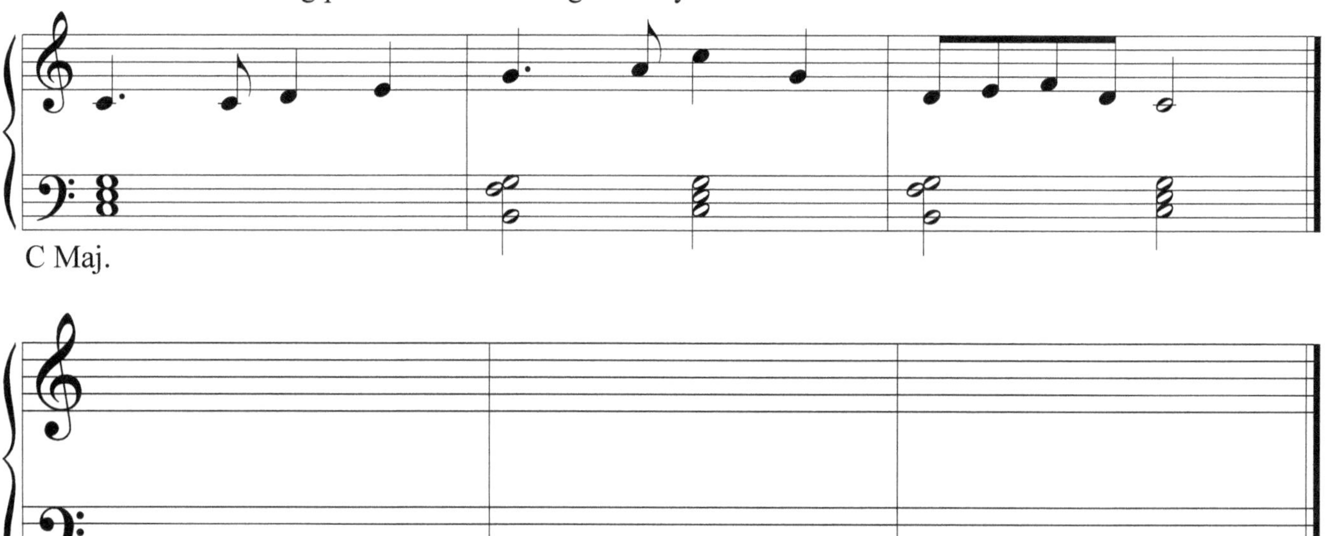

___Maj.

Lesson 9: Ornaments

Musical embellishments called "ornaments" are added to the vocal line to decorate or "ornament" that line.

They are not the main melody notes, and often delay the melody notes, so that when you do hear the main notes they are even more satisfying.

In the Baroque period, singers would improvise ornaments in most pieces, and especially in da capo arias. When the singer would sing the A section the second time, they would add several ornaments so it wasn't an exact repeat of the opening.

Ornaments can be found in all forms of classical music and even music from today. In pop, Jazz, and some Musical Theater music, singers often "riff" or add "runs" to the melody lines of the song. These are modern day ornaments!

Some composers write in the specific ornaments they want the singers to sing. While there are several ornaments, three of the most common ornaments found in Classical music are the Appoggiatura, Mordent, Grace Note, Turn & Trill.

The Appoggiatura: This is an accented, non-harmonic note that resolves stepwise to a harmonic note, often written in small type.

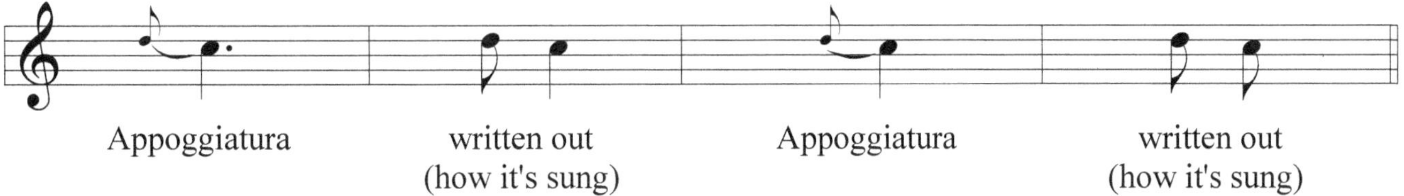

Appoggiatura — written out (how it's sung) — Appoggiatura — written out (how it's sung)

(The Appoggiatura always gets its full value, and this value is subtracted from the note of resolution.)

The Mordent: This is an ornament where the main note and the note below are sung quickly in succession before returning to the main note.

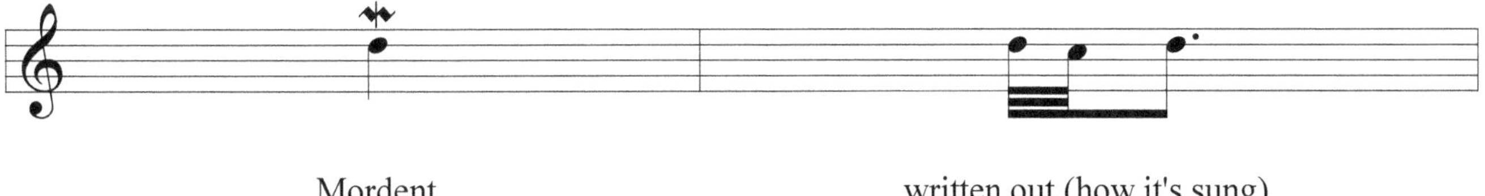

Mordent — written out (how it's sung)

The Grace Note: This is an unaccented ornament consisting of a short note immediately before a longer-lasting note. Grace notes are written in small type, with a slash through the stem.

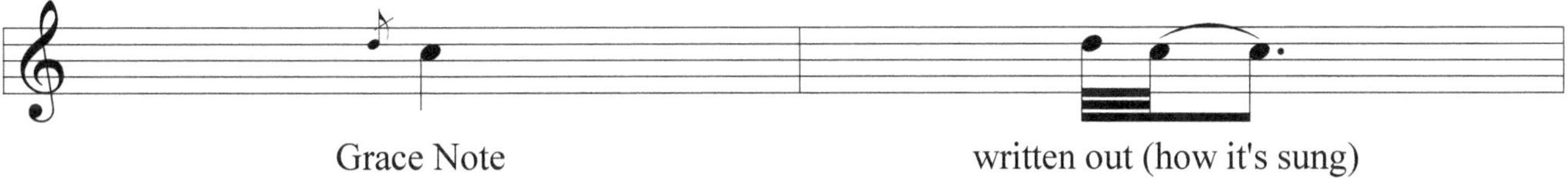

Grace Note — written out (how it's sung)

A Grace note is a small note with a slash through the stem, while an Appoggiatura is a small note that does not have a slash through the stem.

The Turn: This is an ornament consisting of a 4-note figure: the note above, the note itself, the note below, and the note itself. It is executed two different ways depending on whether the turn is over the main note or between it and the next note.

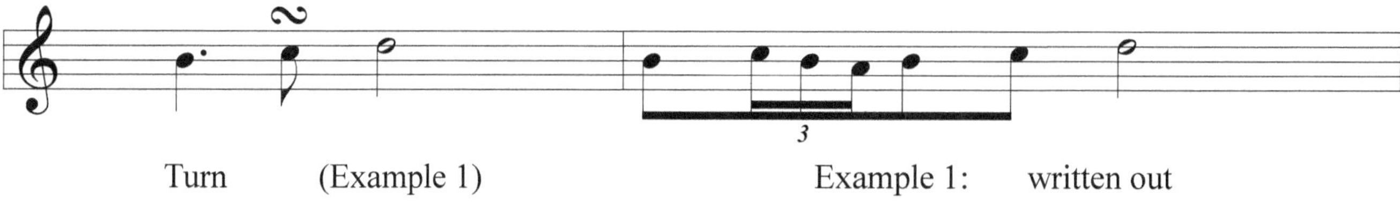

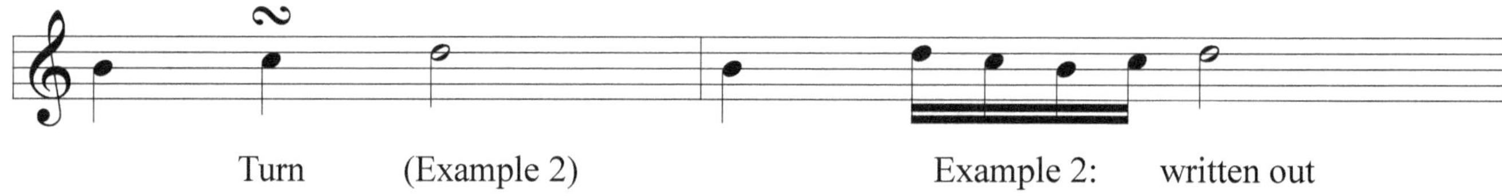

The exact speed and rhythm at which the notes of a turn are executed can vary according to the style and tempo of the piece.

The Trill is an ornament consisting of the rapid alternation of two adjacent notes: the main note and the note either a half or whole step above or below it. It is designated above the note to be trilled either by a *tr* or ⁓⁓ (both of these signs are used today).

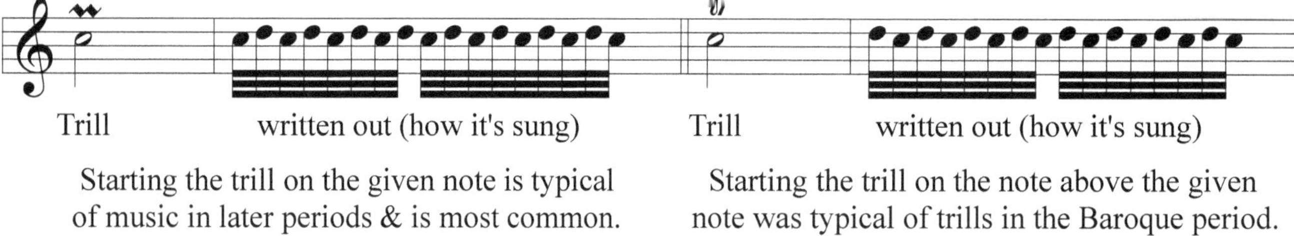

Starting the trill on the given note is typical of music in later periods & is most common.

Starting the trill on the note above the given note was typical of trills in the Baroque period.

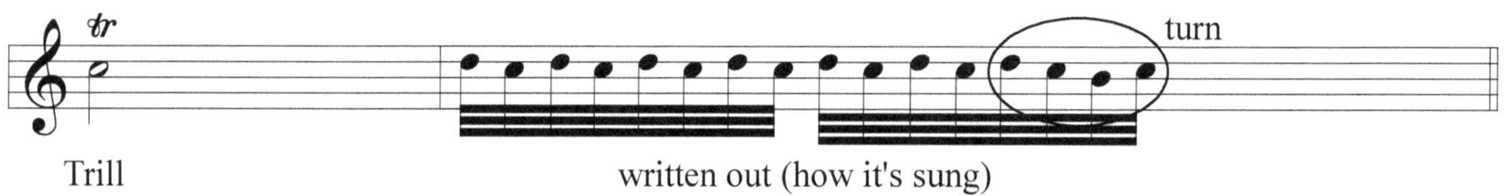

This is an alternative trill, common to the Baroque period, that ends in a turn.

Trills often start slow and become more rapid. This depends on the singer's preference and on the song being sung. The number of alterations between notes changes depending on the length of the note and the tempo of the song. There are additional trills that vary according to musical period and composer.

A Trill (⁓⁓) and Mordent (⁓|⁓) look almost identical, but a Mordent has a line through the center of the symbol.

Here's an example of each ornament within a piece of music...

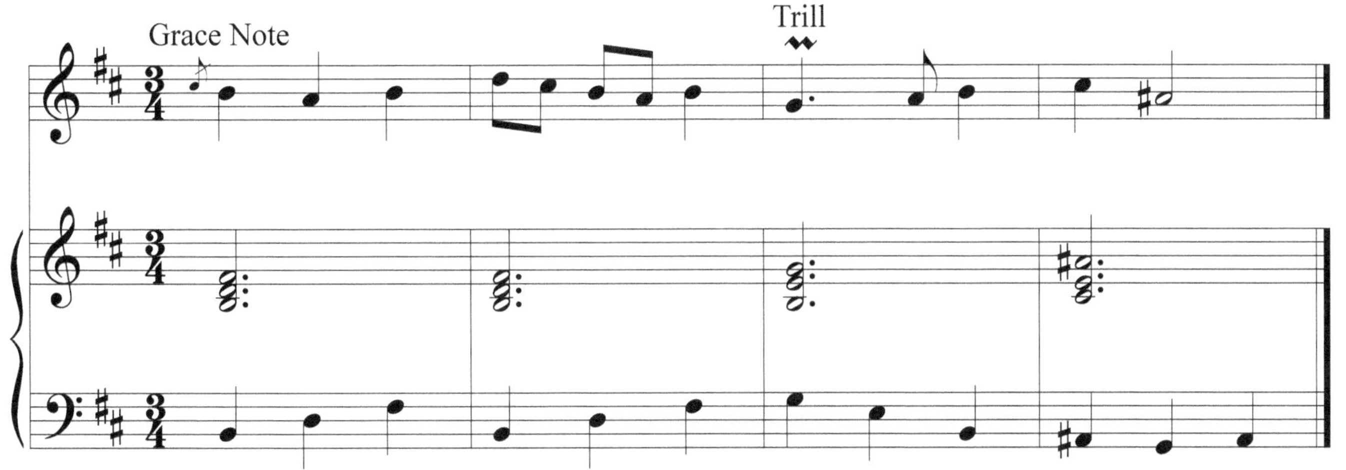

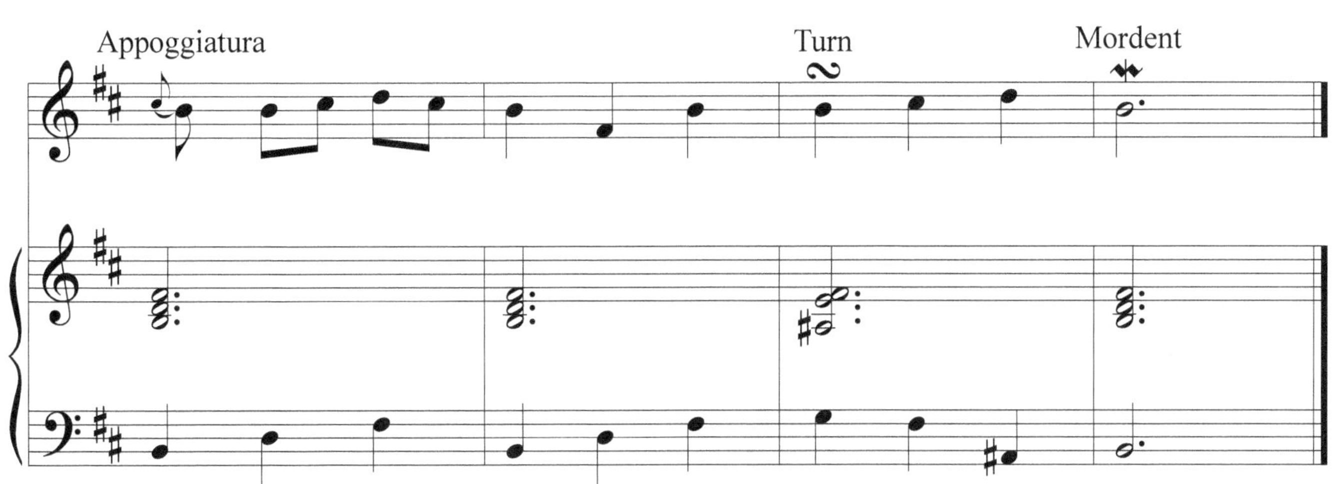

Review: Lesson 9

1. Ornaments are only included in music from the Baroque period. (Circle True or False)

True False

2. Ornaments are part of the main melody in music. (Circle True or False)

True False

3. Singers often add ornaments to what type of song? (Circle your answer)

Folk Songs Da capo Arias

4. Draw a line connecting the ornament on the left to its correct written out version on the right.

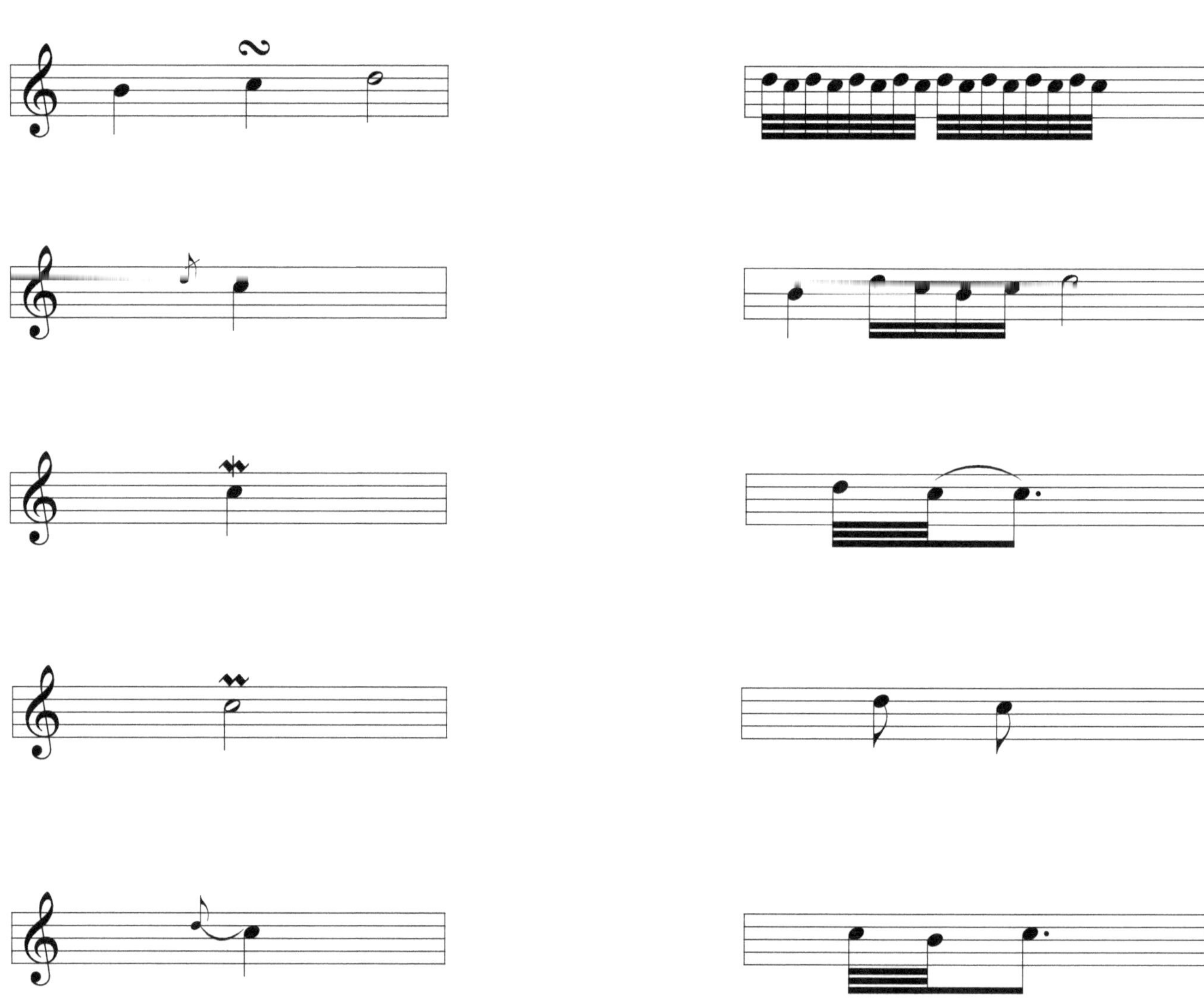

5. Write the name under each ornament in the following musical example: Trill, Appoggiatura, Mordent, Grace Note or Turn.

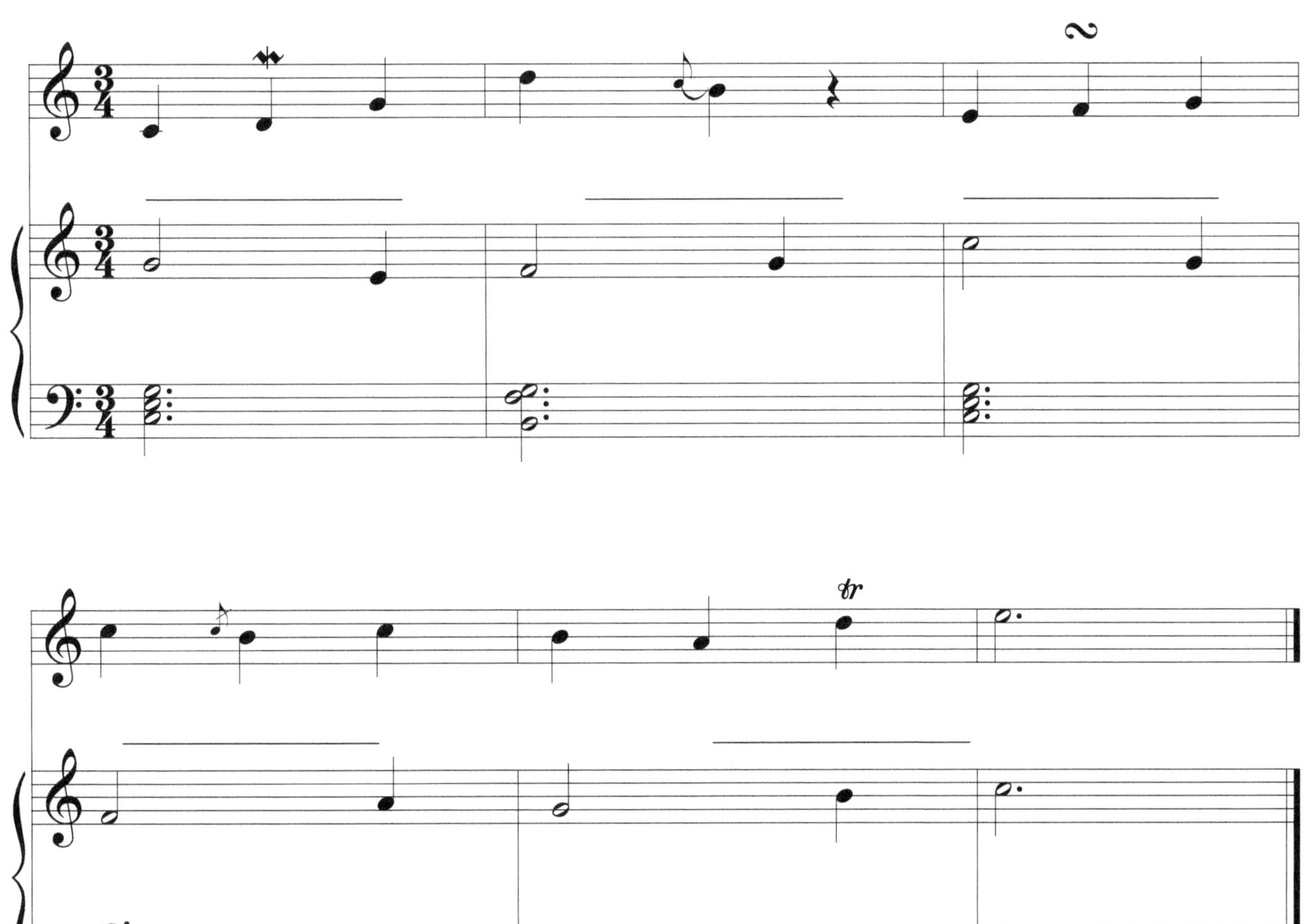

Lesson 10: Conducting Patterns

As singers, we will, at one point or another, sing in front of a conductor. This may be with a choir, jazz ensemble, in a musical or as a soloist. Conductors not only keep the orchestra/band in time, but they also cue all entrances for singers and instrumentalists. Conductors also connect the instrumentalists and singers together with their energy and keep the dynamics uniform in the song.

One of the best ways to understand how to follow a conductor is to actually be able to conduct. Conducting connects your body to music in a different way than singing as a soloist. It helps you feel the beats and rhythm in the music and is something you can do when learning any new song. When conducting, the palms of your hands should face the floor. Often your right hand keeps the beat while your left hand conducts dynamics and cut offs.

In this Level, you will learn the most common conducting patterns: 2/4, 3/4 & 4/4.

<u>2/4 Time</u>: "Down ⟶ up"

1. You begin with your hands together in front of you (figure A).
2. Then you bring your hands down to your waist level, and bring them out (figure B).
3. Lastly, bring them back up in front of your body to the starting position.

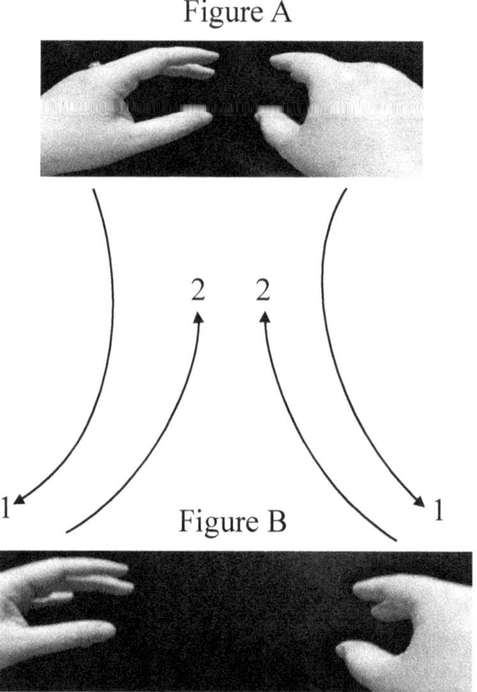

The left hand motion creates the shape of the letter J, while the right hand motion creates a backwards J.

3/4 Time: "Down ⟶ Out ⟶ Up" You can say "Tri-an-gle" as you conduct this pattern as well.

1. You begin with your hands together in front of you.
2. Bring both hands straight down to your waist level.
3. Bring both hands out, like a capital L.
4. Bring both hands back up to the starting position.

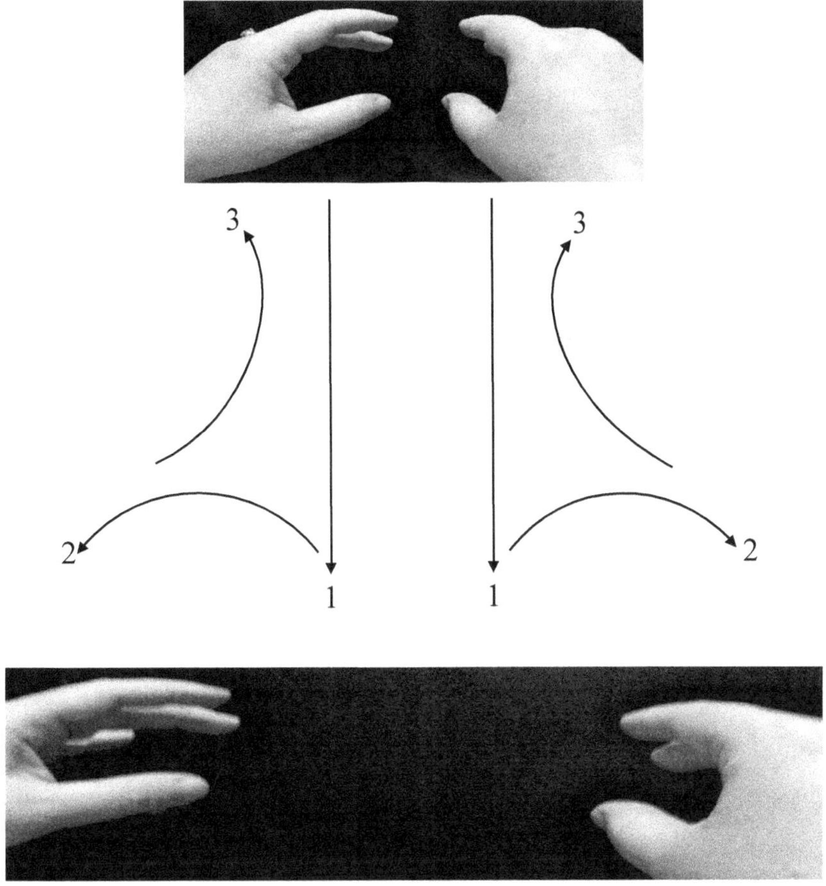

Notice that the lines your hands follow have a bit of an arc to them.Your hands have a small bounce between positions to make each beat clear.

4/4 Time: "Down ⟶ In ⟶ Out ⟶ Up"

1. You begin with your hands together in front of you (a little bit further apart than in 2/4 & 3/4).
2. Bring your hands straight down to your waist level.
3. Bring your hands together in front of your waist.
4. Bring your hands out like a capital L.
5. Bring your hands back up to the starting position.

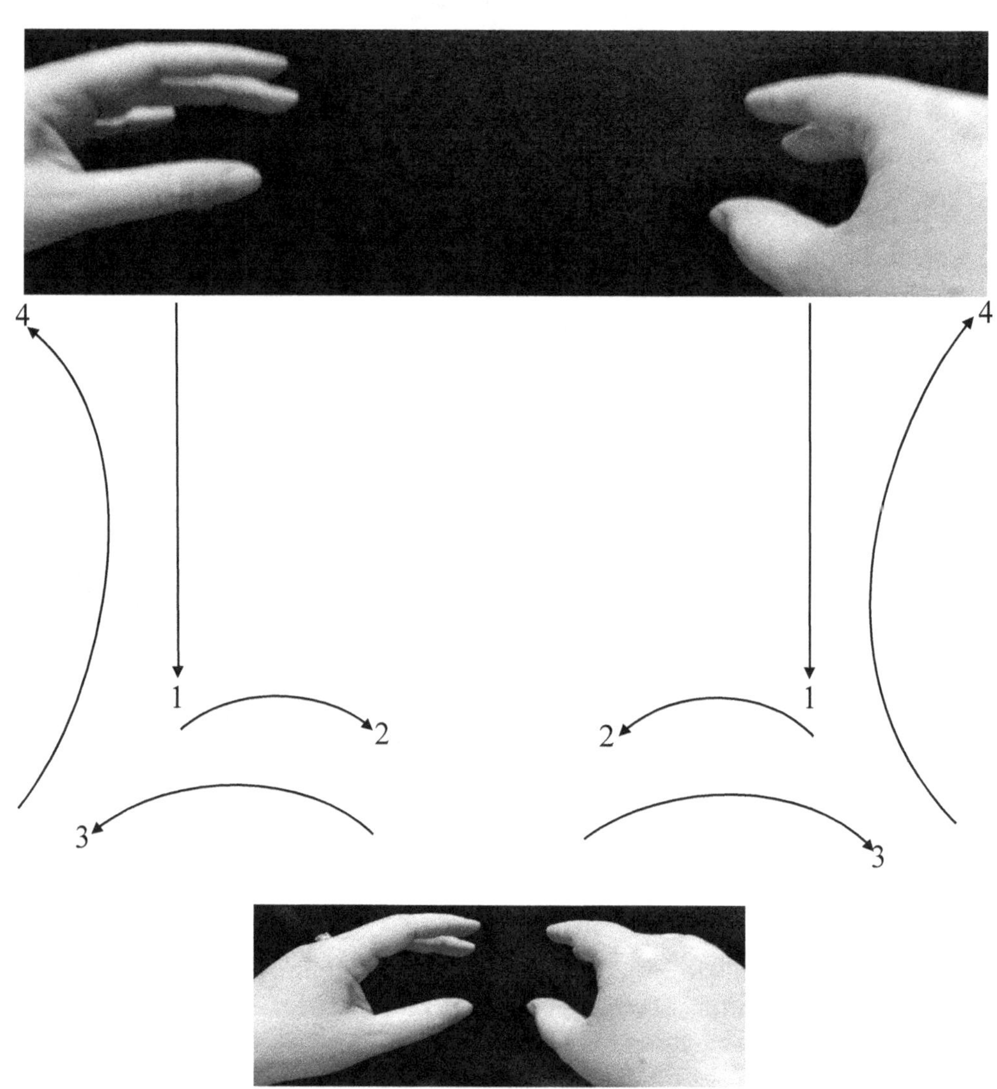

Review: Lesson 10

1. Match the correct conducting catch phrase on the left with the correct time signature on the right.

a. "Down-In-Out-Up" ______2/4

b. "Down-Up" ______3/4

c. "Down-Out-Up" ______4/4

2. Draw conducting patterns beneath the following time signatures. Use lines with arrows to show the directions your hands go. Add numbers to show the order of directions.

2/4

3/4

4/4

Review: Lessons 6-10

1. Add accidentals to create the requested chords. The Major chord is given.

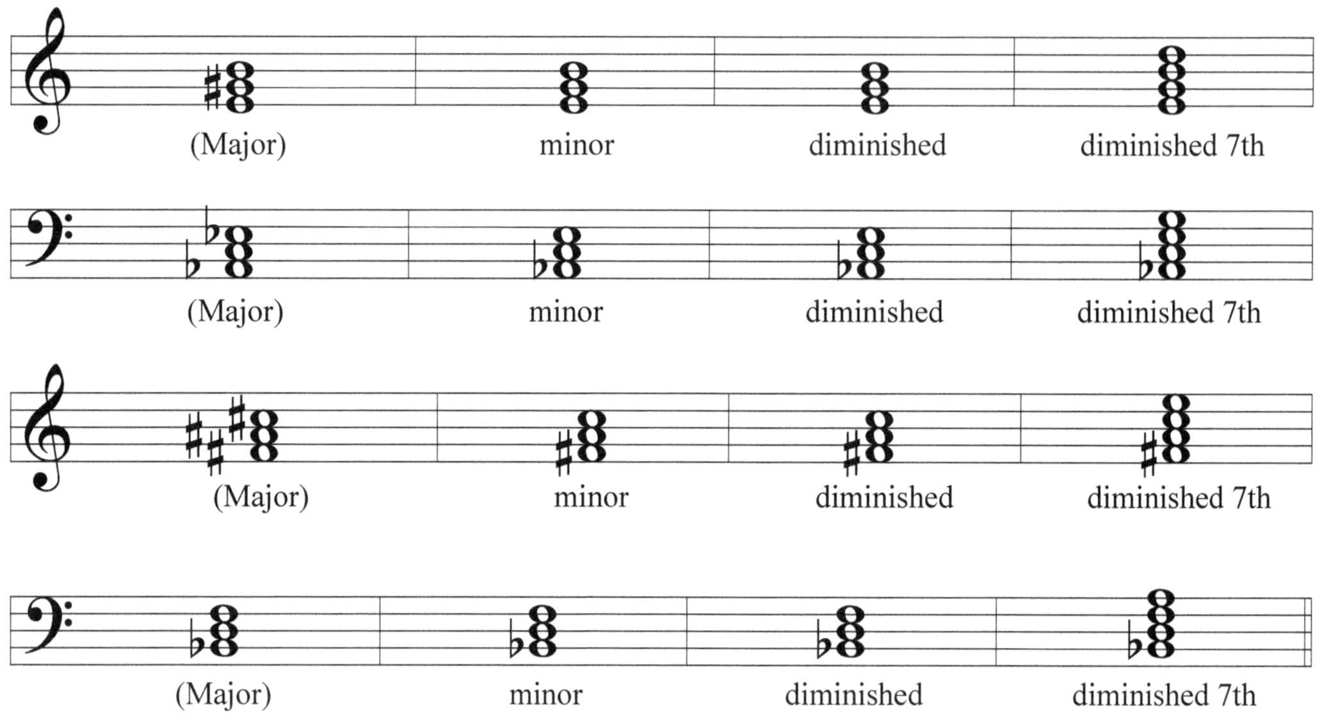

2. Draw the 1st, 2nd and 3rd inversions of the given **diminished 7th** chord. Be sure to add in the necessary accidentals.

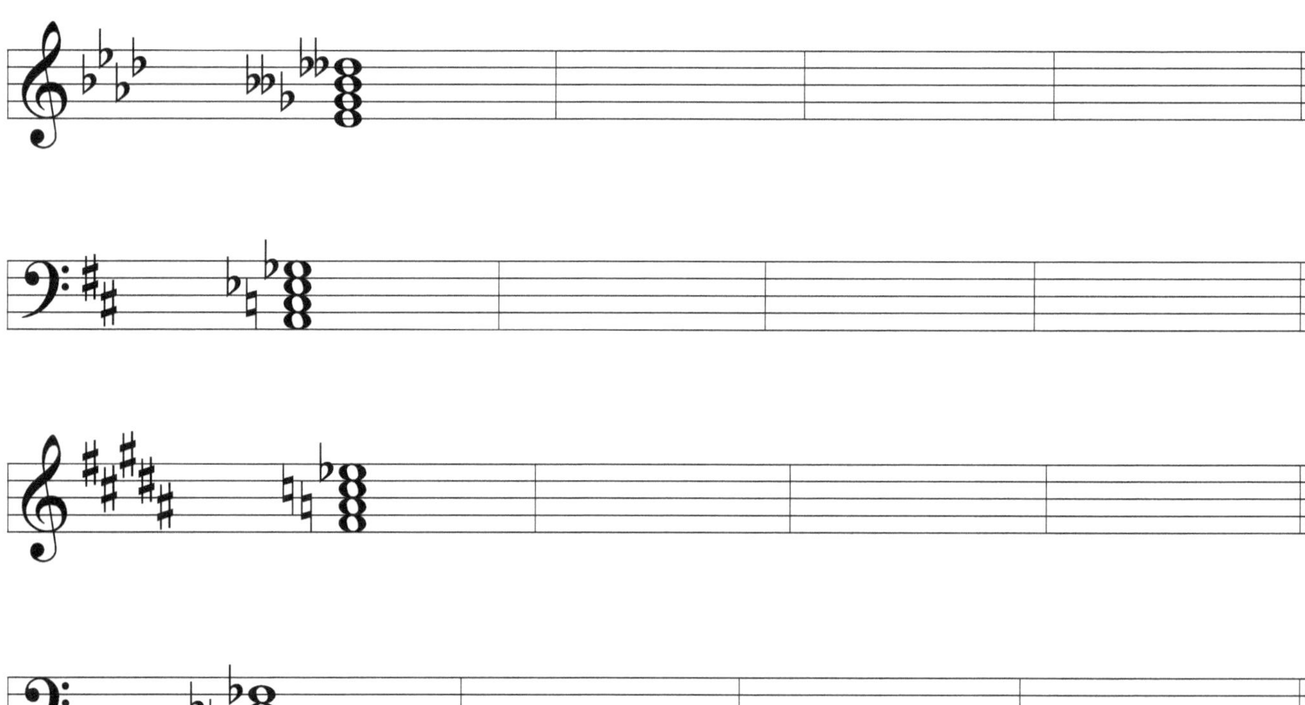

3. Transpose the following melody to the key of E Major.

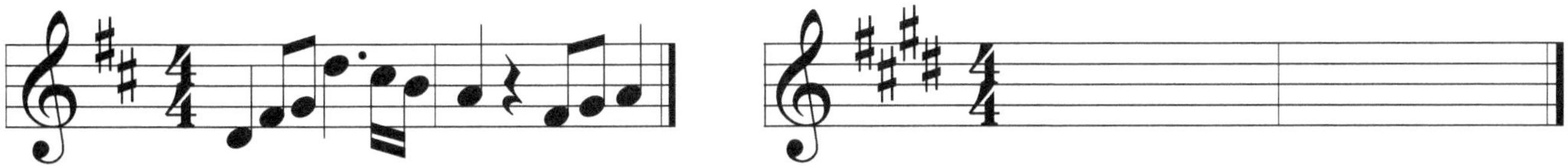

4. Add a note, the interval of a 6th lower to each of the existing notes in the following melody.

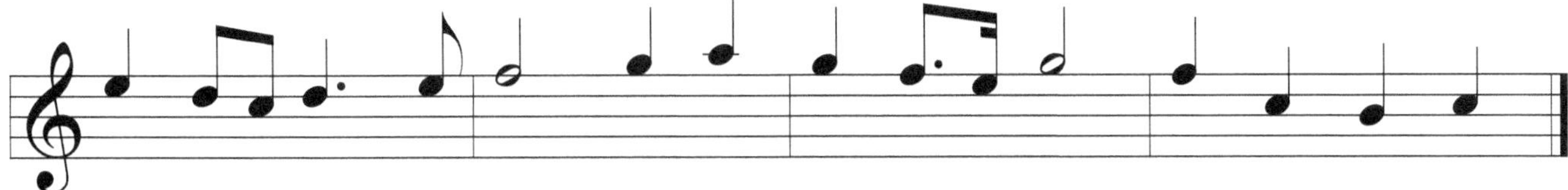

5. Add a note, the interval of a 3rd higher to each of the existing notes in the following melody.

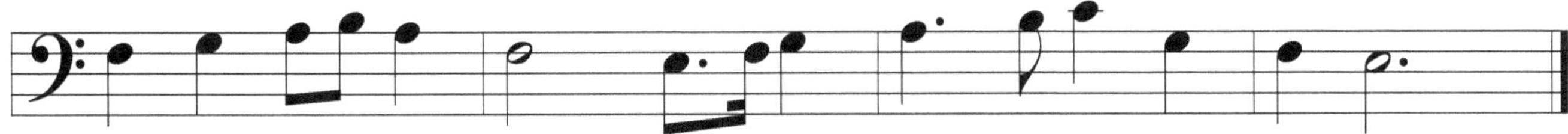

6. Draw a line connecting the ornament on the left to its correct written out version.

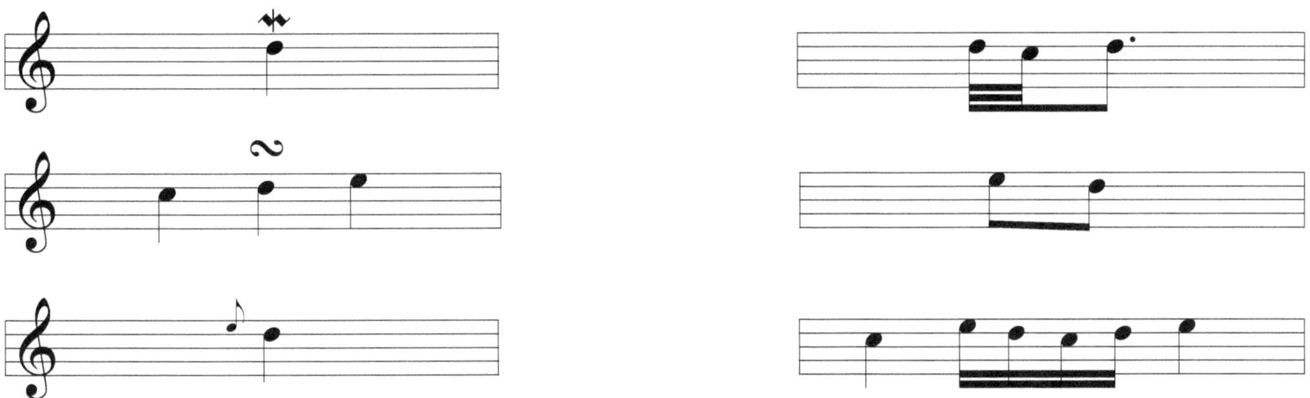

7. Draw conducting patterns beneath the following time signatures. Use lines with arrows to show the directions both of your hands go. Add numbers to show the order of directions.

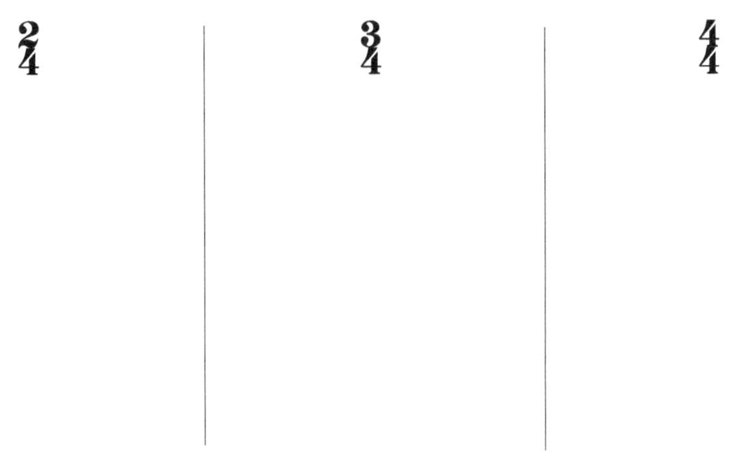

Lesson 11: Vocal Diction & IPA

Every time we sing a song, we are telling a story. As singers, we have to be exceptionally clear with how we pronounce the words of our songs, or our audience will not understand us and our story will not be told.

If you reference a dictionary in any Latin based language (English, Italian, French, German, Spanish, Latin, etc.) you will see some symbols next to the words. These symbols make up the International Phonetic Alphabet, or IPA. The IPA represents the sounds of a language. In fact, the IPA represents nearly any vowel or consonant made by human beings!

In this lesson, we'll focus on the main sounds in the IPA. You will learn what the letter looks like in our language, what the IPA symbol for that letter is, and what it sounds like.

Before we look at the symbols, make a couple of sounds so you can see all of the different positions your tongue moves to in order to make each sound.

Say "ah" as in the word "father," and "ee" as in the word "meet." You'll notice that when you say "ah," your tongue is at the bottom of your mouth, and when you say "ee" the center of your tongue moves to the roof of your mouth, while the tip remains down and behind the bottom teeth. When singing, we must be aware of any tension in our tongue, and ensure that it is in the proper position for creating accurate vowel sounds.

Practice saying the sounds in each of the charts on the following pages and the foreign word that contains the sound/English equivalent. Typing these words into Google Translate or another translation app can help you hear how it should sound.

Check that your tongue and lips are in the position described in the last column.

Below is a chart of the vowels introduced in Levels 1, 2, & 3.

Practice looking at each symbol, then say the english word and pay attention to the tongue and lips position described in the third column.

IPA SYMBOL	SOUND IN ENGLISH WORD	IPA SPELLING OF WORD	TONGUE/LIPS PLACEMENT
i	ski	[ski]	Center of tongue is high Lips relaxed
ɛ	led	[lɛd]	Low tongue Lips relaxed
ɑ	father	[ˈfɑðər]	Low tongue Lips relaxed
o	obey	[oʊˈbeɪ]	Low tongue, tip behind bottom teeth Rounded lips
u	goose	[gus]	Low tongue, tip behind bottom teeth Rounded lips
ɪ	kit	[kit]	High tongue, sides touching top teeth Lips relaxed
e	egg (first vowel sound you hear)	[feɪs]	High tongue, sides touching top teeth Lips relaxed
ə	afraid	[əˈfreɪd]	Mid tongue, tip behind bottom teeth Lips relaxed
æ	cat	[kæt]	Mid tongue, tip behind bottom teeth Lips slightly horizontal
ʊ	book	[bʊk]	Low tongue, tip below bottom teeth Lips relaxed & slightly pouted
ʌ	strut	[strʌt]	Low tongue, tip behind bottom teeth Lips relaxed
ɔ	forest	[fɔrəst]	Low tongue, tip behind bottom teeth Lips slightly rounded

Note: The schwa (ə) and the "uh" vowel (ʌ) are very similar. The schwa (ə) is unaccented and not stressed, while the (ʌ) is open and emphasized, like in the words "money or "under."

Below is a chart of the vowels and consonants introduced in Levels 4-6.
Practice looking at each symbol, then say the english word and pay attention to the tongue and lips position described in the third column.

oʊ (diphthong: 2 vowel sounds)	goat	[goʊt]	Low tongue, tip behind bottom teeth Lips open then rounded
aɪ (diphthong: 2 vowel sounds)	price	[praɪs]	Low tongue then high tongue tip behind bottom teeth then sides touching top teeth Lips tall then relaxed
ʤ	jar	[ʤɑr]	High tongue on hard palate tip behind top teeth Lips rounded
ʎ	million (but keep tongue flat, and tip behind top teeth)	[mɪljən]	High, flat tongue tip behind top teeth Lips relaxed
ʃ	ship	[ʃɪp]	High tongue sides touching top teeth Lips rounded
ɲ	canyon	[kaɲjon]	High tongue Tip touching hard palate Lips relaxed
h	ham	[hæm]	Low, flat tongue Open, wide mouth Lips relaxed
ŋ	sing	[siŋg]	High tongue Middle touching soft palate Lips relaxed
ð	this	[ðɪs]	Mid tongue Tip between teeth Lips relaxed
ç	hue	[çju]	High tongue Middle touching hard palate sides touching top teeth Lips relaxed
x	loch (but don't let tongue touch the roof of your mouth)	[lɑx]	High tongue back arched towards soft palate with air Lips open, slightly rounded
ts	bats	[bæts]	Low tongue Tip between front teeth Lips relaxed
aʊ (diphthong: 2 vowel sounds)	shout	[ʃaʊt]	Low tongue then high tongue tip behind bottom teeth then sides touching top teeth Lips tall then rounded

Below is a chart of the vowels and consonants introduced in Levels 7-8.
Practice looking at each symbol, then say the english word and pay attention to the tongue and lips position described in the third column.

ɑ̃	on (but with nasal sound)	[ɑn]	Back of tongue is high Tip behind bottom teeth Lips tall slightly rounded
ɛ̃	land (but with nasal sound)	[lænd]	Tongue is flat and wide Tip behind bottom teeth Lips spread horizontally
ʒ	vision	[vɪʒn]	Sides of tongue touching teeth in middle of mouth Lips slightly rounded

IPA SYMBOL	UMLAUT EQUIVALENT	FOREIGN LANGUAGE WORD EQUIVALENT	TONGUE/LIPS PLACEMENT
y	ü	German: "über" French: "fut" Does not exist in Italian or English	Center of tongue is high Lips are rounded say "Ee" with "Oo" lips
ø	ö	German: "schöne" French: "feu" Does not exist in Italian or English	An open sound as in "hook" or "hurt" with taller lips, shaped like "oh."
ɛ	ä	German: "hätte" French: "belle" English: "fed" Italian: "bello"	Low tongue Lips relaxed

Review: Lesson 11

1. Check the English word that contains the same sound as the given IPA symbol.

ð ___Pot ___That	ʃ ___Shoot ___Say	oʊ___Boot ___Boat	æ___Pat ___Paint	ɑ̃ ___Rats ___Fond
ŋ ___Spring ___Not	j ___Yes ___Just	ɔ ___Floor ___Goat	ə ___Feet ___About	ɛ̃ ___Band ___Bond
h ___Hot ___Shine	ʤ___Does ___Jerk	ʌ ___Vex ___But	e ___Late ___Pet	ʒ ___Measure ___Buzz
ɲ ___Never ___Canyon	aɪ___Mice ___Late	ʊ ___Look ___Gut	ɪ ___Fit __ Bite	aʊ___Bout ___Fat
o ___Over ___Cot	ɑ ___Fat ___Bother	ɛ ___Breed ___Pet	i ___Fee ___Hit	ç ___Honor ___Heat
ts___Hats ___Tang		u ___Loose ___Mutt	x ___Hoch ___Pox	

2. Connect each IPA symbol with the correct lip position & tongue position.

LIPS POSITION	IPA SYMBOL	TONGUE POSITION
Rounded Say "Ee" with "Oo" lips	ø	High
Relaxed	ɛ	Sides touching teeth in middle of mouth
Relaxed	i	Low Tongue
Open "hook" sound with tall lips, shaped like "oh"	y	Center of tongue high

3. Check the correct IPA spelling for each of the given English words.

Yet	___ jɛt ___ yet	Oven	___ovan ___ʌvən	Fat	___fæt ___fait
Moose	___moss ___mus	Flee	___fli ___flɛ	Around	___uhraund ___əraʊnd
Let	___lɛt ___let	Flower	___flaʊər ___flawir	Just	___ʤʌst ___yʌst
Bother	___bɑðər ___buaðer	Sing	___sinj ___sɪŋ	Shut	___ʃʌt ___chʌt
Mit	___mit ___mɪt	Onion	___ʌnjən ___ɔnjən	Boat	___baut ___boʊt

Lesson 12: Italian, Latin, Spanish, German & French Diction

When you first learn a song in a foreign language, Italian and Latin are two of the easier languages to pronounce. Below are some rules for speaking/singing words in Italian and Latin that can help you learn how to prounounce the text in your songs.
It's also a great idea to use a translation app or website to hear someone pronounce the foreign language text as well.

Italian/Latin Diction

As with any language, practicing speaking this language with an Italian accent will help with pronunciation. IPA is included in parentheses after each Italian/Latin word.

Remember: No diphthongs!
•*Core* (kore) is pronounced Core-A, but without the E sound at the end of A.
Another example is *Mio* (mˈio) is pronounced Mee-oh but without the oo sound and the end of O.

•I's are pronounced like E's. (ie) *Ma'mi* (mami) is pronounced Mamee

•All R's are rolled or flipped. If you cannot roll your R's, try something similar to a D. *Caro* (karo) would sound similar to *Cah-doh*, then add a little less pressure to the roof of your mouth. Your tongue touches the top of your hard palate behind your top front teeth for the first letter.
**Two great practice exercises to learn how to roll your tongue is to say "Podda tea" over and over again, or try saying"Tah-dah" over and over again.

•A "C" followed by an E or I is pronounced as a "CH." (ie) *Facil* (fatʃil) is pronounced Facheel.
Also *Dolce* (doltʃe) is pronounced Dole-cheh.
•A "CH" combo is pronounced as a K. (ie) *Chiaro* (kjaro) is pronounced Kee-ah-ro.

•When a word has a double consonant, you stop on the first consonant then continue. The best example of this is the word "*Pizza*" (piddza). It's not pronounced PEEZA, it's pronounced PEETSA.
Also *Quella* (kwella) is Kwell-lah.

•A "G" if it's before an e or an i is a soft g. (ie) *gentil* (dʒentil) is pronounced jenteel, *Giardi* (dʒardi) is pronounced Jar-dee. Notice the "i" is silent when it falls between G and another vowel. The same rule applies when an "i" falls between C and another vowel as in "*ciao.*" ch-ow
•A "G" followed by an "L" is silent. (ie) *scegliera* (ʃeʎʎera) is pronounced shay-lee-err-ah.
•A G followed by an H is pronounced as a Hard G...*Lunghezza* (luŋgettsa) is pronounced Loon-get-tsa.

•*Que* (kwe) is pronounced Kway.
•*Che* (ke) is pronounced Kay.

•An S followed by a C is pronounced as an SH. (ie) *s'angoscia* (ssaŋgoʃʃa) is san-go-shah.
•If an S is followed by a CH it's pronounced as SK. (ie) *scherzosa* (skertsoza) is scare-tso-za.
•A single S between two vowels is pronounced as a Z. (ie) *ascosa* (askoza) is pronounced ah-sko-za.
•An SC before e or i is pronounced as an SH. (ie) *scegliera* (ʃeʎʎera) is pronounced shay-lee-err-ah.

•An H at the beginning of a word is silent. (ie) *Hanno* (anno) is pronounced Ahn-no.

•A Z is pronounced like TS. (ie) *Danza* (dantsa) is pronounced Dawn-tsa.

•An "A" is pronounced as an "AH"

Spanish Diction

When singing in Spanish, pay special attention to where the composer is from. Spanish pronunciation differs slightly depending on the country. It's always best to listen to a recording, if possible, of a singer or speaker who is from the same country as the composer.

Remember: No diphthongs!

Noche is pronounced No-chay, but without the E sound at the end of A.

Another example is *Mio* is pronounced Mee-oh but without the oo sound and the end of O.

•Roll all R's that begin a word.
•Flip all R's at the end of a word.
•Roll or flip all R's in the middle of a word depending on how it is usually pronounced.

•The "C" sound is different in Spanish from Spain as opposed to Spanish from Mexico and other countries. The Spain "C" is pronounced with a th sound like a lisp (ie) *hacer* is pronounced Hather. In Mexico, it's just an "S" sound (ie) *hacer* is pronounced Ha-ser.

•Double LL's are pronounced as a Y. (ie) *Llega* is pronounced Yeah-gah.

•T's and D's use a flatter tongue, more dentalized. These two consonants are not as bright as we say them in English. Example: *todos* is toe-those, and **not** toe-dohs.

•Pay special attention to accents, and pronounce them as spoken.

•Pronounce J's with a small puff of air, in order for it to be audible, similar to an H. (ie) *Reja* is pronounced Ray-ha.

•Always hold the first vowel when singing a word with a diphthong.

•*Que* is pronounced as Kay.
•*Che* is pronounced as Chay.

•An ñ is pronounced as in the word Ke**nya**.

•A Y (the letter that stands for the word "and") is pronounced as an E, as in "key."

•E's are pronounced as the IPA symbol "e" as in "Pay" when in the middle of a word.
•E's are pronounced as the IPA symbol "ɛ" as in "let" when at the beginning of a word.

•I's are pronounced as E's. *Mi* is pronounced as Mee.

•G followed by an i or e is pronounced with the H sound like *gente* hente or *Ginastera* Hinastera.
•G followed by a u is a hard G as in *gusta* goos-tah

German Diction

As with any language, practicing speaking this language with a German accent will help with pronunciation.

In German, vowel combinations will form sounds similar to diphthongs. "Blau" is pronounced <u>*Blah-oo.*</u> *Much like the sound in the word "**Ou**ch."*

•W's are pronounced as V's. (ie) *Werden* is pronounced <u>Vair-duhn.</u>

•V's are pronounced as F's. (ie) *Vater* is pronounced <u>Faht-uh.</u>

•IE combinations are pronounced as an E. (ie) *Lied* is pronounced <u>Leed.</u>

•EI combinations are pronounced as an I. (ie) *Mein* is pronounced <u>Mine.</u>

•E's at the ends of words are open, using the same sound as a schwa (ə). *liebe* = <u>Lee-buh.</u>

•ü is called an Umlaut (the two dots above a vowel). If you see this over a "u" form an "oo" with your lips, and say an "E." Think of saying "ee" on this inside.

•ä is prounounced like an A as in <u>Maid.</u> (ie) *Mädchen* is pronounced <u>Met-hun.</u>

•ö is pronounced as in the word "hurt" but with an open R. (ie) *öffnen* = <u>erf-nen.</u>

•A Z at the beginning or end of a word is pronounced as a TS. (ie) *Zart* is pronounced <u>Ts-art.,</u> <u>*Herz* is pronounced Hair-ts</u>

•A "D" at the end of a word, or when followed by another consonant at the end a root stem is pronounced as a T. (ie) *Und* is pronounced <u>Oont.</u> (ie) *Bildnis* is pronounced <u>Built-niss</u>

•A "D" at the beginning of a word or followed by a vowel is pronounced as a D. *Kinder* =<u>*Kin-duh.*</u>

•A "B" at the end of a word is pronounced as a P. (ie) *Selb* is pronounced <u>Zelp.</u>

•A CH at the end of a word is pronounced with a lot of air, much like the sound of a hissing cat, as in the word *ich.* *

•Roll or flip all R's in the middle of a word. Open R's at the end of words, using the same sound as a schwa (ə). (ie) *immer* is pronounced <u>imm-uh.</u>

•S's followed by a consonant is sounded as an SH. (ie) *stehn* is pronounced <u>Shtain.</u>

•S's followed by a vowel are pronounced as a Z. (ie) *sei* is pronounced <u>Z-ah-ee</u> (rhymes with high)

•E's are pronounced like an A as in <u>Ate.</u> (ie) *den* is pronounced <u>Dane.</u>

•J's are pronounced as a Y. (ie) *Jäger* is pronounced <u>Yay-guh.</u>

•ß is a double S, "SS"

*The CH sound at the ends of words varies depending on what part of Germany you are from. Some pronounce it with a high middle tongue and similar to the hissing of a cat, others pronounce it more like a "shh." Whatever you choose, remain consistent in your German repertoire.

French Diction

As with any language, practicing speaking this language with a French accent will help with pronunciation.
All R's are forward and flipped when singing French. No back R's as when speaking French.

Remember: No diphthongs: "Les" is Lay without the e sound at the end.

**Much of French involves nasal sounds. You do not pronounce a lot of the ends of words. Instead you end them with a nasal sound. (ie) "Dans"= Don (without closing the N-touching the back of your tongue to the roof of your mouth). Nasals in IPA are indicated by a squiggly line: ɑ̃ this is called a "tilde."

•Ends of words that are not pronounced are "s" "eil" "iens" "t" "ent" "ng" •*Sommeil=Somay Tes-Tay Rayonnais=Ray-oh-nay*
•You do pronounce some endings of words if the following word starts with a vowel. *(vous avez)-* is pronounced Voo-zAh-vay

•An E at the end of a word is the neutral vowel (schwa) much like "uh" (ie) *image*=E-mah-j (g is pronounced like the S sound in the word measure). Other endings of words that have the neutral sound are: Es, eurs, re, ge, le, se
(When spoken, you do not say the schwa at the end of a word, but when singing, the final syllable is typically under a note that must be sung.)

•If an X is at the end of a word and followed by a word that starts with a vowel, it's pronounced as a Z. (ie) *yeux etaient* = Yoo-zA-tay

•The combination *heur* is like saying "earth" (with an open R and a dropped jaw)
(ie) *l'heur* = lehr (with a dropped jaw)

•An accent over an e that is pointing up to the right is pronounced as an A.
(ie) Hélas=A-lass

•U's have an E sound in them. (ie) *nues* = new-uh

•Some ends of words are pronounced as an A. (ie) "ais" and "aient"

•*Oi*=W (as in *oui*-we) *Toi*=Twa *Voix*=vwa

•An I at the beginning of a word is nasal. *Incline*=Un-clean (without closing the first n).

•An N proceeded by a vowel is nasal. (ie) *Long*=Lon (Nasal N without closing it).
(ie) *Silence*=See-lon-s (again without closing the N).

•An X at the end of a word is an Oh sound. (ie) *berceaux*=bare-so

•H's are silent (ie) *Hélas*=A-lass.

•*Qui*=Key

Review: Lesson 12

1. Check the correct IPA spelling for each of the given Foreign language words.

French

- Que ___ kə / ___ kway
- Printemps ___ prɪntamps / ___ prɛ̃tɑ̃
- Le ___ lə / ___ lai
- Penché ___ pɑ̃ʃe / ___ penʃə
- Voit ___ voite / ___ vwa
- Est ___ ɛ / ___ ɛst
- Sous ___ su / ___ souz
- Parler ___ parler / ___ parle
- Nous ___ nu / ___ nuz
- Quand ___ kɑ̃ / ___ kwand
- Bois ___ baɪs / ___ bwa
- Amour ___ amur / ___ amore

German

- Leise ___ laɪzə / ___ laize
- Einsam ___ aɪnzam / ___ ɛanzam
- Über ___ oobə / ___ ybə
- Mein ___ main / ___ maɪn
- Die ___ di / ___ dai
- Heißer ___ haiffə / ___ haɪsə
- Mir ___ miə / ___ mɪə
- Duft ___ dʊft / ___ duhft
- Und ___ ʊnd / ___ ʊnt
- Wach ___ vax / ___ vok
- Dich ___ dɪç / ___ dik
- Fräulein ___ frɔʏlaɪn / ___ fraulen

Spanish

- Porque ___ poɾke / ___ porkə
- Estoy ___ istoi / ___ estoi
- Majo ___ mago / ___ maxo
- Llega ___ ʎega / ___ lega
- Siempre ___ saiempre / ___ sjempɾe
- Quiero ___ kjeɾo / ___ kweero
- Mira ___ miɾa / ___ mɪra
- Cuanto ___ kanto / ___ kwanto
- Cantar ___ kantaɾ / ___ kentar
- Que ___ ke / ___ kwe
- Dolorosa ___ doloɾosa / ___ dolaroza
- Noche ___ notʃe / ___ nochae

Italian/Latin

- Dolce ___ dolche / ___ doltʃe
- Tutto ___ tutto / ___ teutto
- Que ___ kwe / ___ kə
- Caro ___ koro / ___ karo
- Amore ___ amore / ___ amoure
- Che ___ ke / ___ kə
- Troppo ___ tɾˈɔppo / ___ troopo
- Dolor ___ doloɾ / ___ daloɾ
- Piacer ___ pjatʃeɾ / ___ pyatcheɾ
- Bella ___ bella / ___ bɛlla
- Gioja ___ goya / ___ dʒoja
- Luci ___ lutʃi / ___ lusi

Lesson 13: Sight-Singing

In order to learn a song, singers learn to read both rhythmic patterns and notes (melody) on the staff. Singing a melody for the first time is called "sight-singing." Below are some rhythmic examples using the notes introduced so far.

Hint: When singing rhythmic examples, take a breath on the rests: then you won't miss them! *Tap* and *say* the beats, then sing the examples on La (choose any pitch that suits your voice).

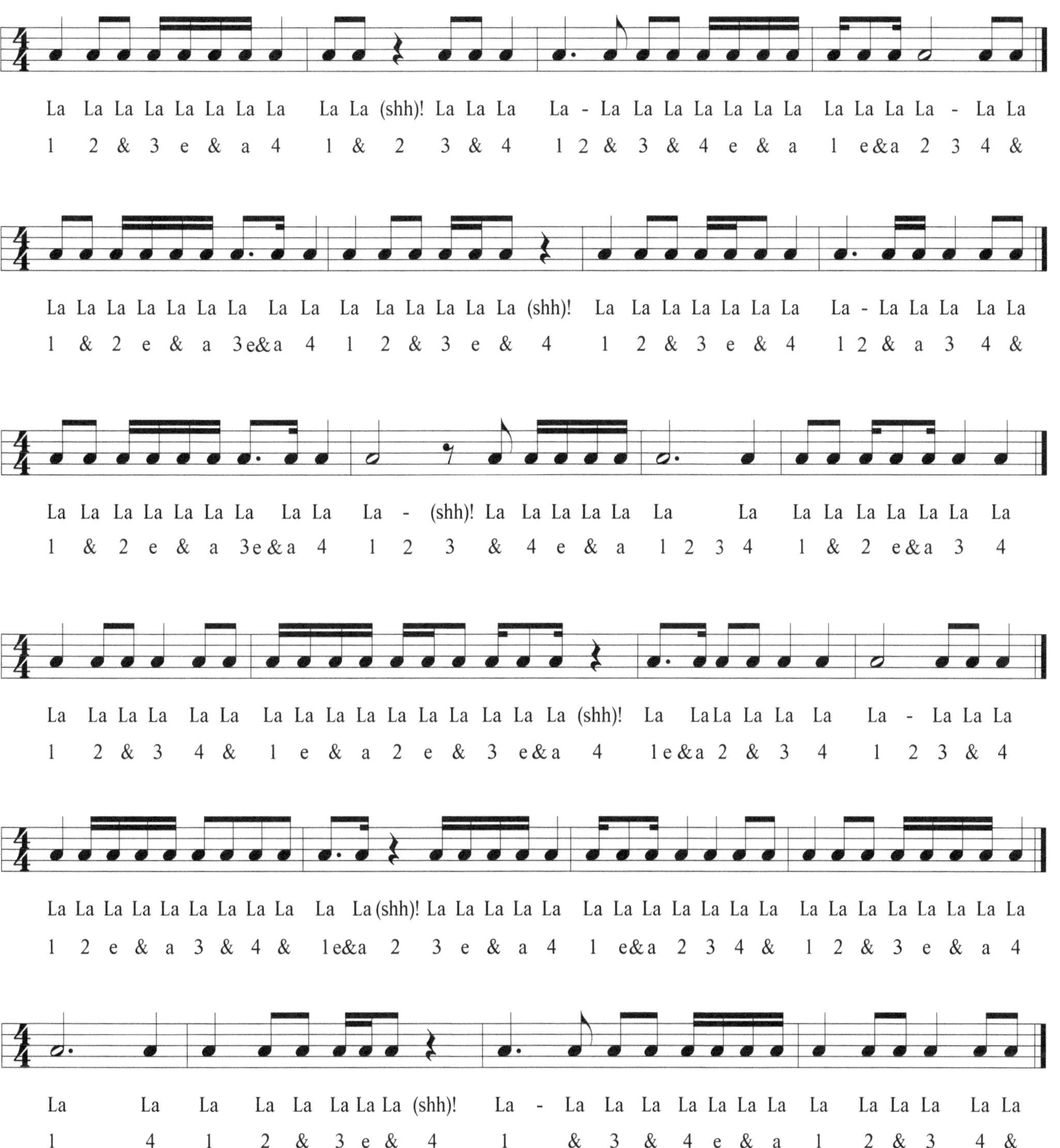

Melody & Solfege

Solfege is a system of assigning a syllable to each note of a scale, just like in the song "Do-Re-Mi" from the musical *The Sound of Music.*
Solfege is a useful tool when sight-singing. Moveable "Do" is when "Do" matches the **root** of whatever key you're in.

In this Level, you will be introduced to melodies in a **melodic minor** key, in the range of an octave. When singing a Melodic minor scale, the solfege is slightly different. When the music ascends, the 3rd note of the scale is lowered, but the 6th note and 7th note are raised (the same as in a Major scale). When the music descends, the 3rd, 6th & 7th notes are lowered, which is exactly the same as a natural minor scale. The altered solfege represents the different notes and sounds that are in a minor scale.

Solfege for an **ascending melodic minor** scale is: Do-Re-Me-Fa-Sol-La-Ti-Do. You may also use the solfege that relates to the relative Major key: La-Ti-Do-Re-Mi-Fi-Si-La.

Solfege for a **descending melodic minor** scale is: Do-Te-Le-Sol-Fa-Me-Re-Do. You may also use the solfege that relates to the relative Major key: La-Sol-Fa-Mi-Re-Do-Ti-La. The following melodies are all minor.

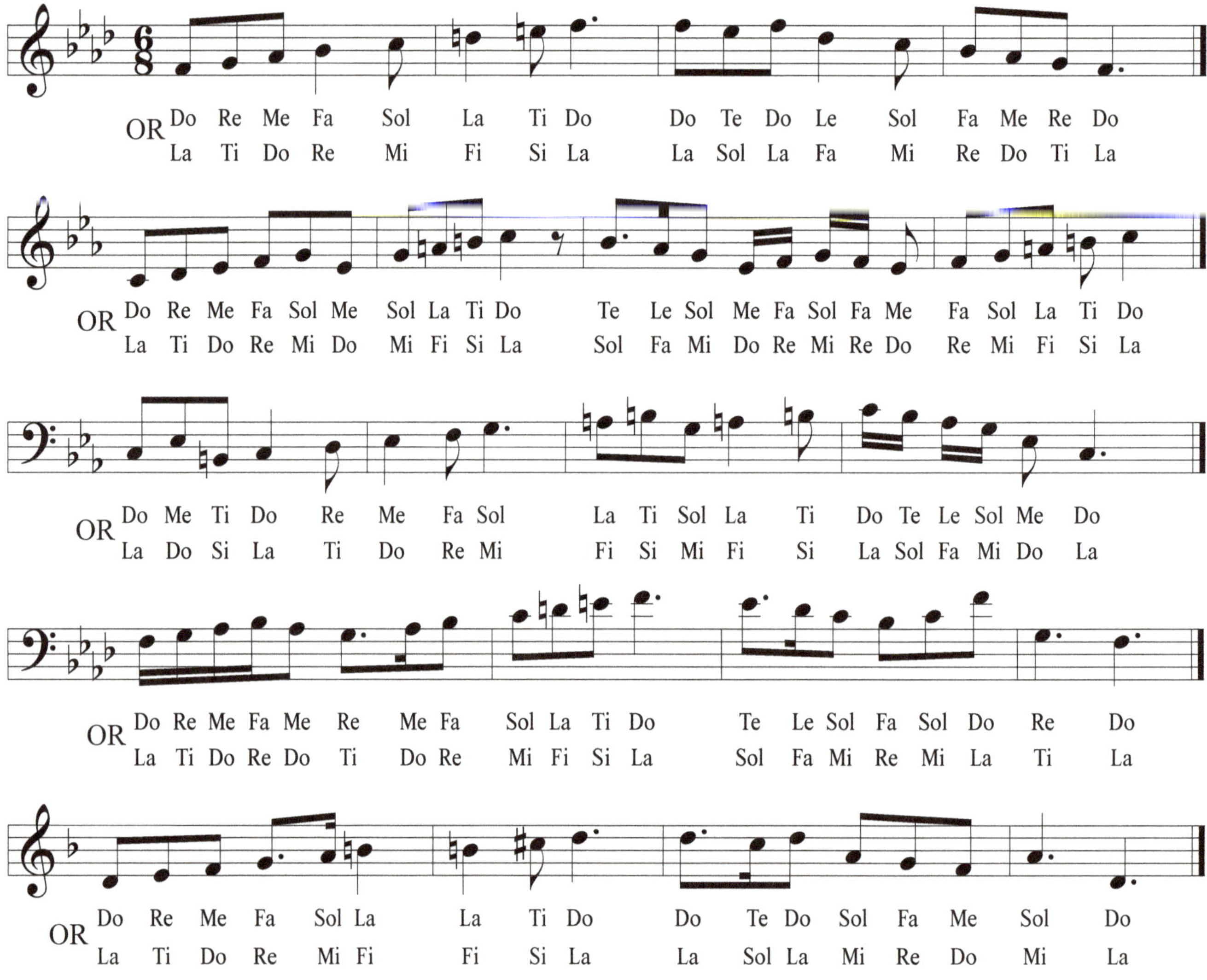

(Me is pronounced "May," Le is pronounced "Lay" Te is pronounced "Tay.")

Review: Lesson 13

1. For the following melodies, write the note names, solfege & beats underneath the notes. Pay special attention to the key signature (Major or minor). Choose either "moveable Do" (where Do is the root of the minor key) or use the solfege as it relates to the Major key. Both examples have been provided for you. Practice singing the examples when you are done!

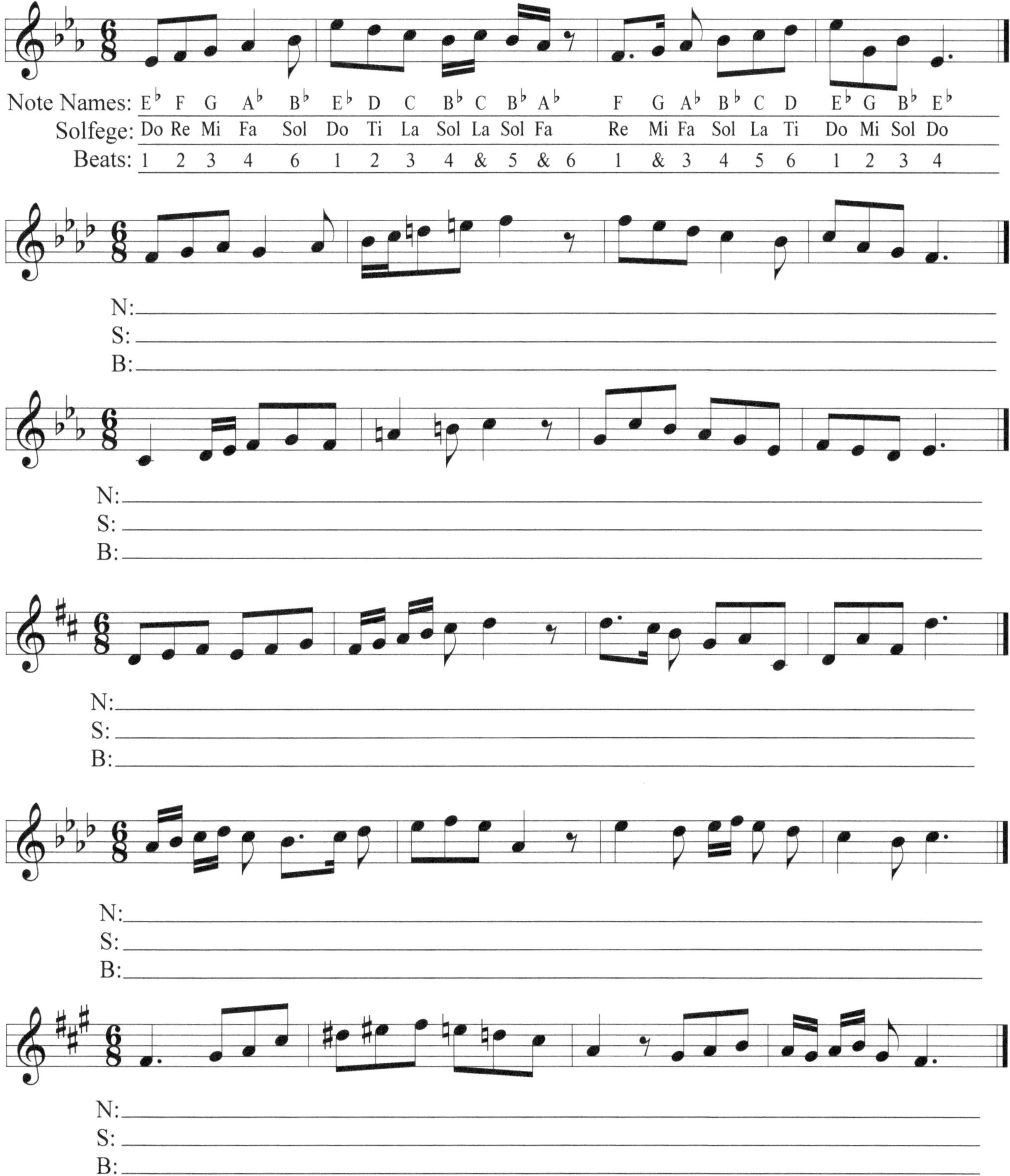

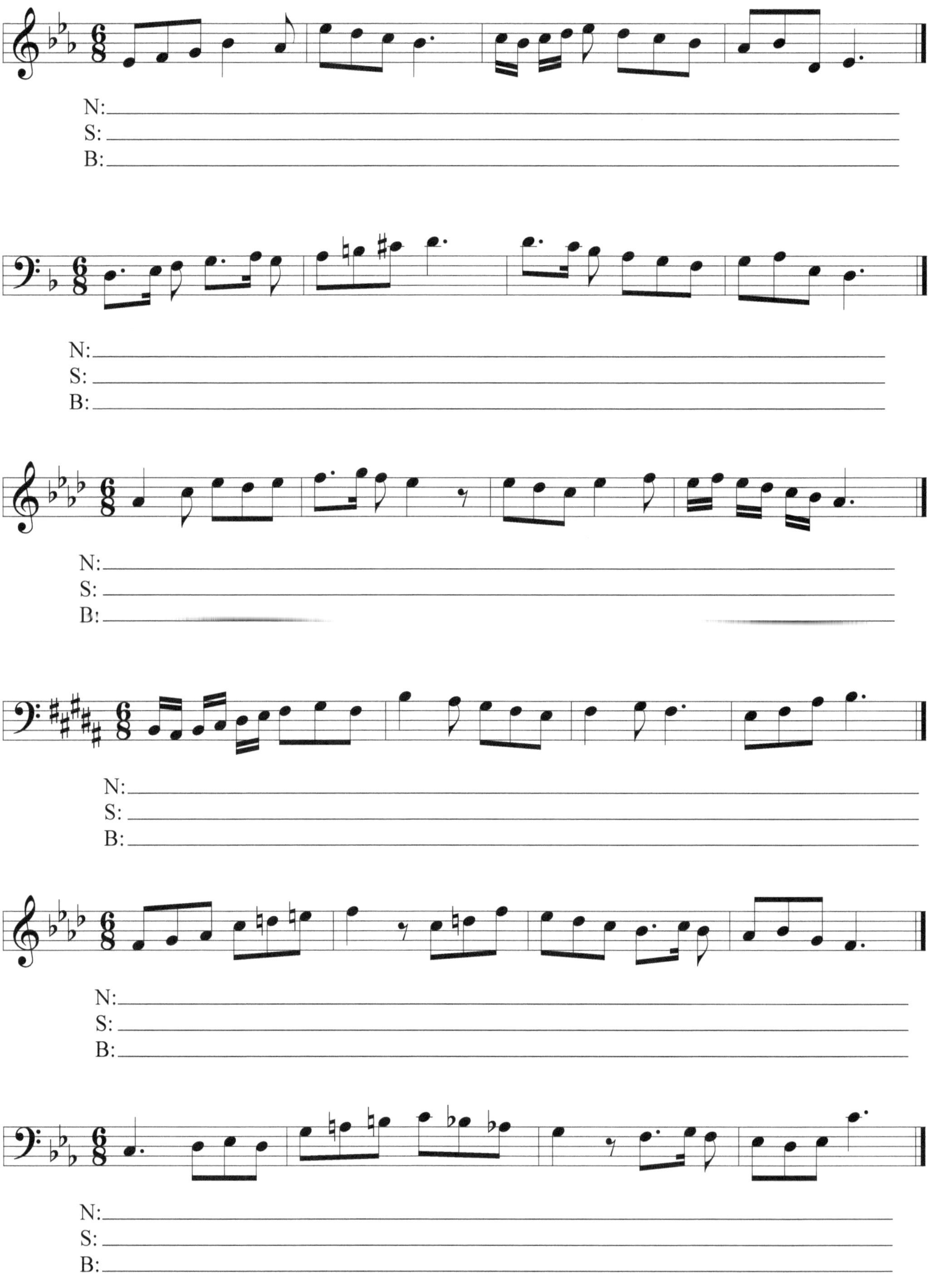
N:
S:
B:
N:
S:
B:
N:
S:
B:
N:
S:
B:
N:
S:
B:
N:
S:
B:

Lesson 14: Musical Terms

A crucial part of understanding music is being able to recognize and define musical terms. Below is a list of terms covered in this level.

descant - a melodic line harmonizing with and usually written above a given melody

doloroso - sorrowful

embellishment - ornaments added to music

falsetto - a high, artificial voice used for notes that lie above the normal register

genre - a distinct type of composition; in vocal music, opera, operetta, oratorio, art song, & musical theatre are all separate genres

giocoso - humorous

harmony - one or more notes, which form a second part under a melody

maestoso - majestically

marcato - stressed, accented

melisma - several notes sung to one syllable

messa di voce - a crescendo and decrescendo on a sustained tone

morendo - fading away

portato - halfway between staccato and legato

song cycle - a group of related songs unified by theme or lyric

sotto voce - quietly, in a soft voice

stringendo - hurrying the tempo, increasing the tension

transposition - to write or perform a musical work in a key other than that in which it was written

turn - (∾) an ornament consisting of a 4-note figure: the note above, the note itself, the note below, and the note itself. It is executed two different ways depending on whether the turn is over the main note or between it and the next note.

vibrato - repeated fluctuation of pitch

Review: Lesson 14

1. Check the definition that matches the given term.

a. messa di voce
___ the average vocal range of a piece
___ a crescendo and descrescendo on the same tone

b. portato
___ halfway between staccato and legato
___ stressed, accented

c. marcato
___ stressed, accented
___ majestically

d. falsetto
___ high, artificial voice for notes above the normal register
___ fading away

e. morendo
___ humorous
___ fading away

f. sotto voce
___ quietly, in a soft voice
___ several notes sung on one syllable

g. tessitura
___ changing from one key to another
___ the average vocal range of a piece

h. vibrato
___ repeated fluctuation of pitch
___ hurrying the tempo

i. song cycle
___ singing the same verse several times
___ a group of related songs unified by a theme

j. stringendo
___ hurrying the tempo, increasing the tension
___ halfway between staccato and legato

k. melisma
___ stressed, accented
___ several notes sung to one syllable

l. giocoso
___ majestically
___ humorous

m. descant
___ a melodic line harmonizing with and usually written above a given melody
___ fading away

n. doloroso
___ sorrowful
___ quietly, in a soft voice

2. Complete the following crossword puzzle using the terms from this level.

Level 9 Crossword

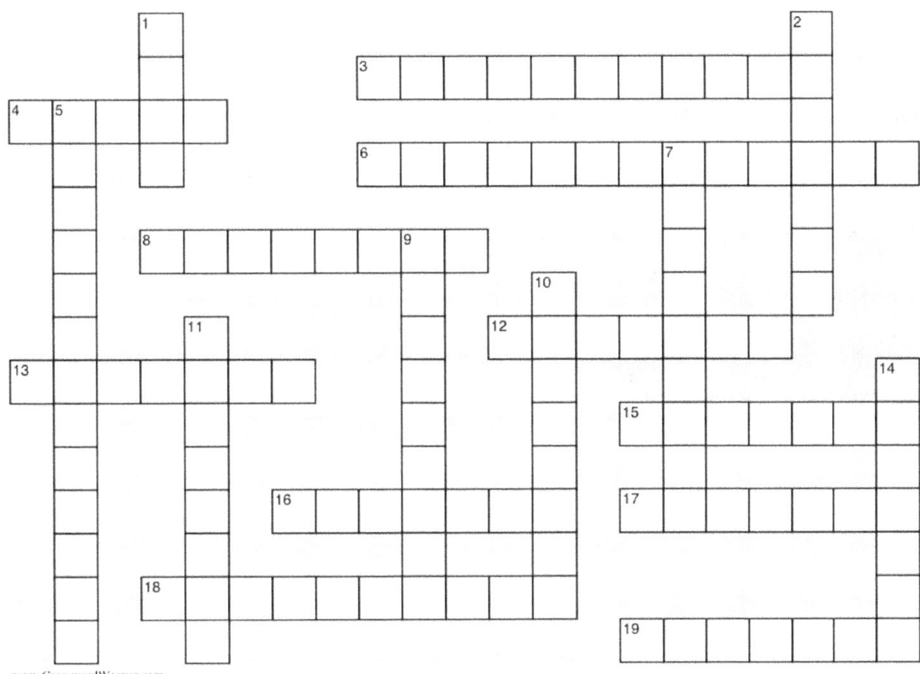

ACROSS

3 a crescendo and decrescendo on a sustained tone (three words)
4 a distinct type of composition; in vocal music, opera, operetta, oratorio, art song, & musical theatre are all separate genres
6 to write or perform a musical work in a key other than that in which it was written
8 sorrowful
12 one or more notes, which form a second part under a melody
13 repeated fluctuation of pitch
15 fading away
16 humorous
17 a melodic line harmonizing with and usually written above a given melody
18 hurrying the tempo, increasing the tension
19 stressed, accented

DOWN

1 an ornament consisting of a 4-note figure: the note above, the note itself, the note below, and the note itself. It is executed two different ways depending on whether the turn is over the main note or between it and the next note.
2 several notes sung to one syllable
5 ornaments added to music
7 quietly, in a soft voice (two words)
9 a group of related songs unified by theme or lyric (two words)
10 majestically
11 a high, artificial voice used for notes that lie above the normal register
14 halfway between staccato and legato

crossword created at:
www.CrosswordWeaver.com

Lesson 15: Spotlight on Composers

An important part of music education is learning about the history of music. Studying composers allows for understanding the music we sing and why it was written the way it was. In this level, you will learn about Samuel Barber, Amy Beach & Pyotr (Peter) Tschaikovsky.

SAMUEL BARBER

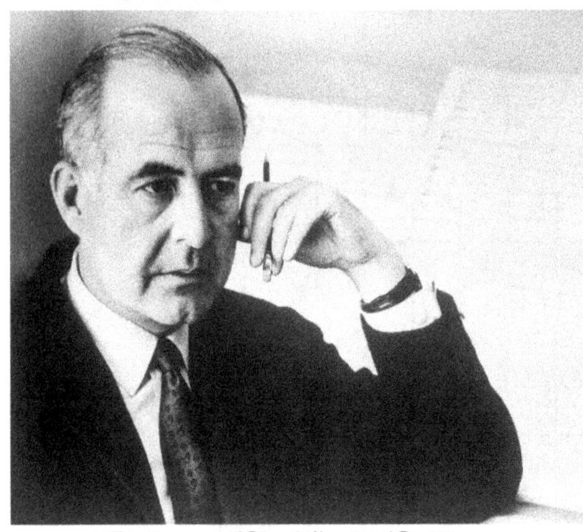

Bettmann/Contributor/Getty

Samuel Barber was born in the Contemporary period of music on March 9th, 1910 in West Chester, Pennsylvania. Barber showed incredible talent at a young age, writing his first musical when he was seven. He also attempted to write an opera when he was ten. By the age of 12 he was already an organist and when he was 14, he entered the Curtis Institute in Philadelphia where he studied piano, voice and composition.

Barber's mother was a pianist and his uncle, Sidney Homer, was a composer of American art songs. It was his aunt, Louise Homer, a lead singer at the Metropolitan Opera, who influenced Barber's interest in voice.

As a teenager, Barber met Gian Carlo Menotti, who became his life partner, and also wrote music with him. It was also during his teenage years that the founder of the Curtis Institute, Mary Louise Curtis Bok, introduced Barber to his lifelong publisher, the Schirmer family.

During his twenties, Barber wrote several successful compositions including his "Adagio for Strings." This piece has since been used in several movies, including *Platoon.* Famous artists performed his pieces including Vladamir Horowitz, Francis Poulenc & Leontyne Price. His pieces contained "polytonality" and employed several time signature changes, thus making his music challenging to sing well.

In 1958, Barber won the Pulitzer Prize for his first opera *Vanessa.* He won another Pulitzer Prize in 1963, for his "Concerto for Piano and Orchestra." Barber also wrote over 60 vocal songs including the famous song cycle *Hermit Songs.* His most famous vocal composition *Knoxville: Summer of 1915,* was written for soprano and orchestra, with text by James Agee. The success of this piece caused several to name Barber as one of the twelve most accomplished composers for voice.

Barber died of cancer on January 23rd, 1981. He was 70 years old.

Best Known Vocal Works:
(Opera) - ***Vanessa*** (1957), ***A Hand of Bridge*** (1959), ***Anthony and Cleopatra*** (1966)

(Song Cycles) - ***Mélodies passagères*** (1950), ***Hermit Songs*** (1953), ***Despite and Still*** (1968)

(Songs) - **"The Daisies," "Dover Beach," "Beggar's Song," "A Nun Takes the Veil," "The Secrets of the Old," "Sure on this Shining Night," "The Crucifixion," "The Monk and His Cat," "The Praises of God," "Un cygne," "Tombeau dans un parc"**

AMY BEACH

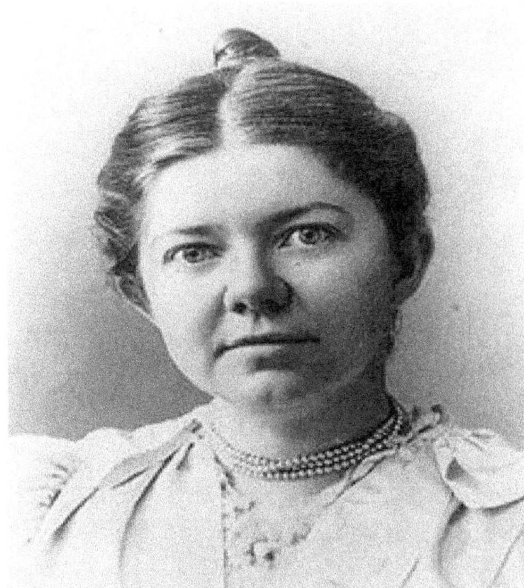
Courtesy of Library of Congress

Amy Beach is an American composer who is considered to be from three different periods of music; the Late Romantic, Impressionistic & Early 20th Century. She was born on September 5th, 1867 in New Hampshire and was a child prodigy. By the time she was one, she could sing forty songs accurately and by age two, she could improvise a countermelody with her mother. She taught herself to read when she was three and was composing music when she was four. By the time she was seven, she was already giving public recitals playing Beethoven, Chopin and her own pieces.

In 1883, she appeared as a soloist with the Boston Symphony Orchestra. She married Dr. Henry Harris Aubrey Beach in 1885 and devoted herself to composition, per her husband's wishes. Her first major success was the *Mass in E-flat Major* which was performed in 1892 by the Handel and Haydn society. She also composed *Jubilate* for the dedication of the Woman's Building at the Columbia Exposition in 1893.

Beach's husband died in 1910, which allowed her the freedom of touring both Europe and America as a pianist and composer. She performed her own compositions and earned the reputation as America's leading woman composer. Her music has been compared to Brahms and Rachmaninoff, but she also used polytonality and whole tone scales in her compositions.

Beach is most well known for her vocal songs. One of her most famous songs is "The Year's at the Spring," from the song cycle, *Three Browning Songs, Op.44.* Beach passed away on December 27, 1944 due to complications from heart disease. On July 9th, 2000, her name was the only woman's name to be added to the granite wall, at Boston's famous Hatch Shell. She was also inducted into the "Classical Music Hall of Fame and Museum" in Cincinnati, Ohio.

Best Known Vocal Works:
(Songs): Over 150 songs including, **"Allein!" "Autumn song," "Chanson d'amour," Come, ah Come,""I Know not How to Find the Spring," "My love is like a Red, Red Rose," "Sea Song," Take, O Take those Lips Away," "The Thrush," "The Year's at the Spring"**

(Opera): ***Cabildo*** (1932)

PYOTR (PETER) TCHAIKOVSKY

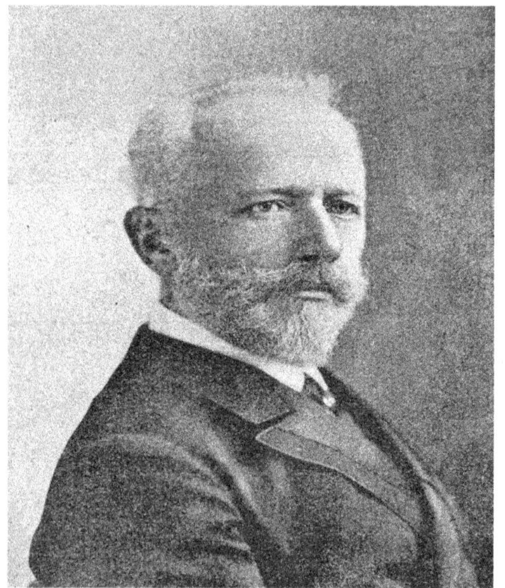
© Oleg Golovnev/Shutterstock.com

Pyotr Ilyich Tchaikovsky was born in the Romantic period of music on May 7th, 1840 in Russia. He began piano lessons when he was five years old and was able to play as well as his teacher within three years. His parents sent him to boarding school when he was 10, which was to train him to be a civil servant. After his mother passed away in 1854, Tchaikovsky turned to composing, writing a waltz in her memory. His father paid for piano lessons for his son, and he graduated from the boarding school at the age of 19.

In 1862, Tchaikovsky went to the Saint Petersburg Conservatory. He studied under Nikolai Zaremba and Anton Rubinstein (the founder of Saint Petersburg Conservatory). By 1863, he gave up his civil service career and studied music full-time, graduating from the Conservatory in 1865.

Tchaikovsky became a professor of Music Theory at the Moscow Conservatory, and he wrote his first well-known piece: the overture for *Romeo and Juliet.* He also wrote the score for the ballet *Swan Lake* (1875) and the opera *Eugene Onegin.*

Between 1877 and 1890, Nadeshda von Meck (a wealthy widow and patron of the arts) was Tchaikovsky's patron and confidante. They exchanged over 1,000 letters during these years, and she was insistant that they never meet face to face. She believed in Tchaikovsky's talent and paid him 6,000 rubles a year making it possible for him to resign from the Moscow Conservatory and focus on composition. She became a close friend to Tchaikovsky but had to end their relationship in 1890 when she became ill and began to have financial difficulties.

In 1880, Tchaikovsky wrote the *1812 Overture* which remains to be one of his most well known pieces. He also was asked to stage a new production of his opera *Eugene Onegin* in Russia, which was a huge success. He also wrote the scores for the ballets, *The Nutcracker, Swan Lake* and *Sleeping Beauty* and wrote 106 vocal songs.

Tchaikovsky died on November 6th, 1893 only nine days after the premiere of his Sixth Symphony, also known as the *Pathétique*. The cause of his death is undetermined.

Best Known Works:
1812 Overture, Romeo and Juliet, Serenade for Strings, along with Six symphonies, Three ballets, four Concertos, string quartets and piano works.

(Opera): 10 operas including, ***Eugene Onegin, The Enchantress,*** and ***Queen of Spades***

(Vocal Songs): 106 songs including, **"Gypsy's Song," "Gentle Stars Shone for Us," "Nur wer die Sehnsucht kennt," "16 Songs for Children"** (arranged for voice & piano and voice & orchestra).

Review: Lesson 15

1. Fill in the correct answer to the questions about Samuel Barber, Amy Beach & Pytor Tchaikovsky.

Samuel Barber

a. What country does he represent?______________________________

b. What musical period does he represent?________________________

c. What is the name of the famous family who were his publishers?____________________

d. What is the name of his Pulitzer prize opera that premiered in 1958?

____

e. What is the name of his most famous vocal composition for soprano & orchestra, with prose by James Agee?___________________________________

f. Name his piece that has been used in several movies, including "Platoon."_____________________

Amy Beach

a. What country does she represent?____________________________

b. Which 3 musical periods does she represent?____

c. She was a soloist with what Symphony Orchestra?___________________________________

d. Name her first major composition which was performed in 1892.__________________________

e. Name her most well-known song from the cycle "Three Browning Songs, Op.44."

____

f. As of 2011, Beach is the only woman composer's name on the wall of what famous theater in Boston?________________________________

Pytor Tchaikovsky

a. What country does he represent?_________________________

b. What musical period does he represent?________________________

c. Who was Tchaikovsky's patron and confidante?_______________________________

d. Name the three ballets he composed.____

e. Name his teacher, who founded the Saint Petersburg Conservatory.________________________

f. He died nine days after the premiere of which of his works?____________________________

Level 9 Review Test

Answer the questions on the next page about the musical example below. (15 points)

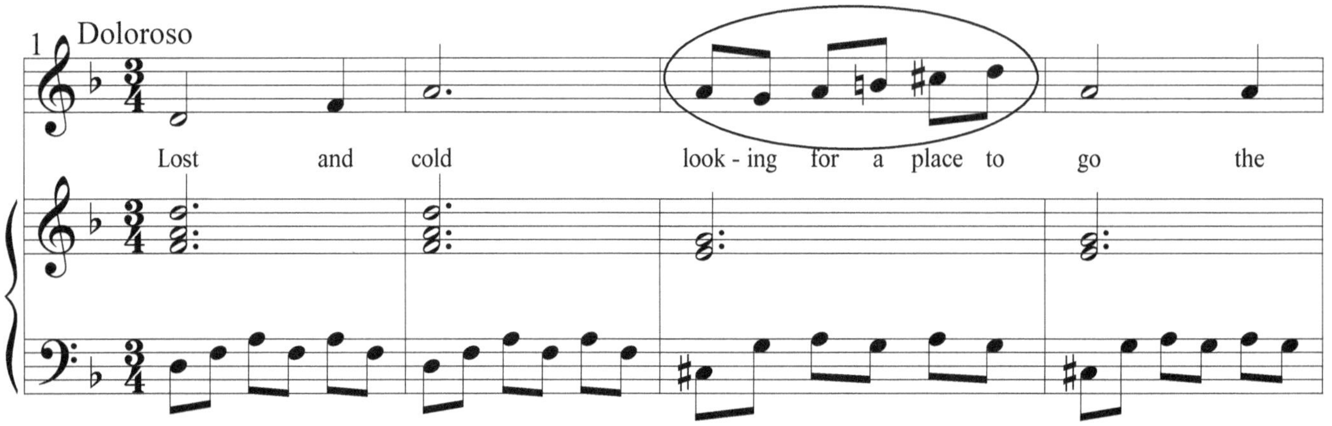

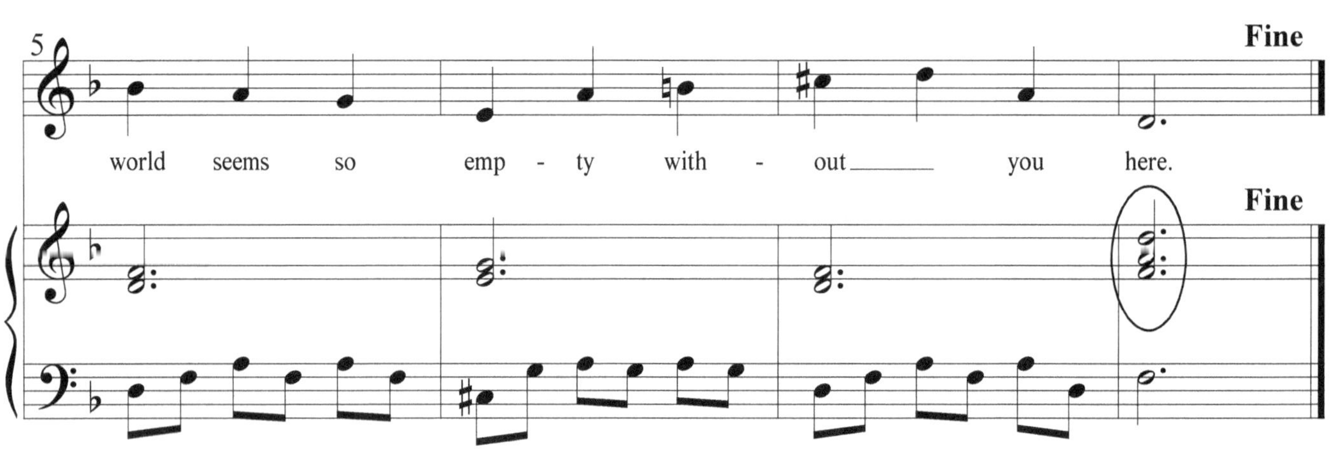

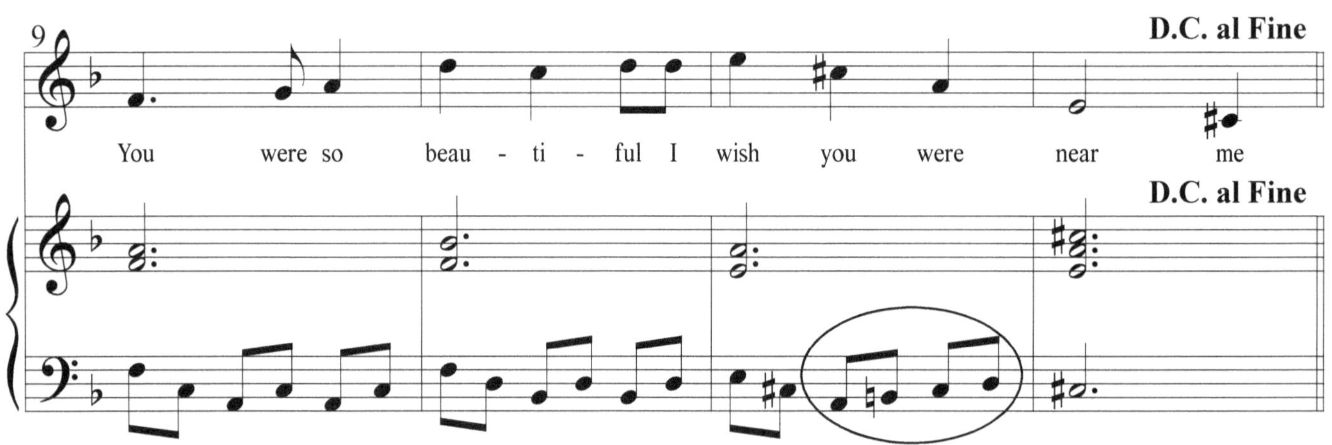

1. What minor key does this song begin in? _____f minor

_____d minor

2. What Major key does it modulate to in m. 9? _____B♭ Major

_____F Major

3. What type of minor scale do you see (circled) in m.11? _____Harmonic

_____Melodic

4. Which measure has the first Dominant 7 chord (broken) in the Bass clef? _____1

_____3

5. What is the Roman Numeral for the circled chord in measure 8? _____ iv

_____ i

6. What inversion is the circled chord in measure 8 in? _____1st

_____2nd

7. Name the solfege for the circled notes in the vocal line in measure 3.

_______ _______ _______ _______ _______ _______

8. How should this song be sung, based on the term above the vocal line in m.1? _____joyfully

_____sadly

9. If this song was transposed 1 whole step up, what minor key would it be in? _____e minor

_____f minor

10. How many times will the first and second line (systems) be heard? _____once

_____twice

11. Add the necessary accidentals to the natural minor scales below to create **melodic minor** scales. (4 points)

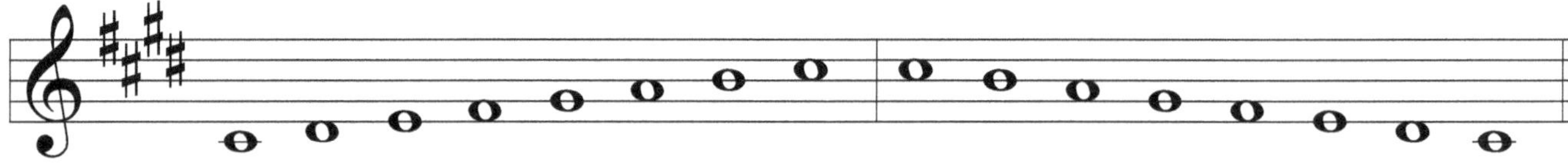

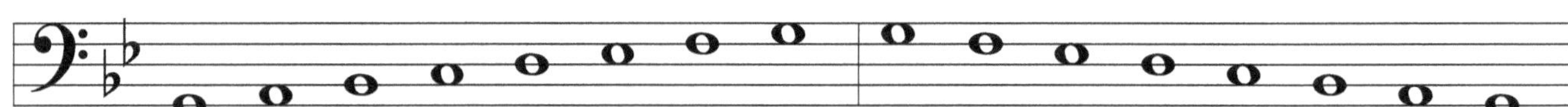

12. Use whole notes and accidentals to complete each scale. Draw an **ascending** scale in the first measure and a **descending** scale in the 2nd measure. Do not use a key signature. (4 points)

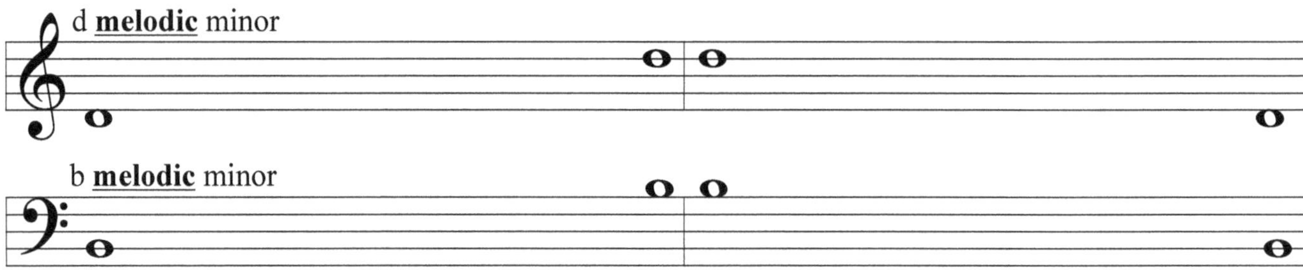

13. Draw the 1st, 2nd & 3rd inversion of the given Dominant 7 chord. (6 points)

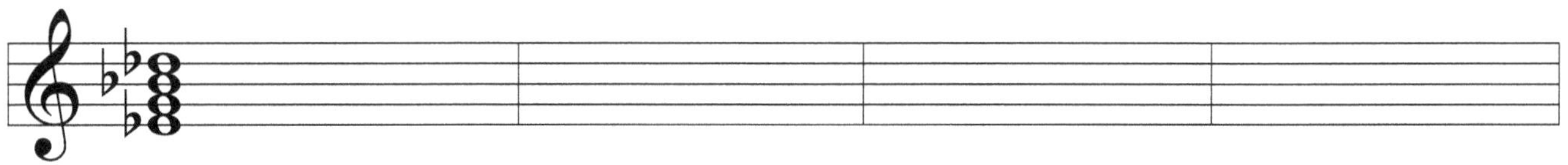

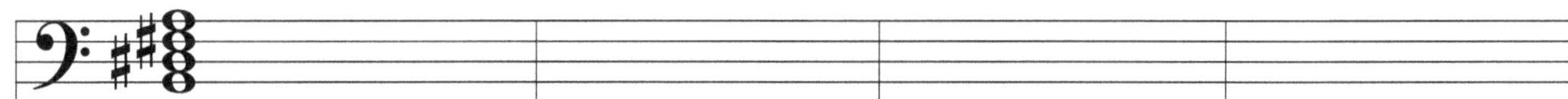

14. Draw a root position **Dominant 7th** chord in each of the following keys. (4 points)

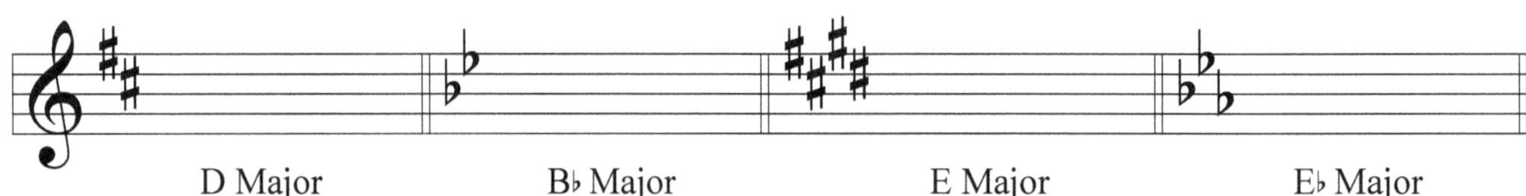

15. Check the correct inversion for the following Dominant 7th chords. (5 points)

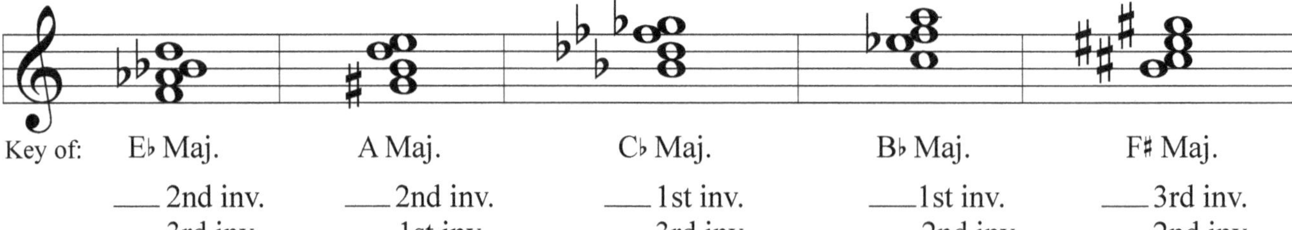

16. Name the Major key to which each of these Dominant 7th belongs. (4 points)

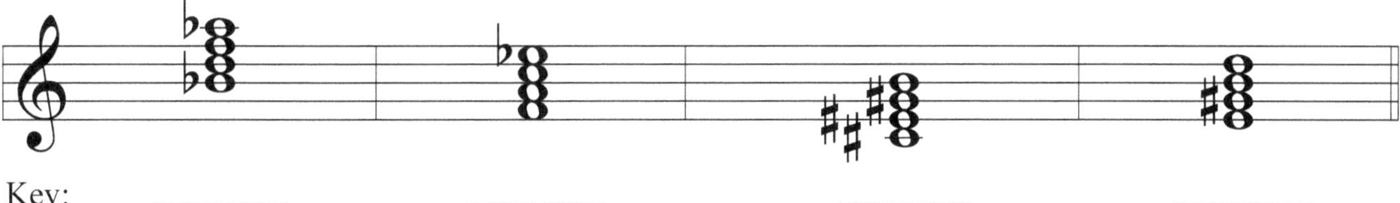

17. Draw the 1st, 2nd and 3rd inversions of the given **Dominant 7th** chord. (4 points)

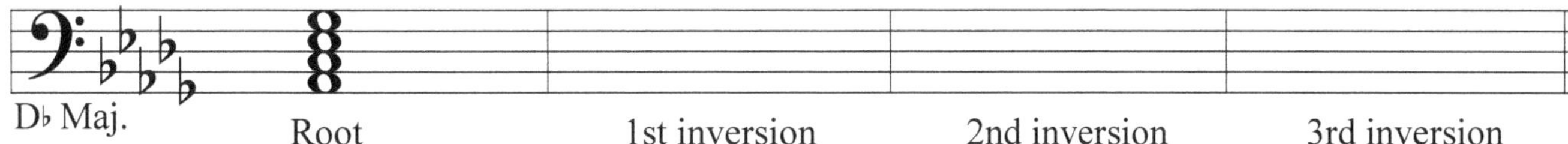

18. Write each triad in the requested inversion. Add the necessary accidentals to each triad. (4 points)

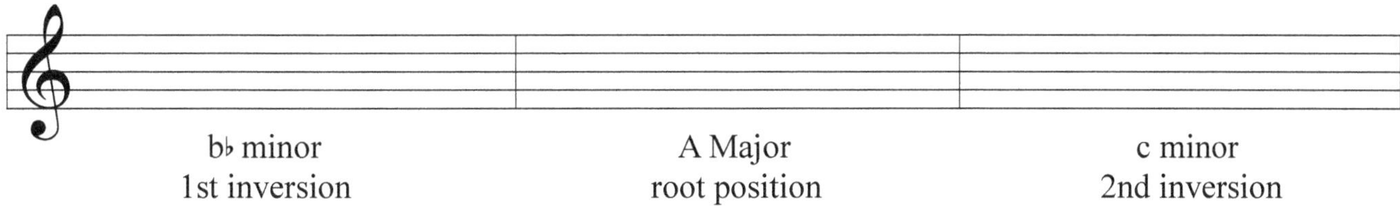

19. Add accidentals to create the requested chords. The Major chord is given. (3 points)

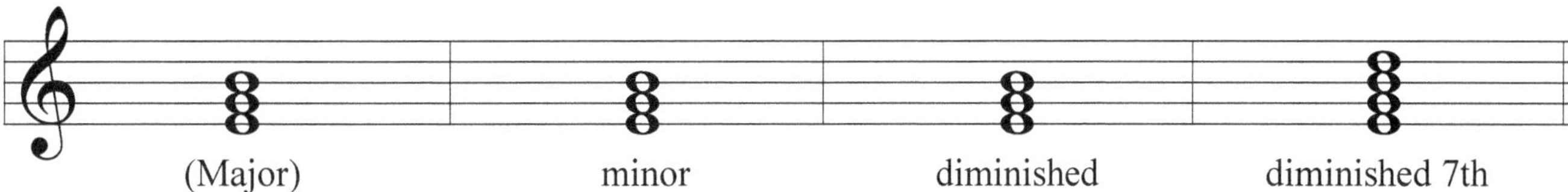

20. Draw the 1st, 2nd and 3rd inversions of the given **diminished 7th** chord. (4 points)

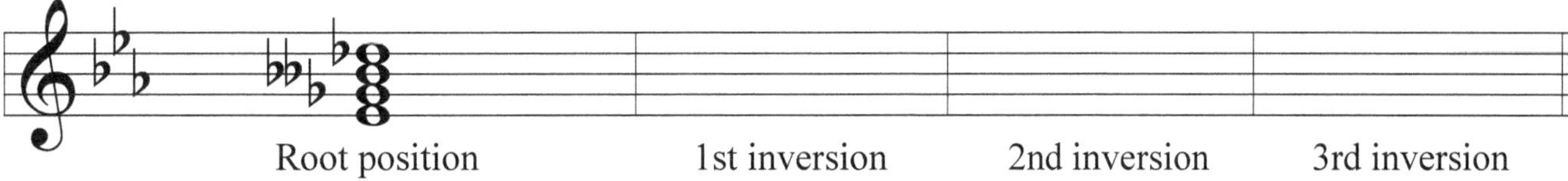

21. Choose the correct name for the following ornaments. (5 points)

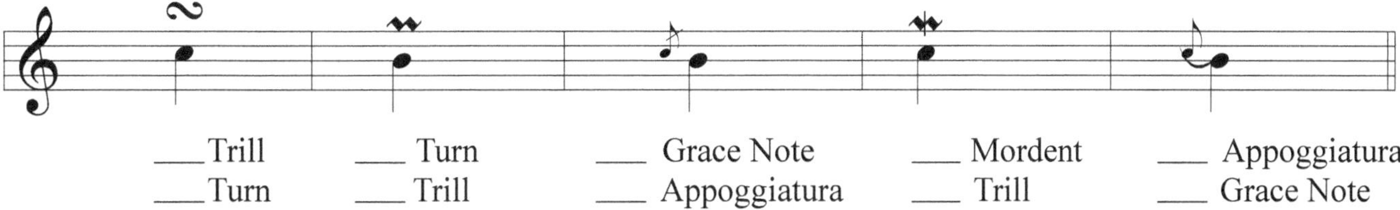

22. Add a note, the interval of a 3rd higher, to each of the existing notes in the following melody. (4 points)

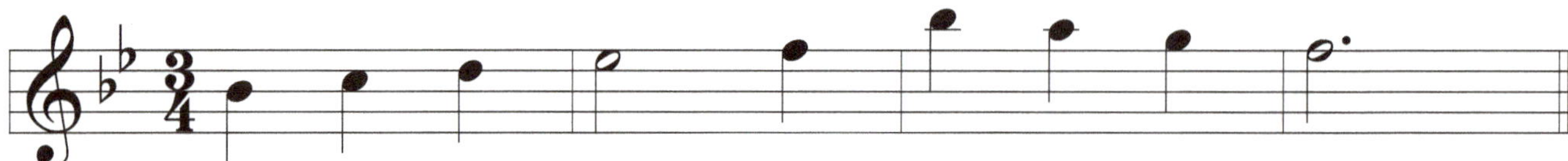

23. Add a note, the interval of a 3rd lower, to each of the existing notes in the following melody. (4 points)

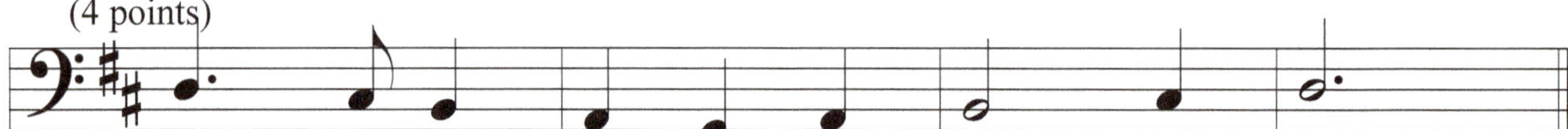

24. Add a note, the interval of a 6th higher, to each of the existing notes in the following melody. (4 points)

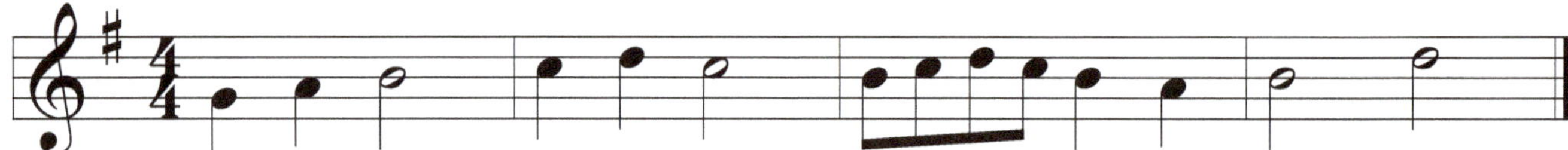

25. Add a note, the interval of a 6th lower, to each of the existing notes in the following melody. (4 points)

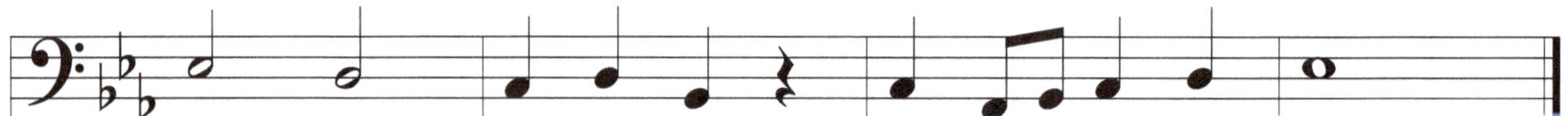

26. Transpose the following melody down by one whole step. Be sure to add the new key signature, and follow the intervals in the given example. (4 points)

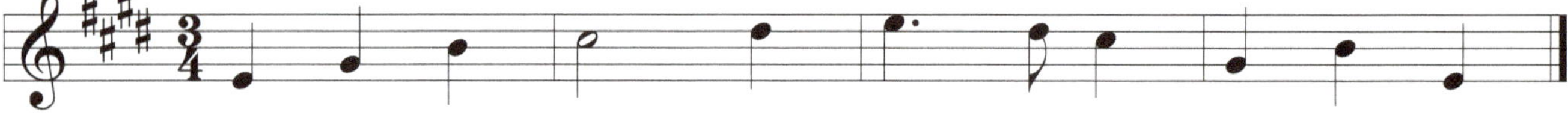

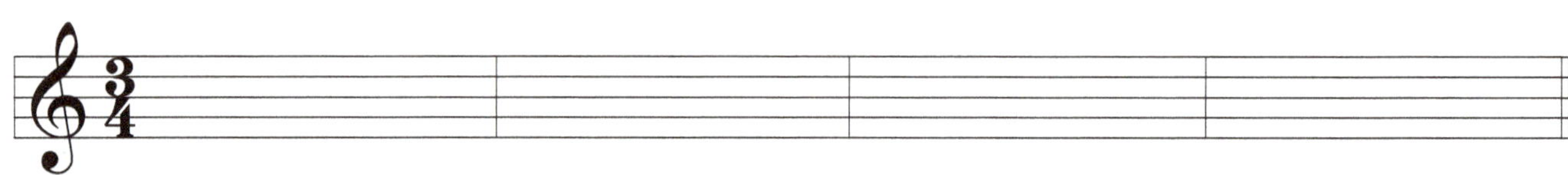

27. Transpose the following melody up by a Perfect 4th. (4 points)

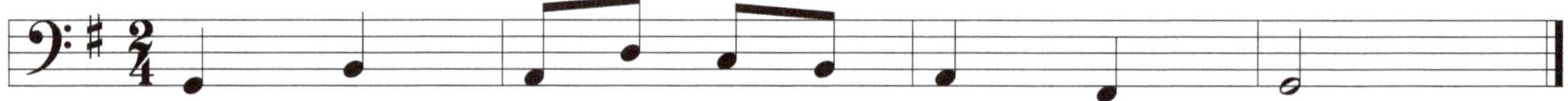

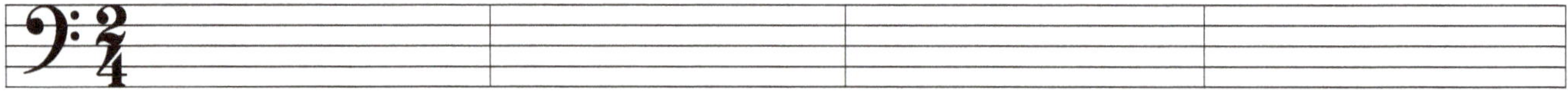

28. Draw conducting patterns beneath the following time signatures. Use lines with arrows to show the directions your hands go. Add numbers to show the order of directions. (3 points)

2/4

3/4

4/4

29. Add **one** note to the end of each measure to complete this rhythmic pattern. (4 points)

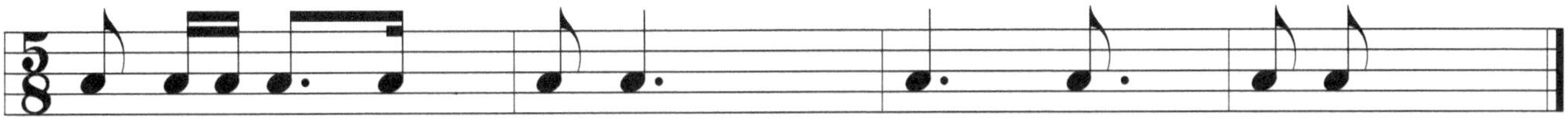

30. Add three bar lines and a double bar line to this rhythm. (4 points)

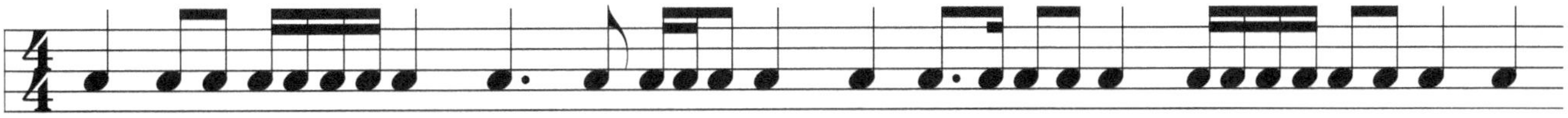

31. Write the solfege under the notes in the following melodic minor example. (4 points)

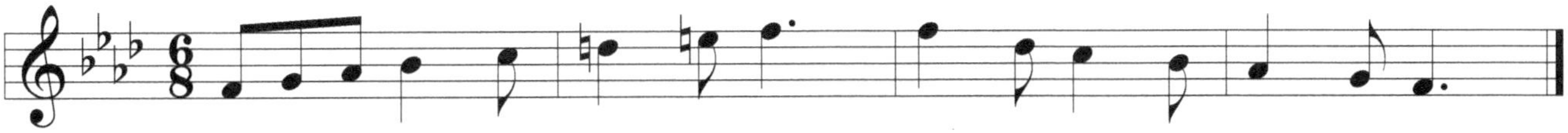

32. Choose the correct IPA spelling of the following foreign language words. (8 points)

Spanish

Quiero ___kjeɾo
___kwiero

Llamo ___ʎamo
___lamo

Italian/Latin

Quella ___kwella
___kella

Chiamo ___ʃiamo
___kjamo

German

Leise ___leizə
___laɪzə

Mein ___maɪn
___meɪn

French

Quand ___kwa
___kɑ̃

Suis ___su
___sɥi

33. Fill in the correct answer using the musical terms in this level. (5 points)

a. _____________________ means halfway between staccato and legato.

b. _____________________means hurrying the tempo, increasing the tension.

c. A _______________________is a melodic line harmonizing with and usually written above a given melody.

d. _______________________means "humorous" in Italian.

e. __________________________means to write or perform a musical work in a key other than that in which it was written.

34. For the following questions about Barber, Beach or Tchaikovsky write the correct word or composer. (10 points)

a. Barber won a Pulitzer Prize for his first opera, ____________________.

b. This composer could sing forty songs accurately by the age of one.________________________

c. Beach appeared as a soloist with the ____________ Symphony Orchestra.

d. This composer wrote the score for the ballet *The Nutracker.*______________________________

e. Barber wrote the song cycle _____________ *Songs.*

f. This composer wrote the song cycle *Three Browning Song, Op.44.*_______________________

g. Tchaikovsky had a wealthy patron by the name of ____________________________.

h. This composer wrote the famous piece, "1812 Overture."_________________________________

i. Barber had his song "Adagio for _______________" in the movie *Platoon.*

j. This composer wrote over 150 songs for voice, including "The Year's at the Spring."

_____________________________.

Final Score:_________________/124 answer key begins on the next page

Level 9 Review Test: Answers

Answer the questions on the next page about the musical example below. (15 points)

1. What minor key does this song begin in?

_____ f minor

_X_ d minor

2. What Major key does it modulate to in m. 9?

_____ B♭ Major

_X_ F Major

3. What type of minor scale do you see (circled) in m.11?

_____ Harmonic

_X_ Melodic

4. Which measure has the first Dominant 7 chord (broken) in the Bass clef

_____ 1

_X_ 3

5. What is the Roman Numeral for the circled chord in measure 8?

_____ iv

_X_ i

6. What inversion is the circled chord in measure 8 in?

_X_ 1st

_____ 2nd

7. Name the solfege for the circled notes in the vocal line in measure 3.

Sol Fa Sol La Ti Do

OR

Mi Re Mi Fi Si La

8. How should this song be sung, based on the term above the vocal line in m.1

_____ joyfully

_X_ sadly

9. If this song was transposed 1 whole step up, what minor key would it be in?

_X_ e minor

_____ f minor

10. How many times will the first and second line (systems) be heard?

_____ once

_X_ twice

11. Add the necessary accidentals to the natural minor scales below to create **melodic minor** scales. (4 points)

12. Use whole notes and accidentals to complete each scale. Draw an **ascending** scale in the first measure and a **descending** scale in the 2nd measure. Do not use a key signature. (4 points)

d **melodic** minor

b **melodic** minor

13. Draw the 1st, 2nd & 3rd inversion of the given Dominant 7 chord. (6 points)

14. Draw a root position **Dominant 7th** chord in each of the following keys. (4 points)

D Major | B♭ Major | E Major | E♭ Major

15. Check the correct inversion for the following Dominant 7th chords. (5 points)

E♭ Maj. 2nd inversion | A Maj. 1st inversion | C♭ Maj. 1st inversion | B♭ Maj. 2nd inversion | F♯ Maj. 3rd inversion

16. Name the Major key to which each of these Dominant 7th belongs. (4 points)

Key of: E♭ Major | B♭ Major | F♯ Major | A Major

17. Draw the 1st, 2nd and 3rd inversions of the given **Dominant 7th** chord. (4 points)

Root | 1st inversion | 2nd inversion | 3rd inversion

18. Write each triad in the requested inversion. Add the necessary accidentals to each triad. (4 points)

b♭ minor 1st inversion | A Major root position | c minor 2nd inversion

19. Add accidentals to create the requested chords. The Major chord is given. (3 points)

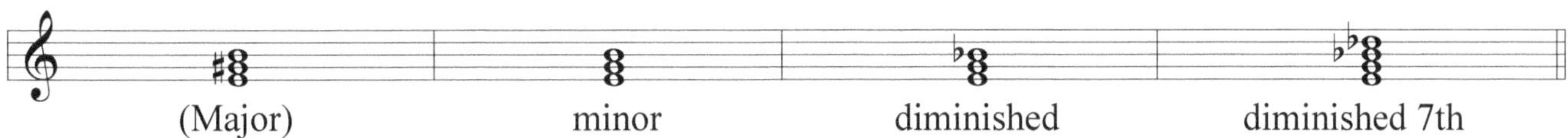

20. Draw the 1st, 2nd and 3rd inversions of the given **diminished 7th** chord. (4 points)

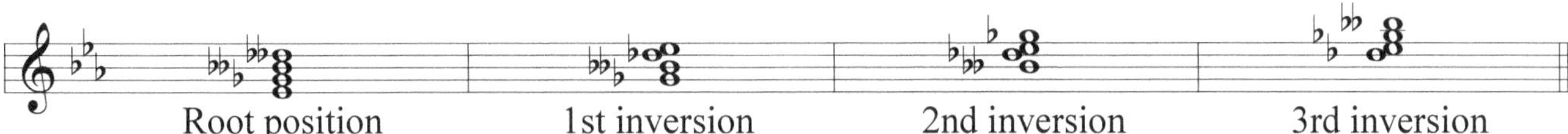

21. Choose the correct name for the following ornaments. (5 points)

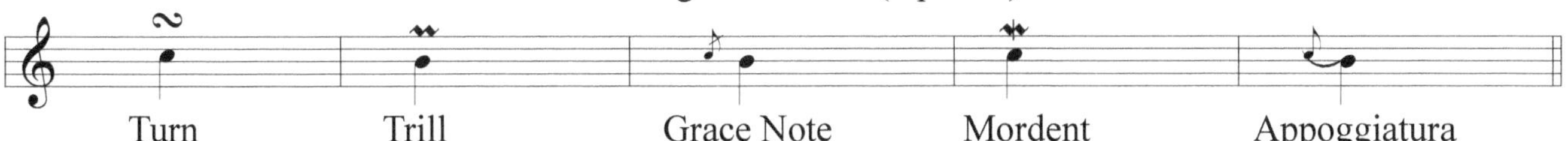

22. Add a note, the interval of a 3rd higher, to each of the existing notes in the following melody. (4 points)

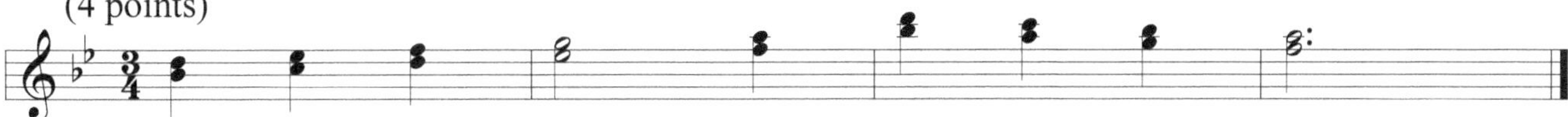

23. Add a note, the interval of a 3rd lower, to each of the existing notes in the following melody. (4 points)

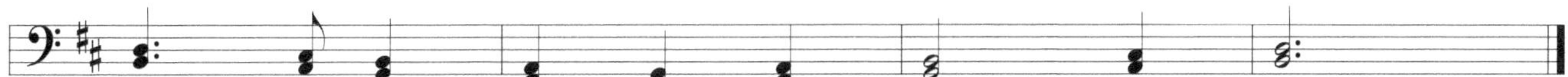

24. Add a note, the interval of a 6th higher, to each of the existing notes in the following melody. (4 points)

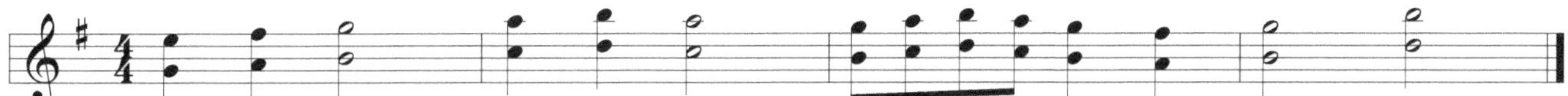

25. Add a note, the interval of a 6th lower, to each of the existing notes in the following melody. (4 points)

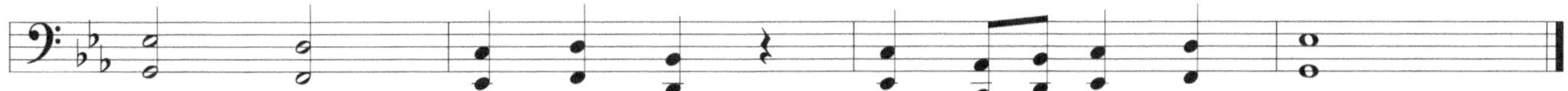

26. Transpose the following melody <u>down</u> by one whole step. Be sure to add the new key signature, and follow the intervals in the given example. (4 points)

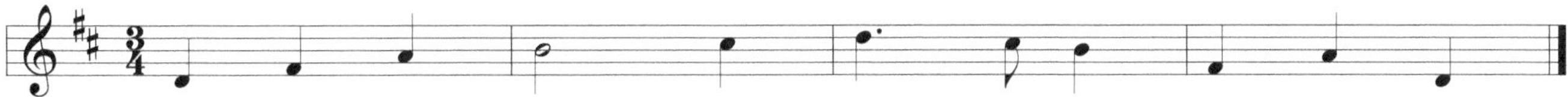

27. Transpose the following melody <u>up</u> by a Perfect 4th. (4 points)

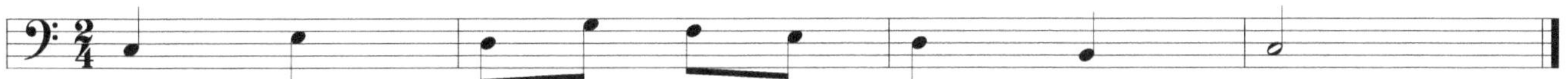

28. Draw conducting patterns beneath the following time signatures. Use lines with arrows to show the directions your hands go. Add numbers to show the order of directions. (3 points)

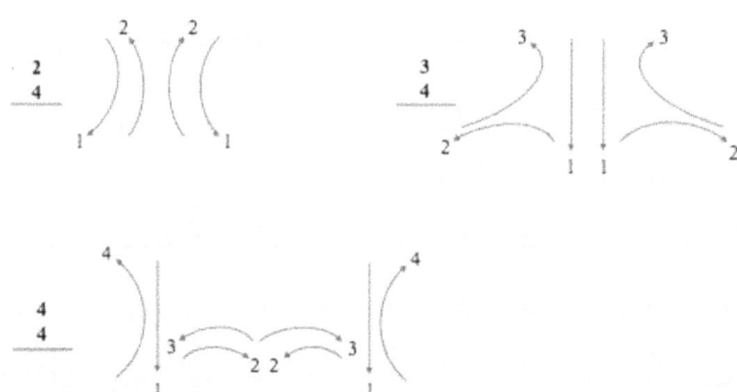

29. Add **one** note to the end of each measure to complete this rhythmic pattern. (4 points)

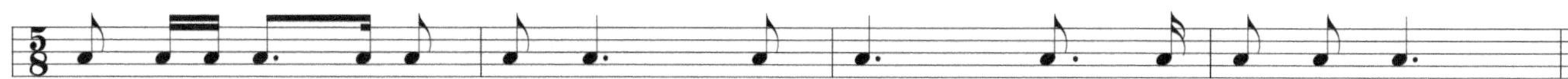

30. Add three bar lines and a double bar line to this rhythm. (4 points)

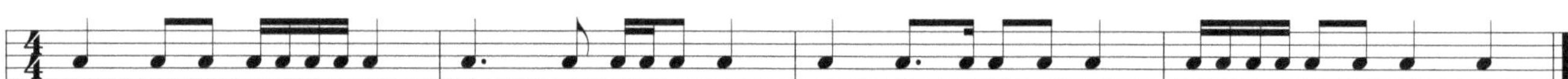

31. Write the solfege under the notes in the following melodic minor example. (4 points)

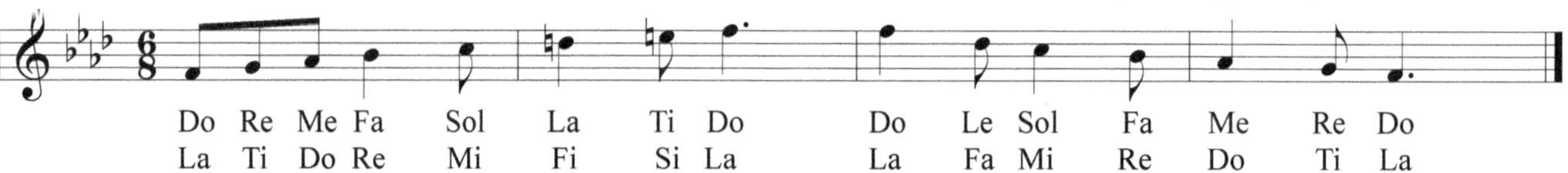

32. Choose the correct IPA spelling of the following foreign language words. (8 points)

Spanish

Quiero=kjeɾo Llamo=ʎamo

Italian/Latin

Quella=kwella Chiamo=kjamo

German

Leise=leizə Mein=maɪn

French

Quand=kã Suis=sɥi

33. Fill in the correct answer using the musical terms in this level. (5 points)

a. ___portato___ means halfway between staccato and legato.
b. ___stringendo___ means hurrying the tempo, increasing the tension.
c. A ___descant___ is a melodic line harmonizing with and usually written above a given melody.
d. ___giocoso___ means "humorous" in Italian.
e. ___transposition___ means to write or perform a musical work in a key other than that in which it was written.

34. For the following questions about Barber, Beach or Tchaikovsky write the correct word or composer. (10 points)

a. Barber won a Pulitzer Prize for his first opera, ______Vanessa______.

b. This composer could sing forty songs accurately by the age of one.______Beach______

c. Beach appeared as a soloist with the ___Boston___ Symphony Orchestra.

d. This composer wrote the score for the ballet *The Nutracker.*______Tchaikovsky______

e. Barber wrote the song cycle ____Hermit____ *Songs.*

f. This composer wrote the song cycle *Three Browning Song, Op.44.*______Beach______

g. Tchaikovsky had a wealthy patron by the name of ______Nadeshda von Meck______.

h. This composer wrote the famous piece, "1812 Overture."______Tchaikovsky______

i. Barber had his song "Adagio for ____Strings____" in the movie *Platoon.*

j. This composer wrote over 150 songs for voice, including "The Year's at the Spring."

______Beach______.

REFERENCES

Grout, Donald. *A History of Western Music.* New York, NY: W.W. Norton & Company, Inc., 1996.

Moriarty, John. *Diction.* Boston, MA: E. C. Schirmer Music Company, 1975.

Music Teachers' Association of California. *Certificate of Merit Voice Syllabus.* San Francisco: Music Teachers' Association of California, 2011.

Piston, Walter. *Harmony, Fifth Edition.* New York, NY: W.W. Norton & Company, Inc., 1987.

Plantinga, Leon. *Romantic Music, A History of Musical Style in Nineteenth-Century Europe.* New York, NY: W.W. Norton & Company, Inc., 1984.

Randel, Don Michael. *The Harvard Biographical Dictionary of Music.* Cambridge, Massachusetts: The Belknap Press of Harvard University Press, 1996.

Randel, Don Michael. *Harvard Concise Dictionary of Music.* Cambridge, Massachusetts: The Belknap Press of Harvard University Press, 1978.

Rushton, Julian. *Classical Music, A Concise History from Gluck to Beethoven.* London, England: Thames and Hudson Ltd., 1986.

The New Grove Dictionary of Music and Musicians. http://www.oxfordmusiconline.com., 2011

www.ingramcontent.com/pod-product-compliance
Lightning Source LLC
LaVergne TN
LVHW061251100826
845148LV00008B/1095

9781524914448